The Unique Life of a
Ranger

SEASONS OF CHANGE
ON BLAKENEY POINT

AJAY TEGALA

Cover image © Dan Sunderland

First published 2022

The History Press
97 St George's Place, Cheltenham,
Gloucestershire, GL50 3QB
www.thehistorypress.co.uk

© Ajay Tegala, 2022

The right of Ajay Tegala to be identified as the Author
of this work has been asserted in accordance with the
Copyright, Designs and Patents Act 1988.

British Library Cataloguing in Publication Data.
A catalogue record for this book is available from the British Library.

ISBN 978 1 8039 9029 3

Typesetting and origination by The History Press
Printed and bound in Great Britain by TJ Books Limited, Padstow, Cornwall.

Trees for LYfe

Dedicated to

Bob Pinchen (1865–1943)
Professor Francis Oliver (1864–1951)
Billy Eales (1883–1939)
Ted Eales (1918–92)
Reginald Gaze (1894–1974)
Joe Reed
Graham and Marilyn Lubbock
who all dedicated many years to the protection of Blakeney Point.

And everyone who has helped protect the Point in any way –
in particular, those I have had the pleasure of working alongside,
and family and friends to whom I have never managed to adequately
explain what it is like to live and work on Blakeney Point.

In memory of

Simon Aspinall, John Bean, Ray Greaves,
Ben Collen, Martin Woodcock, Steve Trudgill
and my Grandad: Peter Haywood

Young grey seal pup. (Ajay Tegala)

Headland of Blakeney Point showing local place names. (Ajay Tegala)

1. Hood
2. Long Hills
3. Yankee Ridge
4. Pinchen's Creek
5. Beach Way
6. Landing ridge
7. Lifeboat House and Old Lifeboat House
8. Plantation and laboratory
9. Main dunes
10. Great Sandy Low – location of ternery: 1901–18
11. Near Point – location of ternery: 1919–99
12. Gap
13. Stanley's Cockle Bight
14. Middle Point
15. Beach colony – location of ternery: 2019–21
16. Far Point – location of ternery: 2000–15
17. Tip – location of ternery: 2016–18

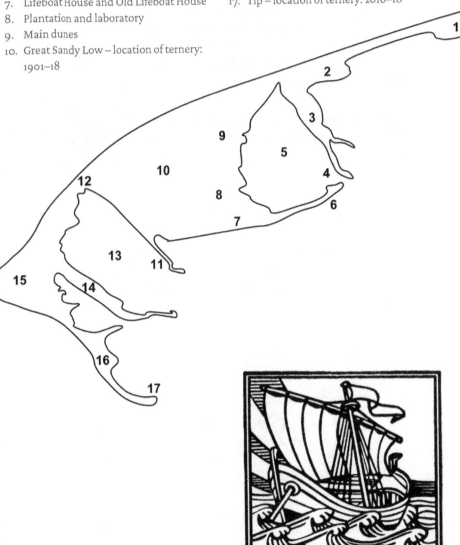

This medieval ship emblem has appeared on several Blakeney Point publications.

Contents

About the Author

AS A WILDLIFE PRESENTER, Ajay Tegala shares his passion for the natural world. His credits include *Springwatch* and *Inside the Bat Cave* (both BBC Two). As a countryside ranger, Ajay is grounded in the world of nature conservation. At the age of 15, he decided to become a conservationist after a week's work experience at Wicken Fen.

Ajay grew up in East Anglia and went on to complete a degree in Environmental Conservation and Countryside Management at Nottingham Trent University, alongside volunteering on the north Norfolk coast at Blakeney Point. He went on to become the Point's full-time ranger, protecting shorebirds and seals as well as inspiring countless visitors.

www.ajaytegala.co.uk

Foreword by Megan McCubbin

THE BRITISH COASTLINE IS a landscape characterised by drama and intrigue. The land lies exposed to the blanket of waves that, gentle or powerful, continue to re-shape its features. It's here that a very select, very special group of wildlife make their home. The intertidal and coastal habitats are some of the most inhospitable in the world as species must be able to thrive in the ever-changing hot, cold, wet, dry and salty environment it presents. Visiting these environments is enchanting and a wonderful day out – but it's another thing entirely to dedicate your life to understanding its patterns and to protect its wildlife.

Ajay Tegala has dedicated much of his time working as a ranger on an isolated, internationally important nature reserve: Blakeney Point, where Norfolk meets the North Sea. He lived in a former lifeboat station at the end of a 4-mile shingle spit and worked with a small team of colleagues and dedicated volunteers to protect vulnerable ground-nesting birds during their breeding season, including rare terns migrating from Africa.

Ajay writes so eloquently, bringing to life the stories that have made him the passionate naturalist he is today; from his first visit to Blakeney Point to the many, many sleepless nights safeguarding precious terns from a whole host of potential dangers. With extracts from his diary, you feel as though you are alongside him learning what it takes to be a ranger. You feel the ups and downs as he encounters new species and watches the chicks he so devotedly protected successfully take their first flight.

This intimate and unique window into a small patch of the British coastline is beautifully written. For conservation, it's important to know an area well but to live and breathe it, each and every day throughout the seasons, is something remarkable. Ajay's passion bursts through the pages. And, if you're anything like me, you're left with the urge to grab your walking boots and head out to your local patch so that you can get to know it that little bit more.

Megan McCubbin

Acknowledgements

FOR THEIR SUPPORT DURING my Blakeney days, thanks to Graham and Marilyn Lubbock, Eddie Stubbings and Bee Büche, Chris Everitt, Dave Wood, John Sizer, Richard Porter, Richard Berridge, Barrie Slegg, Paul Nichols and Sarah Johnson, Mike Reed, Joe Reed, Jason Bean, Graham Bean, the late John Bean, Jim and Jane Temple, Bernard Bishop, Keith Miller, the late Ray Greaves, Simon Garnier, Desmond McCarthy, Sally Chandler, James McCallum, Joe Cockram, Pat and Alan Evans, Andrew and Kay Clarke, Iain Wolfe, Al Davies, Andy Stoddart, George Baldock and Alex Green, Victoria Egan, Neil Lawton, Jason Pegden, Lucas Ward, Nick Bell, Stuart Warrington, Matt Twydell, Godfrey and Judy Sayers, Bill Landells, Martin Perrow, Brent and Brigid Pope, Alison Charles, Richard Timson, Simon Gresham, Greg Cooper, Terry Sands, Stuart Banks, Josh Herron, David Bullock, the late Josh Barber, Harry Mitchell, Tony Martin, Faith Hamilton, Sabrina Fenn, Mary Goddard, Anne Casey, Steve Prowse, Carl Brooker, Luke Wilkinson, Ryan Doggart and Wynona Legg, Val MacFall, Leighton Newman and many other locals, volunteers, colleagues and conservationists who I have had the pleasure of working with and learning from. Huge thanks, of course, to my wonderful family, too.

Special thanks to the National Trust, who have been caring for Blakeney Point since 1912 and have employed me in various roles since 2010. Thanks also to University College London, Blakeney Area Historical Society and the Zoological Society of London.

Very special thanks to Harry, Kate, Charlotte and Hannah for encouraging me to write and to Megan McCubbin for kindly writing the foreword. I am extremely grateful to Graham and Marilyn Lubbock, Richard Porter, Ian Ward, Joe Cockram, Pete Stevens, the Trudgill family, Dan Sunderland, University College London and the National Trust for kind permission to use their photographs. Thanks also, for assistance with the editing and publishing process, to David Foster, Gerry Granshaw, Dave Wood, John Sizer, Joe Reed, Martin Perrow, Tony Martin, Isabel Sedgwick, Claire Masset, Nicola Guy, Ele Craker, Lauren Kent and my parents: Bev and TT. Lastly, thanks to the many authors and writers whose works have informed, inspired and motivated me.

Preface

Riding a Tide

WHEN YOU LIVE IN a remote former lifeboat station at the end of a 4-mile shingle spit, surrounded by sea at high tide, protecting internationally important seabird colonies, you're often asked what it's like. Few people have had the privilege and responsibility of living on an isolated, internationally important nature reserve, their every move judged by countless critics. This book gives me the opportunity to share my personal perspective of the joys, struggles and surprises that made life as Blakeney Point's ranger so unique. This is the story of what life as a ranger on one of Britain's prime nature sites is really like.

As soon as I started working on Blakeney Point, I contemplated one day writing about my experiences, from the excitement of monitoring the rapidly growing seal population to the challenges and struggles of protecting ground-nesting birds from a plethora of threats. And in spring 2020, like so many, I found myself with time to look back and reflect. For over a decade, I had been collecting information, keeping diaries of first-hand experiences and memorising stories I had been told.

Each year, hundreds of thousands of visitors come to north Norfolk to enjoy themselves and experience its inspiring landscapes and magnificent wildlife. Just the mention of Blakeney Point is enough to bring a smile to many a face. But I have had the privilege of actually *living* out there, in all weathers. I have gained an insight into the real Blakeney Point in her numerous guises.

I once joked that it would take a book to really explain what I have experienced and learned during my time on the Point. That became a personal challenge in 2020, and eighteen months of pleasure followed, culminating in this book.

Part 1 follows my year as a volunteer assistant warden, experiencing life on the north Norfolk coast for the first time: learning about the wildlife, tides and the complexities of managing a dynamic nature reserve. Part 2 is an account of my first breeding bird season on Blakeney Point itself. Part 3 covers my time as the Point's full-time ranger, from dealing with a major tidal surge to solving a great seal mystery.

The title of the book refers to how the changing seasons influence weather and wildlife in a complex cycle – partly predictable, partly unpredictable. Time and tide have formed, eroded and altered the topography of Blakeney Point, creating a fascinating, ever-changing landscape that is home to a stunning array of creatures who adapt to these changes.

Since Blakeney Point became famous in the Victorian times, our relationship with it has changed. Thankfully, for the last 120 years, it has been protected. The key focus of safeguarding its vulnerable ground-nesting birds has been a constant, but the precise ways in which the Point is managed have developed, just as the whole world has changed.

In the book, I look at the changes I have both experienced and studied, sharing the love I feel for this magnificent, wild stretch of Britain's coastline. This is my tribute to the beauty of Blakeney, to the wildlife and the people to whom it is home.

Ajay Tegala, January 2022

Introduction

Reaching a Point

MORSTON QUAY WAS CLOAKED in a thick sea mist. We crossed a wooden bridge over a tidal creek and boarded an open-topped ferry, which took us out into the disorientating greyness of Blakeney Harbour. Some time passed before a shingle finger appeared in front of us, emerging from the mist. The air was suddenly filled with the noisy cries of black-headed gulls and Sandwich terns, which were nesting behind a string fence line. On the water's edge were dozens of common seals. It was as if we had ascended through the greyness to reach a magical wildlife island.

The boat landed and our feet crunched on shingle as we walked towards the former lifeboat house, clad in corrugated iron painted deep blue. Along the ridge, I spotted several oystercatchers. Their camouflaged eggs were protected by square stringed-off enclosures. To someone familiar with predominantly brown garden birds and inland river fowl, oystercatchers were appealing, with their distinctive pied plumage and carrot-coloured bills, which emitted a piercing call. We were intruders to their nesting grounds.

Inside the Lifeboat House, we glanced at the museum-like display about the birds and plants found in this special environment. Heading back outside, we followed a wooden boardwalk over the undulating dunes towards a bird hide. Completing a circular route, we ended back at the landing stage, where we were collected and ferried back to Morston. An hour on Blakeney Point flies by.

It was a weekday afternoon in early June, during the school half-term holiday. I was 14, and this was my first visit to this part of the Norfolk coast. Like countless others, my family was on holiday in the county and had come to see the seals. The mist made it a mysterious and eerie experience. I felt like I had entered a secret haven, a sanctuary for seals and birds. The memory would never fade.

In the early twenty-first century, the vast majority of ferry passengers come to see the seals. A smaller number are interested in the birds and a smaller number still appreciate the flora. During the late nineteenth century, neither seals nor birds were so appreciated. In fact, both were shot – with guns, rather than cameras.

Most Blakeney bird records from the Victorian era are of specimens secured by the so-called 'gentleman gunners'. These were primarily Londoners who came to Blakeney and Cley to hunt rarities during the spring and autumn migrations. Local taxidermists were kept busy preserving and presenting the skins of birds shot by the collectors.

Horrifyingly large numbers were lost to punt guns. This impacted not only on the migrant birds on passage, but resident and breeding species too. By 1892, the oystercatcher had been completely lost as a breeding species on the Point. There was a growing need for its protection.

Although destructive, the Victorians greatly improved our knowledge and understanding of birds. Being able to examine carcasses in the hand enabled plumage and moult to be studied, which informed the identification guides we use to this day. Victorian ornithologist Henry Seebohm observed – quoting the 'Old Bushman' – 'What is hit is history and what is missed is mystery'.

The year 1901 was a milestone. It marked the foundation of the Blakeney and Cley Wild Bird Protection Society. A group of concerned locals came together to try to better protect the birds that came to the Point during the breeding season. Robert J. Pinchen, a butcher by trade, was appointed as the Point's watcher at a meeting in Cley. According to

Pinchen's book, *Sea Swallows*, he was employed for ten weeks each nesting season on a weekly wage of 15 shillings.

Another gentleman was key to the protection of Blakeney Point. Professor Francis Wall Oliver of University College London (UCL) first visited the Point in 1904 while recuperating from pleurisy. Oliver recognised the value of the saltmarsh and dunes from a botanical point of view, with enormous research opportunities. The university purchased the now derelict Old Lifeboat House in 1910 and it became a field centre.

Oliver made regular field trips to Blakeney. He mapped the distribution of saltmarsh plants in relation to the amount of saltwater flooding they could withstand. In some ways, this work was in the vein of explorer Alexander Von Humboldt, who had done similar work across the globe a century earlier. Along with other pioneering ecologists, including Doctor Sydney Long, Professor Oliver produced numerous papers and scientific journal articles.

The unspoiled expanses of saltmarsh and largely unspoiled sand dunes might not have been protected and made accessible to the public had it not been for Oliver. Following the death of Lord Calthorpe, his north Norfolk coast estate went on the market. This included Blakeney Point. Oliver gained agreement for the Point to be used for botanical studies and to be sold as a separate lot. At his suggestion, the Point was bought by public appeal and transferred to the National Trust in August 1912. Funds had been provided by the Fishmonger's Company and an anonymous donor: banker and entomologist, Nathaniel Charles Rothschild.

Already a bird sanctuary, Blakeney Point had now become the country's very first coastal nature reserve. The National Trust shared UCL's appreciation for the Point's botany, physiography and also its ornithology. Bob Pinchen was kept on as watcher, already having eleven seasons under his belt.

The National Trust had been founded just over seventeen years previously and had managed the country's first nature reserve, Wicken Fen, since 1899. Both Wicken and Blakeney are often referred to as the birthplace of ecology in relation to their respective habitats. Over a century on, the trust's core responsibilities on Blakeney Point are much the same as they were when they acquired it: to protect the terns and other vulnerable ground-nesting bird species.

Four tern species breed on Blakeney Point. All four nest on the ground, laying between one and three eggs in a simple scrape in the sand and shingle. These elegant seabirds migrate to Norfolk from wintering grounds in Africa. Closely related to gulls, terns have more angular wings, forked tails and plunge-dive to catch small fish. In fact, common terns are sometimes called sea swallows because of their tails.

The Sandwich tern is the largest of Blakeney's terns. So named because it was first described in England at Sandwich in Kent, by ornithologist John Latham in 1787. The Dutch name of *grote stern* is perhaps more appropriate as it translates as 'great tern'. In 2012, this was the most numerous breeding tern on the Point, with over 3,000 pairs nesting. However, breeding was not confirmed on the Point until 1920 when the first nest was discovered.

Breeding pairs doubled in 1921, exceeded 100 in 1923 and reached around 300 pairs in 1924. Following their rapid colonisation, 1925 saw breeding numbers fall to just eight pairs. It was noted that the bulk were thought to have deserted to nearby Scolt Head Island, 12 miles west of the Point. Since that time, the north Norfolk Sandwich tern population has regularly switched between Blakeney and Scolt Head. If something made the colony feel unsettled at one site, birds would desert to the other. For a period, Blakeney was the sole breeding site and at other times it was Scolt Head. Rarely was there a year with a completely even split. Historically, there was a great rivalry between the wardens of the two sites.

Throughout the 1960s and most of the '70s, between 1,000 and 2,000 common tern pairs nested each summer. It was in 1978 that the Sandwich tern overtook the common tern as the most numerous breeder.

The common tern has bred on the Point since before Pinchen's time. In his first year as watcher, 140 pairs nested. Numbers increased steadily year on year, benefiting from the protection afforded. Common terns were first documented at Blakeney around 1830 but are more than likely to have been present for some time before this date. As the name suggests, the species has a far larger British breeding population than the Sandwich tern and is more widespread, nesting inland as well as on the coast.

Throughout the 1980s, between 1,000 and 3,000 Sandwich terns nested, but common terns dropped to 200–300. In the 2000s, common tern numbers dropped below 100 pairs in some years. A theory for this significant change is that the Sandwich terns had taken over as the dominant species, pushing the common terns out of the prime nesting and feeding areas and therefore making them less successful breeders.

As well as the common tern, the only other tern species known to have nested on the Point in Victorian times was the little tern, then known as the lesser tern. In 1901, there were about sixty nests. Fast forward 115 years, and breeding numbers were much the same. However, since the Second World War, over 100 nests have been recorded on a number of occasions.

In the 1970s and again in 2011, Blakeney Point supported the country's largest and most productive little tern colony. They are, however, typically inconsistent and very sensitive, frequently suffering very low productivity. Their habit for nesting close to the high-water mark makes them vulnerable to big tides, especially when combined with strong onshore winds.

Since 1922, a small number of Arctic terns have bred at Blakeney each year. Never more than twenty-four pairs have nested in a year, this number is usually below ten and often below five. They are at the southern limit of their breeding range. Although the least common of the four species on the Point, sometimes these are the first species visitors encounter when they board the ferries in Morston Creek.

A fifth species that has previously bred is the roseate tern, Britain's only other breeding tern. Two pairs nested between 1921 and 1930, and single pairs bred in 1939 and 1948. In 1997, a pair nested but the eggs were predated, and another unsuccessful breeding attempt was made the following year. It was only in these fourteen years that five tern species bred at Blakeney, although roseate terns are seen over the Point on passage most years. Black terns are also seen on passage most years, they bred inland in East Anglia until 1885.

Methods of protecting and counting the terns have evolved since Pinchen's time. He would mark nests with sticks. Visitors would be allowed to walk inside the colony, looking out for the sticks to avoid trampling on eggs. Although tolerant to a certain degree, this did disturb the terns. People would picnic in the colony, causing birds to leave their nests for long periods and thus making the eggs vulnerable to chilling or overheating, depending on weather conditions, as well as giving predators the opportunity to take eggs.

After the Second World War, warden Ted Eales introduced fencing. According to his memoirs, he found some metal wire washed up on the beach. He had the idea to create a wire fence around the ternery to keep people out. This method is used to this day, albeit with road pins and baler twine instead of metal wire.

Fences and signs alone are not sufficient to protect the vulnerable terns. Especially as tides reduce the area available to fence without the risk of being washed away. A physical presence is needed to ensure nobody accidentally strays too close to the breeding colonies.

Watcher Bob Pinchen in the early 1920s. (National Trust)

Warden Ted Eales in the late 1940s. (John Trudgill)

This means that the job of the Point watcher-come-warden-come-ranger and their assistants involves keeping careful watch on the ternery between early April and mid-August. Stationed on the beach at low tide, they can direct seal-seeking visitors as far away from the nesting area as possible, following the water's edge.

This may sound simple, but often visitors accidentally stray too close to the terns. Excited by the experience of seeing seals, visitors can easily forget about the inconspicuous ground-nesting birds and some simply don't register them at all.

The majority of visitors to the Point arrive by boat from Morston, landing for just thirty minutes to an hour. In this short time, they are not able to reach the beach – and the ternery is usually cut off by the tide, even if they do. A much smaller number of people make the 4-mile trudge westwards from Cley beach. An even smaller number wade across the harbour through thick mud and tidal creeks. Their route and timing have to be carefully chosen, with local knowledge of the dangers. Even if this specific knowledge is gained, the harbour changes from year to year, with creeks moving and sediment shifting. Tide timetables are only useful to a point, as onshore winds can cause the harbour to fill up earlier. This is nature in truly dynamic form.

Albeit far fewer in number than they once were, bait diggers come to know the many moods of the 'fickle maiden' that is Blakeney Point. Wind strength and direction can alter the speed at which the tide rolls in and out. When out digging for mud-dwelling worms to be used as fishing bait, up to a mile from terra firma, bait diggers must be constantly aware of their surroundings, carefully choosing the right moment to beat a hasty retreat. Time and tide wait for no one.

Part 1

Beginnings –
A Year on the Coast

1

Minding the Gap

EARLY ONE JULY MORNING, Graham steered the powerboat along Morston Creek into Blakeney Harbour. Dozens of other boats were moored in the harbour; some were fishing boats, but most were pleasure craft. By far the largest was *Juno*, a massive sailing barge majestically dominating the harbour with its size and beauty. Barely a decade old, her design was inspired by the Thames cargo barges that were common along the east coast up until 100 years ago.

Half a decade since my first seal trip, I was now on my second trip through the harbour, during my second day as a volunteer assistant warden. Two-thirds of the way through an Environmental Conservation and Countryside Management degree, I was embarking on a placement at Blakeney National Nature Reserve to develop my skills and experience.

Cley-born Graham has lived his whole life in rhythm with the changing seasons and shifting sands, working on the reserve since the mid-1980s. He started out as a seasonal assistant warden on Blakeney Point, returning for a second season before securing a permanent role based primarily on the mainland sections of the nature reserve.

On this occasion, Graham was managing the Point for a day. He and I were holding fort while Point-based warden, Eddie, and the two seasonal assistants attended a course on dealing with confrontation.

Graham explained how all of the many mooring buoys were connected to their moorings on ropes. These ropes can get wrapped around boat propellers if they are steered too close to the buoys. That is one of the reasons why 'all good wardens carry a knife', something he would go on to tell me many times.

Although very much at home steering the boat, Graham was cautious. He had a respect for the environment that came from years of experience. You can't always see what's beneath the water at high tide, but the floor of the harbour is a network of channels and banks. Straying too far from the main channels can lead to propellers being damaged from scraping the bottom and boats can all-too-easily become, quite literally, stuck in the mud.

We followed a line of sunken willow branches, which marked the course of Pinchen's Creek, named after the Point's first warden. Pinchen and his family would spend the summer months based in a houseboat moored on the edge of this creek. In fact, a piece of wood from one of his old houseboats, the *Britannia*, remains behind the ferry landing stage, completely overlooked by the majority of visitors.

The saltmarsh beyond was a haze of purple with common sea-lavender in peak bloom, the most vivid colour in the landscape. On that Tuesday in early July, the first high tide was early in the morning and second was in the early evening, with low tide around midday. This is known to locals as a split tide: the ideal conditions for going out to the Point by boat for the day. Every other Sunday there is a split tide. Between mid-April and mid-October, during the interwar years, these were known as Point Sundays.

The ferries now rarely land for more than an hour. But, for much of the twentieth century, locals would sail out on a morning tide to spend the day on the Point. Families would relax on the foreshore and in the sand dunes or go sailing and fishing. Lugworms would be dug on the ebb tide to catch flatfish with. This, along with cockling, was a way of subsidising low weekly earnings.

At the end of the day, families would head home with their pets and primus stoves. They would usually leave their litter behind. From the age of 11, local boy Ted Eales was on the payroll as litter collector. Ted's father, Billy, took over from Bob Pinchen as watcher in 1930.

A split tide worked perfectly for the Point's resident wardens to have the opposite of a Point day – leaving in the morning and returning in the evening. Graham and I were taking their place for the day. The bow of the boat slowly pushed gently into the shingle of the landing ridge and Graham carefully positioned the anchor.

We trudged over the shingle as we headed towards the Lifeboat House. The same route thousands of visitors walk every summer and the one I had walked five summers before. Graham explained that we had now passed the peak of the breeding bird season, the previous three months having been the busiest time for the Point's wardens. Most of the oystercatchers now had young, but some had experienced unsuccessful first and even second nesting attempts, so were still incubating eggs. Our task for the day was to make sure that birds with eggs could incubate them in peace and those with young could tend to them without being disturbed.

There was time for a cup of coffee first. We ascended the concrete steps to the Lifeboat House door. To our left was another set of concrete steps, which led into the visitor centre. Graham led the way into the kitchen, commenting that he couldn't live in a place so untidy as he gestured to the array of items spread across the table. Alongside a teapot and other kitchen items lay copies of *British Birds* magazine, an A4 page-a-day 2009 diary and various office items. It was clear that living and working merged in this building. I felt like an intruder in the wardens' home.

A wooden-panelled wall and sliding door separated the living quarters from the visitor centre. Pinned to it were a wide variety of invertebrate identification charts: moths, butterflies, dragonflies, bees and grasshoppers. Also pinned to the wall was a cartoon drawing of a bird blowing a trumpet, captioned 'Trumpeter Finch'.

The kettle whistled on the gas hob and Graham asked if I wanted coffee or tea. As we sipped our hot drinks, he outlined the plan for the day. We would alternate between the beach and the Lifeboat House area, swapping over every hour. First, he would take me to the beach and set me off on 'gap' duty.

Walking over the boardwalk towards the beach, Graham mentioned that the recycled plastic boards had only been laid the previous autumn. He explained how the old wooden boards would get slippery when wet and rotted fairly quickly, whereas the recycled plastic – made from old milk crates – should last much longer and provided better grip. Indeed, it blended in well and didn't look out of place. There were already lichens growing on the boards in places.

At the end of the boardwalk, we continued in a straight line towards a ridge of sand dunes called Far Point. Extending from Far Point, sits Middle Point, a block of dunes to the west. Graham pointed behind us to the end of the dunes we had just crossed on the boardwalk: there stood Near Point, where an old wooden hide was visible in the distance.

He explained how, over the years, the Sandwich terns had shifted their nesting position as the spit had grown in length, favouring the westernmost tip. Graham peppered his commentary with jokes. It was a laugh a minute, with humour injected at every opportunity. I had known him just twenty-four hours, but I already knew I enjoyed his company. He had a sense of fun, balanced by true passion for his part of the north Norfolk coast.

Low tide on the beach near the gap: all sand and sky, August 2009. (Ajay Tegala)

Through a gap in the dunes, the inky blue North Sea was visible. The gap had been worn by the footsteps of the many people taking the most direct route to the beach. A line of orange string held up by rusty metal stakes led almost to the water's edge. A short way to the left, there was an upside-down plastic fish box positioned up in the dunes, overlooking the beach. This was to be my post for the first of many hours 'on gap'.

Everyone who works or volunteers on the Point during the tern breeding season becomes familiar with the gap. The fish box has since been upgraded to a wooden garden chair, but the job remains the same. This is the best location to meet visitors who have walked up the Point from Cley. Whether they have followed the beach all of the way along, or cut into the dunes to the boardwalk then headed back out to the beach, this is the point where the two routes converge.

Graham explained that the tide would recede almost as far as the distant wreck marker post, which looked nearly half a mile ahead of us. He pointed out a marker buoy about the same distance to our left. This was the furthest I was to let anyone walk along the Point. I was to ask walkers to stick as close to the shoreline as possible. This way, they would be able to get a decent view of the seals without disturbing the nesting little terns on the beach. Confident that I would speak to every visitor who made it to the gap, Graham left me to keep watch.

The little tern has the highest level of legal protection of all four tern species nesting on the Point. Their rarity affords them listing under Schedule 1 of the Wildlife and Countryside Act of 1981. It is a criminal offence to disturb, intentionally or recklessly, an adult and their young on or near their nest. That year, fifty-six little tern nests had been recorded on the beach and the first chicks – half a dozen of them – had been observed only the previous day.

At low tide, seals haul out on the opposite side of Blakeney Channel to the Point, known as Stiffkey West Sands. Visitors can therefore see them from the opposite side of the water without disturbing them. That said, by far the best way to see the seals up close is on the ferry trips from Morston. The seal ferries conveniently help to protect the seals and nesting birds by providing a disturbance-free but breathtaking way for millions to appreciate the wild wonder of the Point.

As I sat waiting for the first walker of the day to appear, I took in the beauty of my surroundings. The white dots of terns and gulls flew above the deep blue of the sea. The sound of the gently lapping waves was very relaxing – although I did not feel completely relaxed because I had responsibility, a job to do. These were my first moments as a warden. As a 19-year-old student, this would shape the rest of my life, although I didn't realise it at the time.

More than half an hour had passed before the first visitor came into view on the beach. I headed down from my vantage point, following the fence line to the shoreline. The solitary walker, in his late twenties, saw my green, branded polo shirt and began asking about the reserve and its wildlife. I was not yet knowledgeable enough to answer all of his questions, but politely communicated where he could walk to safely see seals. Having had part-time jobs centred around giving good customer service, my conversation with the walker flowed naturally and the necessary information was imparted.

Satisfied he had grasped the directions I had given, I returned to the fish box to keep watch for more people. I also followed the suggestion I had been given and tentatively kept watch on the walker, through a pair of Minox binoculars I had been provided with. He reached the buoy that marked the limit of public access and lingered there a while before eventually starting to head back along the same route he had arrived, just as I had requested. If he had continued further along the beach beyond the buoy, I would have had to jog swiftly over and ask him to return.

The reason access was limited to that particular buoy was so that visitors did not stray beyond the view of the watching warden. Merely a few hundred metres further along the beach was the very tip of the Point, where about a third of the nation's Sandwich terns were feeding their chicks. The majority of these chicks were not yet capable of flight. In fact, that same day, the very first juvenile Sandwich tern of the season was heard calling over the Lifeboat House.

As well as the West Sands, at low tide a small number of seals would often haul out on the end of the Point. If someone was to walk too close to them, they would dart into the sea. This prevents them from resting, digesting their food and healing any wounds. Such disturbance also reduces the chances of the ferry trips seeing as many seals at the next high tide, thus spoiling the enjoyment of others as well as disturbing a protected wild mammal.

Graham arrived five minutes early. He had just been on a careful walk a short way off the boardwalk and found a partridge nest containing ten eggs. He showed me the photograph he had taken and explained this was the reason that people should not stray from paths. I left Graham at the gap and returned to the Lifeboat House to explore its lookout tower at his suggestion.

At the top of the stairs stood a simple wooden ladder screwed to the wall. As I climbed up, it creaked slightly. I pushed open the hatch and entered the lantern, where an old armchair and telescope were located, along with a few tomato plants, benefiting from the greenhouse-like conditions. This was clearly the perfect place to keep watch on the Point and the harbour. Hours could easily be lost observing the geography of the landscape.

As the harbour emptied, areas of bare mud, green saltmarsh vegetation and silvery-white shingle were becoming exposed. Saltwater rippled seaward through the main channels, with the moored boats facing the direction of the outward tide. On the exposed mudflats and marshes, small wading birds probed with their bills, searching for worms and crustaceans beneath the surface. Distant car windscreens glistened in the sun, parked on Morston Quay. The pine trees between Wells and Holkham were visible to the west and Cley coastguard shelter could be picked out to the east.

An hour later, I returned to the gap. By now, the tide had pulled out much further and a considerable expanse of sand had been exposed. Graham encouraged me to try to count the seals every hour as the tide went out. That way, I would appreciate how many more of them hauled out as the sand was exposed. Meanwhile, he headed to Pinchen's Creek to make sure the boat was still afloat as the tide dropped. The further out from the high water mark it could be pushed, the sooner it would be afloat again on the next tide and the earlier we could use it again. Otherwise, we would have a longer wait for the water to get higher and Graham didn't like to wait around too much, if he could help it.

During his lunch break, he had wandered carefully onto the salt-marsh and plucked a few handfuls of Salicornia, or glasswort, known more commonly as samphire and sometimes referred to as 'poor man's asparagus'. He told me to give it a good wash to get the mud and salt off, boil it for ten minutes and add vinegar if I fancied. Technically, it is illegal to uproot any wild plant on the reserve, but Graham explained how locals hadn't done any harm by taking small amounts. Sustainable gathering of samphire had occurred for generations and become part of north Norfolk culture. However, high-end restaurants had now discovered it. If I spotted anyone gathering large amounts for commercial use, then I would need to take a photograph as evidence and report it.

At dead low tide, I wandered down to Pinchen's Creek. It was now almost completely empty, its steep sides clearly visible. There were a few marks in the mud where boat propellers had evidently scraped the bottom. I was fascinated by how different the harbour looked at low tide and also the number of birds that were feeding on the saltmarsh now that it had been uncovered, like a curtain lifting.

The main sand dunes are a vastly different place to the marsh. Cushions of grey green cladonia lichen crunch underfoot, dried by the sun. The antler-like branches of the lichen earn it the nickname reindeer moss. When it rains, the lichens rehydrate, softening and changing colour to a deeper green. The shingly lows of the dunes are dominated by tiny tussocks of coarse grey hair-grass, a nationally rare plant of which Britain has more than 25 per cent of the world's population.

I'm not sure what Graham's first impressions of me were. Probably a quiet, slightly shy 19-year-old, clearly with limited experience of boats or coastal environments. But perhaps someone keen to listen and learn, willing to get stuck in and develop as many skills as possible; someone eager to soak up the wisdom of those who had grown up surrounded by coastal wildlife. I know he appreciated having an extra person on the ground; an extra pair of eyes and hands to help keep a lookout and protect the reserve he cared so much for; an extra voice to speak to visitors ... and a fresh set of ears to listen to his jokes and 'true stories'!

2

The Freshes

IN THE EIGHTEENTH CENTURY, a four-storey tower windmill was built north of Blakeney Church, at Friary Farm. The 32ft-high flint tower overlooks Blakeney's freshwater grazing marshes, an area of reclaimed saltmarsh that was enclosed by a sea wall around 1650.

Corn was ground in the windmill throughout the nineteenth century, but in January 1912, the Blakeney miller was declared bankrupt, and it came into the ownership of Lord Calthorpe, who also owned Blakeney Point. When he died, there were plans to convert the windmill into a residential house. However, it has laid derelict for over a century. It was left to the National Trust in 1983, who maintain the building in the hope that it may be possible to restore it one day.

During the 1990s, the Blakeney National Nature Reserve office and workshop was moved from Morston to Friary Farm. After half a decade of planning, a single-storey flint building was built adjoining the flint wall that surrounds the old windmill. It imitated a previous building, shown in old photographs, of which only the original base remained. The reserve now had volunteer accommodation on the mainland.

The first residential volunteer to stay there, Reuben, went on to become an RSPB – Royal Society for the Protection of Birds – reserve manager at Leighton Moss in Lancashire. He kept in touch with Graham and his wife, Marilyn, who started working for the trust around the same time. Marilyn had taken up a six-month post doing administration at the Blakeney reserve office in 1998 and ended up working there for more than two decades.

I arrived at Friary Farm on a sunny Sunday afternoon, winding my way around the luxury static caravans to the Blakeney reserve office adjacent to the caravan park. Seasonal warden Chris met me and gave me a key for the volunteer accommodation beside the windmill. He directed me to the room beside the kitchen, stating that the other bedroom was for the lads on the Point to use on their days off.

That evening, seasonal Point warden Richard had a night off. Richard had spent the previous summer as a seasonal warden on the Farne Islands in Northumberland, also managed by the National Trust. He spent most of his days off birdwatching on the Point, in search of rare migrants. But now that the spring migration was truly over, he was using his weekly days off as a chance to explore the Norfolk coast.

We walked the short distance to Friary Hills. These had been formed by glacial deposits at the end of the last ice age. There was a time when the sea reached right up to the base of them, where wharves were created for boat building and repairs. Standing on top of a bench to see over the mass of gorse, we looked out over the Blakeney Freshes. Richard casually commented how it wasn't a bad back garden. This was to be my back garden for the next year.

Before me lay a patchwork of lush, green fields, silvery water and swishing reeds dotted with bushes. The Great Barnett, formerly a tidal creek, carries water from the River Glaven through the middle of Blakeney Freshes and out into the harbour through a culvert. The water levels are carefully managed throughout the year to create optimum conditions for breeding waders and overwintering wildfowl.

Over the course of my year volunteering on the reserve, I went on many walks along the coastal path around Blakeney Freshes. From the hills, one morning, I was treated to my first view of an otter. It bounded across an open field before disappearing into the reeds.

On a cold evening in February, after hours of searching, I finally caught my first view of a special bird I had longed to see for years – the bittern. A magic, milestone moment.

As a child, I had enjoyed identifying birds on the River Welland and at the Peakirk Waterfowl Gardens. Grey Herons were my favourite – seeming so big to a small child. I flicked through my parents' *Field Guide to the Birds of Britain and Ireland* and saw the other birds in the heron family: purple heron, spoonbill and bittern. I made it my mission to one day see them all in the wild.

The spoonbill was relatively easy to see during my first week in north Norfolk. I went to Cley Marshes, lifted up the hide flap and there was one on a scrape. Bingo! Although it did tease me by initially keeping its bill tucked away as it rested.

On the edge of Blakeney Freshes is a small wildfowl collection: a selection of exotic ducks with clipped wings owned by the Blakeney Wildfowling Association. It reminded me of Peakirk. Richard hated it, saying that people come to Blakeney and the first birds they see are non-native species in captivity. Conversely, the Point's other seasonal warden, Paul, pointed out that a lifelong appreciation and interest in birds can begin with the opportunity to easily access and observe them up close. It quickly became clear to me that, within the small and close-knit Blakeney team, there was a range of different opinions of what conservation meant. I could usually see both sides.

Over the course of my first few weeks at Blakeney, I spent much time on the Freshes with Chris and Graham, learning my way around – which ditches had crossings, which didn't, where we could and couldn't drive the various estate vehicles, which fields the trust owned and who the various other local landowners were.

One of the owners had built a private boardwalk into the reeds where the 'ping' of calling bearded tits (or 'bearded reedlings', as Chris called them) could be heard. These small, moustached birds are more often heard than seen, staying out of sight on windy days, tucked away in the safety of the reedbed – and most days seem to be windy on the Norfolk coast.

Chris taught me that birdwatching – in particular, his monitoring of breeding birds – is about patience and being able to relax into it. Much better to wait patiently in the same spot than to keep frantically dotting around and missing, or even disturbing, what you are trying to observe.

Three years previously, the north-east corner of Blakeney Freshes had become separated by a wide man-made channel. Shingle from

Blakeney Point getting pushed into the River Glaven, where it enters Blakeney Harbour, was increasing flood pressure further upstream. Cutting a wide new channel a few hundred metres south enabled more water to be washed out to sea more quickly, solving this problem.

The result was a sort of no-man's-land between the Point and Freshes: Chapel Island. So named due the flint foundations of a medieval building on the slightly raised ground of Blakeney Eye, Faden's 1797 map of Norfolk marks the building as 'chapel ruins'. A map from 1586 shows a man with dog and rabbits, suggesting it may have been a warren lodge. The discovery of a coin, found during excavations ahead of the river realignment, suggests that it may have been a toll building where ships were charged and possibly also blessed before heading out to sea. Indeed, Cley had one of the country's busiest ports between the fourteenth and seventeenth centuries.

An unforgettable moment occurred during my first few days on the Freshes. I walked along the edge of the Great Barnett, through the rough grass. Suddenly, a large bird emerged from behind a tussock, just a few metres ahead of me. Seemingly as shocked as I was, it took to the air clumsily, half-flying towards the reedbed. I knew instinctively that this was one of the juvenile marsh harriers that had hatched nearby, now developed enough to fly but still mastering the art. Practically making eye contact with such a rare bird was awesome, but the encounter also gave me a greater appreciation for how vulnerable young birds are, even large raptors.

Managing natures reserves is a fine art of balancing access and conservation. Giving everyone access to nature is so important. Sir David Attenborough famously stated, 'No one will protect what they don't care about, and no one will care about what they have never experienced.'

Throughout my time at Blakeney, I encountered the many ways people can experience wildlife: from the stunning seal trips to the miles of footpaths offering wild views. Like my colleagues, I shared my enthusiasm and growing understanding of the reserve with visitors, encouraging them to support our conservation work. But the marsh harrier experience highlighted the importance of ensuring certain areas are free from human access for the benefit of wildlife. Some creatures really do need space away from people.

Except for the old cart track, which intersects the eastern side of the Freshes, there is no public access onto them. The coastal path, running along the top of the sea wall, gives walkers pleasant views from a safe distance. Wildlife can behave naturally, providing dogs are kept under close control, as dogs are seen by birds as predators.

They are also seen as predators by cattle. In contrast to the relative wilderness of Blakeney Point, the Freshes are very much a managed habitat. As well as controlling the water levels and creating ponds for wildfowl and waders, the grass height is managed for their benefit. This involves cattle grazing between May and October using local tenants.

On my early orientation walks around the Freshes, I was taught how to behave around the cattle. Always closing gates and ensuring they are securely shackled was obvious, as was identifying the bull in the herd. It was also very important not to get between calves and their mothers.

The farmers were responsible for daily welfare checks and any supplementary feeding, which was more for the benefit of being able to handle them than for their diet as there was ample vegetation for them to eat. Whenever we brought the HiLux or Land Rover Defender onto the fields, the cattle would associate it with being fed, so passing through gates needed to be swift and smooth to avoid being followed too closely.

The ditch between field numbers 6 and 7 was shallow in summertime and frequently crossed by the herd. On one occasion, a calf making the crossing had strayed into a deeper section of the ditch and become stuck. Chris and I found it. By this time, the rest of the herd had moved on, leaving it alone, tired and weak from struggling. The owner was called immediately and was nearby, so he was able to come and save its life. Such is the diversity and unpredictability of a warden's job, often being first on the scene of unexpected incidents. Fortunately, this one had a happy ending. To prevent any further danger to the cattle, we placed several large flints along the crossing point to reduce the depth of the water.

Where grazing cattle are involved, ragwort control is necessary to prevent them ingesting it. This is most prescient when grass is being harvested for hay, as dried ragwort is more likely to be eaten than fresh plants growing in fields, which most livestock tend to instinctively avoid. Although ragwort is an important nectar and food source for many insects, uprooting this toxic plant is a job almost every conservation volunteer will experience. I was already acquainted with it from previous work experience at Deeping Lakes with the Lincolnshire Wildlife Trust.

On the last Sunday of July, Chris and I were assisted by the Norfolk National Trust volunteer group. Pulling ragwort is better done in a group as it increases effectiveness and motivation. The group knew from experience that tea, coffee and cake helps, too. One member was actually heard to complain at the disappointingly low amount of ragwort available to pull. Indeed, we finished early and spent the remainder of the afternoon walking the coast path and picking litter. Sadly, litter picking is a never-ending job. Chatting to the volunteers as we worked, many of them remarked how lucky I was to be at the start of a year in this truly wonderful location.

I was indeed very grateful and excited, although, in truth, I was still settling in and finding my feet. Living alone for the first time and adjusting to north Norfolk life, it took a few weeks for the place to really get under my skin. But, slowly and surely, it really did – more profoundly than I had imagined.

3

Back and Forth

THROUGHOUT JULY, I WENT out to the Point by boat once a week. This was to give me a varied experience and also to help increase cover while the wardens took it in turn to use up some of their leave before autumn migration began.

On my second trip, I went on a seal ferry to familiarise myself with their commentary and get better acquainted with some of the ferry staff. Richard was on his own that afternoon, so we took it in turns on the gap, just as I had done with Graham the week before. It is important that there is always a minimum of two wardens on the Point at peak times.

Somewhere around 5 p.m., when Richard was satisfied there were no more walkers heading up the beach, he took me onto Middle Point to watch the terns. Richard confided that he had initially thought Near Point was called 'Nare' Point due to his colleagues' Norfolk accents.

Tucked inconspicuously into the dunes at the end of Middle Point, we watched the colony from a safe distance. The evening air was full of sound: the cries of Sandwich terns and black-headed gulls plus the occasional piping calls of oystercatchers. Terns could be seen flying in with small fish glinting in the sunlight. Through a telescope, I could see a group of juvenile terns on the edge of the colony. I watched carefully to see if I could spot any of them being fed.

As well as witnessing successful tern feeds, I also observed klep-toparasitism: black-headed gulls attempting to steal the fish that the terns were bringing in. This gave an insight into the complex relation-ship between the black-headed gulls and Sandwich terns. A tern may have expended considerable energy flying several miles to procure a fish for their chick, only to have it snatched by a black-headed gull to feed its own young without having to leave the colony to catch it. This means that the terns are more likely to successfully feed their chicks if they choose smaller fish that aren't so easy for the gulls to spot. If a fish has been out of the sea for some time, it must be dipped in water to help it slide down the chick's throat before any gulls have the chance to snatch it from them. The black-headed gulls have a more varied diet than the terns, foraging for earthworms on the mainland as well as stealing fish. They have even been seen to pull fish out of tern chicks' throats.

Although you could be forgiven for thinking the gulls are of no ben-efit to the terns, they do in fact provide a big advantage. Black-headed gulls are much more aggressive towards predators than Sandwich terns. I had seen a BBC wildlife documentary showing Arctic terns dive-bombing Bill Oddie on the Scottish island of Saint Kilda, but Sandwich terns do not behave so boldly. The inconvenience of having occasional fish stolen is outweighed by the security they gain against aerial preda-tors by nesting beside the gulls.

Watching the drama of the colony is so absorbing, especially with hundreds of individuals to observe. Richard, meanwhile, was a little perturbed that the nearby beach colony was very jumpy. Largely con-cealed from where we were sitting by the Far Point dunes, a smaller colony of common and little terns were nesting on the beach. Like the main ternery, we had been protecting this colony all afternoon while on gap duty. It was not clear what was putting the terns up as no bird of prey or crow could be seen.

Having dedicated his summer to protecting the breeding terns, it was clear Richard wouldn't relax until the birds settled. On that occasion, there was no obvious cause for their jumpiness, but he kept watch and made a note of it, with intent to watch them carefully the following day to be absolutely sure that there was not a problem. For example, a small mammalian predator, such as a rat or a stoat, on the ground could be almost impossible to spot from afar.

The tide being far out and the beach exposed, Richard took the quad bike to Cley beach to pick up Point warden Eddie, who was returning from a day off laden with a week's provisions. I sat on a fish box in the trailer behind the quad bike, bouncing along as we travelled over sea-carved bumps across the inter-tidal sands.

Visit number three was particularly eventful, and not just because it was my first time staying overnight in the Lifeboat House. On this occasion, Chris took me out there in the *Whittow*. With us in the boat was Toby, a 17-year-old work experience student from Fakenham College on the penultimate day of his two-week stint.

Chris steered the boat along Morston Creek, veering west into Blakeney Harbour, a route I was now becoming familiar with. We soon spotted a capsized sailing dinghy. As we drew closer, we saw two men in the water. They were older gentlemen and looked quite cold. Keeping calm, Chris pulled up alongside and I helped him pull the men into the boat, one by one.

Newly hatched ringed plover chick on the shingle, July 2009. (Ajay Tegala)

We took them back to Morston Quay as quickly as possible, so they could get dry and warm up. Chris later said that he was quite worried about one of the men, whose lips were turning blue. Thankfully, they were both okay and later sent their thanks to the reserve office.

Toby and I walked up the steps to the Lifeboat House and explained how the supplies we had brought had got wet in the drama. The wardens had some news of their own. A ringed plover nest outside the house had just hatched. I was given special permission to photograph the delightful chick, quickly and carefully – a fluffy ping-pong ball on stilts. As I was approaching it, the adult bird noticed me and gave a warning call. The chick responded by getting down low and blending in with the shingle.

Our group task for the morning – while the tide was still up – was to lay the final section of recycled plastic boardwalk. The main walkway had been completed the previous autumn, but there was a section at the highest point to be made into a viewing platform. We had fun dragging a ready-joined section of boards up the steep incline, trying not to slip over. As we completed the boardwalk, the clouds dispersed, and the temperature rose.

With low tide approaching, I did a stint at the gap, which I described in my diary: 'Absolutely beautiful views of golden sand, blue sea and sky. The sun on my back, a light breeze blowing though my hair. The distant sound of seals.' By now, I was more confident talking to visitors, better able to answer their questions and explain the sensitivities of the site. I had developed a technique of beginning every conversation with a polite opening, which I felt was successful. I recorded in my diary how 'I even spoke to a party of people who were breaking rules by putting up tents. They understood and did not argue.'

Not every instance was to be as smooth as this one. There has to be a blanket no camping rule on sensitive nature reserves such as Blakeney. If you allow one person to bend the rules, others might notice and follow suit. This could lead to increased litter in the dunes, increased disturbance to vulnerable ground-nesting birds, increased trampling of special plants and increased risk of fire, hence the no open fires or barbecues rule.

Indeed, one of the high tide duties is to patrol the landing ridge to ensure no visitors are keeping oystercatchers away from their nests or having barbecues. The dry marram grass in the dunes could easily catch light and fire would quickly spread. This had been a problem on plenty of other sites. For example, further up the east coast, in Northumberland, a floating lantern had set fire to the sand dunes at Lindisfarne, home of the endemic Lindisfarne helleborine.

Some holidaymakers inevitably saw the wardens as killjoys, spoiling their beach fun. However, it was done with good reason. Not to prevent people enjoying themselves but to protect one of the country's key wildlife sites. Our role was not just to protect the reserve but to try and help every visitor appreciate the beauty and fragility as much as possible. The ambitious goal we were all working towards was that one day, everyone visiting any wildlife site would know how to behave and not cause any disturbance.

Another goal for that afternoon, which felt ambitious at the time, was walking from the Lifeboat House to Cley beach and back for the first time. It was a chance for Point warden Eddie to give me a tour of the whole site and at the same time return Toby safely to his mother. The nature of Blakeney Harbour means it only holds enough water to travel by boat between the Point and Morston for a limited window around high tide: up to two hours before and after high water, depending on tide height, wind strength and wind direction.

It is possible to walk off the Point to Cley beach at any state of tide, except during the very fiercest of winter storms. At low tide, the wardens' quad bike and trailer can be used along the sand, but Eddie explained that he tried to use this as infrequently as possible, to save fuel and prevent disturbing the atmosphere. For visitors blissfully enjoying the peace of the place, a noisy quad bike speeding past can be startling and irritating. Besides, walking gives the opportunity to check on the rest of the Point, which can easily be overlooked when the wardens' time is largely occupied at the western end and around the Lifeboat House.

We walked off along the beach, following the water's edge. Eddie pointed out wading birds on the shoreline, which up until now I had only seen pictures of in my bird guide: sanderling, dunlin and turn-stone. He also pointed out birds moving along the coast further out to sea: a small number of gannets in the distance. The more you looked, the more you could see.

Eddie explained that true birdwatchers walk on the shingle ridge rather than the beach, looking for birds among the Suaeda bushes. So, we did this on the walk back, after a Tunnock's chocolate caramel wafer for an energy boost.

'Suaeda' comes from the scientific name for shrubby sea-blite, a dominant plant on the shingle ridge, although nationally scarce. Of Mediterranean origin, here it is at the northern limit of its range. The most northerly bush is at Gibraltar Point, across the Wash on the south-eastern tip of the Lincolnshire coast. Able to withstand occasional tidal inundation and invigorated by shingle burial, it is one of the few plants that thrives in this rare, vegetated shingle habitat. Its thin waxy leaves provide cover for birds in need of shelter having just migrated across the North Sea. This is why Suaeda is the haunt of the birdwatcher, it may hold resting rare birds hidden within it.

We paused briefly near the Watch House. Dating back to 1835, it is the oldest building on Blakeney Point. Built by the Preventative Men, forerunners to Customs and Excise, as a lookout for smugglers, it ironi-cally ended up being used to store contraband. The building was used as a coastguard lookout in both world wars and was manned by the founder of Bean's Boats, William 'Trip' Bean, in the Second World War. After the war, it was used by the Girl Guides for a period, before falling into disrepair. Blakeney Parish Council set up a trust, which organised a fundraising programme to restore the building and turned it into a basic, but unique, holiday rental property, sleeping eight.

The Watch House and surrounding landscape had featured as a location in the dark, satirical 2005 art house mockumentary film, *Brothers of the Head*. The film tells the bizarre story of conjoined twins who spend their childhood at the Watch House and go on to become 1970s rock stars. Author Piers Warren went on to use the Watch House as the setting for his 2011 supernatural thriller *Black Shuck*, a novel about the East Anglian ghostly black dog of English folklore.

Eddie told me that the building is also known as Halfway House because, at one time, it had been halfway along the Point. However, the spit has since grown in length. The location of the house is thought to be approximately where the spit ended around 1500. A sea chart from 1693 shows a small headland of sand dunes level with Morston village.

The Old Lifeboat House was built around 1862 – replacing an earlier one that had fallen into decay – at what was then the end of the Point. Everything west of the new lifeboat house – built in 1898 to house a larger lifeboat – has grown since that time. The Point grew considerably in the first quarter of the twentieth century, which led to the abandonment of the lifeboat house as it was no longer suitably located for prompt launching.

Our bird of the day was spotted in the sand dunes as we approached the headland. Conversation had turned to football when an owl caught our attention, much longer winged than a barn owl and a browner colour, glowing gold in the evening light. A short-eared owl – my first. I failed to capture it with my camera but savoured the moment.

It is a tradition to buy a beer for your accompanying birdwatchers whenever you see a bird species for the first time, known as a 'birding tick' because the bird can be ticked off your list. Miles from the nearest drinking place, Eddie, Paul and Richard had set up their own private pub in the Lifeboat House. Every two weeks, Woodforde's Norfolk Brewery would deliver two polypins of their Wherry ale to the Friary Farm office. From there, it was taken out to the Lifeboat House, either by boat or quad bike. It was stored in the cleaning cupboard, actually in the visitor centre but safely under lock and key.

The supply was such that each warden could have up to four pints an evening without drinking the supply dry before the next delivery. This meant there was usually some spare for guests, although a tally of every pint poured was kept scribbled on a piece of scrap paper pinned to the kitchen wall. As a volunteer, mine was on the house, although I would always take cake or biscuits with me whenever I visited, a sort of unofficial trade for ale and always appreciated by the ever-peckish wardens.

Graham had painted a slightly chaotic picture of the wardens' living conditions, so I was pleasantly surprised by the refined evening I spent on the Point. Tea was always served in a teapot. Paul cooked an evening meal of roast vegetables, Yorkshire pudding and gravy – no meat because Eddie was attempting to be vegetarian like his girlfriend, Bee, so Eddie's days off tended to be a meat feast for his carnivorous colleagues.

After dinner, we stood on the back steps of the Lifeboat House with telescopes. Technically, these were actually at the front of the building, overlooking the harbour towards Stiffkey. Approximately thirty little egrets were observed flying to roost in the trees behind Stiffkey Fen. These were written in the bird log, along with the day's notable bird sightings, listed carefully in taxonomic order. In the background, Classic FM was playing on the radio.

I spent the night in the downstairs bedroom and woke early to the sound of calling oystercatchers. A distinctive call, but far from being synonymous with serenity. Having referred to the mere few slices of bread I had brought with me as 'prison food', Paul rustled up bacon and eggs for breakfast.

In the downtime between jobs, I was encouraged to read from the wealth of books in the Lifeboat House. After flicking through a few recent editions of the *Norfolk Bird and Mammal Report*, I read former warden Ted Eales' memoirs cover to cover. I found it fascinating to learn more about the history of the Point and its protection.

I also picked up a delightful book called *Redshank's Warning*, a sort of *Famous Five*-style story about a family from Newmarket coming to Blakeney on holiday and visiting the Point. It painted the place in an idyllic light and increased my appreciation for the opportunity to stay out there.

Somewhat out of place amongst the natural history books, stood a 1960s edition of Kathryn Hulme's *The Nun's Story*. Paul had gone through it and scribbled comical and slightly tongue-in-cheek alternative chapter titles. I couldn't resist joining in and offered 'Mother Superior ... Daughter Inferior'.

Walking off the Point to Cley beach later in the day, I experienced the phenomenon of the Point's localised microclimate. It was raining hard on the mainland, just half a mile away, but perfectly dry on the spit. A little later, it even appeared to be raining out to sea. I did eventually get wet, shortly before arriving at Cley, where head warden Dave collected me in the HiLux. When he asked me how I found my first night on the Point, I told him how impressed I was with their civilised lifestyle. I wrote in my diary, 'Staying overnight in the Lifeboat House was a great experience ... enabling an insight into the wardens' lifestyles and opinions.'

Three days later, Dave took me out to the Point by boat for a second overnight stint. Walking along the landing ridge to the Lifeboat House in the heavy rain, I met a UCL lecturer and his wife coming out to stay in the Old Lifeboat House for a couple of days to do some research. Eddie's girlfriend, Bee, was holding fort and made us all tea, before helping turn the gas on for the Old Lifeboat House.

Between helping cover gap duty and entering the bird log data onto a spreadsheet, I chatted to seasonal warden Paul about his connection with the Point. This was his third consecutive season.

Eddie had been a seasonal warden the year before Paul started, when Dave was the lead warden on the Point. In the autumn, Dave was promoted to head warden and became mainland based. Eddie, having enjoyed his seasonal contract and made a good impression, became Dave's replacement on the Point. Eddie had suggested that Paul should apply for the seasonal warden role, knowing his ornithological knowledge and personality would be a good fit. Dave also thought that having a familiar face on his team would benefit Eddie during his first season in charge out on the Point: a big responsibility and considerable step up from assistant.

It was clear to me that cooperation and teamwork are so important. From negotiating days off, so that the Point is always appropriately staffed, to maintaining good working and social relationships while living closely together, it seemed to me that the 2009 Point team really gelled. However, Richard later told me that he found it difficult when he started; having high standards, he was a little frustrated that daily life on the Point wasn't as organised and efficient as he felt it could be. However, they clearly all shared an unshakable dedication to protecting the breeding birds and fragile habitats.

They were also enthusiastic about insects. A Robinson moth trap was run overnight for my benefit. Being in the downstairs room, I set my alarm for dawn to cover the trap with a towel to stop any moths escaping before they had been identified. After breakfast, we worked our way through the egg boxes, which the moths were resting in. The common species were pointed out to me, and I tried to make a mental note of their appearance to speed up my identification for future surveys. I helped flick through the identification guides to find some of the more obscure ones. Some individuals had become worn and so were harder to identify. It also became apparent that there was variation within the same species. This was the case for the extremely variable rustic moth, and the aptly named uncertain moth.

I was grateful to have my eyes opened to the world of moths. All too often disregarded as butterflies' dull, nocturnal cousins, they can in fact be just as colourful and beautiful. It takes the dedication of putting a light out at night to encounter a true flavour of their diversity. This was part of the wardens' programme of routine monitoring. Much care was put into identifying each individual moth, with the records collated and submitted to the Norfolk county recorder at the end of the year.

One of the most abundant species on this occasion was the large, pale-brown drinker moth, so named because the larvae supposedly drink drops of dew. We also caught five different species of yellow underwing of varying sizes. Perhaps the most appealing moth was the garden tiger, with its distinctive black, white and orange markings. We had twenty-two of these in the trap. There were also twelve rosy minors, a moth synonymous with coastal habitats. The largest species in the trap was a poplar hawk-moth, an inconspicuously coloured moth, except for flashes of bright red on its underwings.

Some rather impressive moth caterpillars were to be found a short walk away in the Plantation. Planted during the First World War by

Professor Oliver as an experiment to see which tree species would grow well in the dunes, the Plantation became a much-revered spot for bird-watchers as many a tired migrant songbird has appeared there after crossing the North Sea, including numerous rarities.

In the centre stands a stunted sycamore tree. Beneath it, the first watcher's dog, Prince, was buried in 1925. Black pines stand little higher than the sycamore. Self-sown white poplars overhang the perimeter fence. It was feeding on the leaves of these dwarf white poplars that I was shown the impressive caterpillars of the puss moth. When disturbed, the bright green caterpillars rear their heads and shoot extendable pink flagella from their twin tails. An impressive sight for sure. That day, my family took a seal trip and met me out on the Point. I took them to the Plantation and proudly showed them the puss moth caterpillars in all their glory.

Having demonstrated I could engage well with visitors and communicate conservation messages, I became involved in a wider shorebird protection project. The Norfolk Coast Partnership was set up in the early 1990s to focus on pressure arising from an increasing number of recreational visitors and the potential damage it could cause to areas of natural beauty. A new collaborative project between the various conservation organisations along the north Norfolk coast, titled 'Share with Care and be Aware', involved talking to visitors about the vulnerability of beach-nesting birds, such as the ringed plover. Small cards highlighting the key messages were handed out and the hours spent talking to the public were recorded. The Point wardens were able to do this as part of gap duty, but there weren't enough staff to cover the Cley end of the Point.

That is where I came in, along with ornithologist, faithful Point volunteer and all-round naturalist, Richard Porter. I first met Richard at his home, where we were both briefed on the project. He had been head of species conservation for the RSPB, starting out as an investigations officer in the 1970s, making a name for himself by helping to bring to justice egg collectors; people – almost exclusively men – who illegally steal wild birds' eggs for their private collections.

Once acceptable and common, egg collecting became illegal in Great Britain in 1954 due to the undeniable negative impact on bird populations. Richard had been involved in a five-day chase through the Scottish Highlands in pursuit of two men who had raided golden eagle nests.

A contemporary magazine described a 30-year-old Richard Porter as:

> ... perhaps one of the first members of the eco generation, although instead of expressing just vague hippie-like concern with the Earth, he has a very precise objective: to protect the wild birds that fascinated him as a Cockney kid.

Richard was retired but was still very much involved in the world of conservation, on a global scale, with Bird Life International in the Middle East. In particular, the Central Marshes of Iraq. At the time I first met him, he was involved in producing the first bird guide to be printed in Arabic.

Richard would walk up the Point, from Cley beach, as often as he could, recording the butterflies and birds he observed and passing his data on to the Point team. At that time, he was systematically mapping the plants growing along the Point. Throughout my placement year, I went on to help Richard collate and format his plant data to produce abundance maps for the publication of his Blakeney Point plant atlas.

Spending so much time on the reserve for his botanical and ornithological research meant he was ideally placed to help engage with walkers. In fact, Richard has a real talent for communicating to any audience.

I proudly shared how a conversation I had with a lady at Cley beach had lasted almost half an hour, agreeing on the importance of giving wildlife space. My colleagues politely pointed out that this was 'preaching to the converted' and altering the mindset of those who were less wildlife aware was the key to the project's success. I had to up my game.

On 3 August, I took my third and final overnight trip to the Point of the summer, as well as my sixth visit in a month. It marked the beginning of the end of the breeding bird season. I was dropped at Cley beach with my sleeping bag and supplies, where I was met by the quad bike and trailer. About 2 miles or so along the beach, we stopped to carry out our task for the morning: taking down the little tern fencing between the Watch House and the Hood. The name 'Hood' may have come from 'hook' originally, as it was probably a shingle hook on which the present sand dune system was formed.

This area of shingle, vegetated primarily by sea sandwort, had hosted thirty pairs of little terns that summer, who had fledged twenty-one young. With settled weather, no persistent predator problems and apparently moderate prey availability, it had been a pretty good summer and a succinct breeding season for this colony. Little terns are the first of the Point's four breeding tern species to begin their return migration to Africa, vacating the colony from late July onwards.

With no breeding birds or young left within this enclosure, there was no longer a need to exclude visitors from this part of the reserve. I helped wind in the orange baler twine and twist out the rusty metal stakes, which we tied in bundles of ten and loaded carefully into the trailer. The bundles were then stored underneath the Lifeboat House ready to be used again the following spring.

Over the past two weeks, there had been an invasion of hoverflies and ladybirds. They were doubtlessly moving along the coast. That warm and sunny day, as we travelled from Cley beach to the Lifeboat House, we estimated that there were literally millions of marmalade hoverflies and two-spot ladybirds. Sitting at the gap that afternoon, numerous ladybirds landed on me. In their desperation for food, they would actually bite. It was a crazy experience, never before had I ever seen half as many. The wardens told me that back in May, there had also been a painted lady invasion, when they estimated a peak of 18,500 butterflies came in off the sea in a single day. Bee had been out surveying in a boat and seen a long string of them flying above the sea.

Between 4 and 5 in the afternoon, I was on gap duty. The sunshine was glorious, and the beach was quiet. At precisely 4.40 p.m., I officially became 20 years old. I marked the end of my teen years with a solitary dip in the sea. On returning to the Lifeboat House, I casually mentioned that I was at last no longer a teenager and we had a few drinks accompanied by a Swiss roll for a birthday cake. I noted in my diary, 'The night was rounded off with a perfect glimpse of the moon reflected in the sea.'

4

Holiday Season

WITH AUGUST UNDER WAY and the summer holidays in full swing, most of the next four weeks were spent helping the team at Morston Quay. The car park and information centre were managed by wardens Graham and Chris, alongside three visitor reception assistants: Ray, Penny and Kim. They were a great team and welcomed the hundreds of daily visitors with excellent customer service and good humour.

The information centre was built in 1984, the year Graham first worked on the reserve. Since then, he had spent countless hours conversing with visitors there, answering their questions, enhancing their experience and helping them board the ferry trips to see the seals. By far the most commonly asked question was, 'Where do I pick up the ferries?' To which Graham would sometimes respond by jokingly saying that the ferries weighed a ton, therefore picking them up was not recommended.

By the end of the twentieth century, the majority of seal trips went out of Morston Quay rather than Blakeney. This was because Blakeney Quay was progressively silting up, making it shallower and therefore harder to launch ferries safely and reliably. There had been attempts to dredge the channel, but it became clear this would have to be done regularly to become effective, fighting against a natural process.

Some ferry companies launched occasional trips from Blakeney on spring tides and some still sold their tickets on Blakeney Quay, although most of the trips went from Morston. This often caused frustration when cars had paid to park at Blakeney and then had to pay again at Morston for the seal trip itself, as the parking tickets are not transferable between the two locations. (National Trust members can, however, park at both places for free.) Sometimes tourists would arrive at Morston in a frantic state, racing to get their boat in time, having sped along the coast road from Blakeney. Our mission was to help these people to park, relax and get to their boat.

I quickly learned the four companies and what colours their boats and smocks were. Bean's have white boats with an orange rim. There were two brothers, John and Graham, sons of 'Trip' Bean, who had started Bean's Boats in the mid-1930s with his brother, Kitch. Graham Bean sold his tickets on Blakeney Quay and John from his cottage in Morston. So, seal trippers needed to know which Bean they had booked with in order to get on the right boat. Graham Bean's crew wore orange smocks and John Bean's crew wore blue smocks.

Temple's Seal Trips have also been operating since the first half of the twentieth century. They wear red smocks and have white boats with a red rim. Jim Temple took over the business from his father, William, in the late 1960s. The family have a long connection with the Morston Anchor Inn and sell their tickets from there.

Bishop's Boats have two grey former lifeboats with a red rim. Their tickets were sold on Blakeney Quay. Bishop's Boats started in 1965, running people from Blakeney Quay to Blakeney Point and, over time, had branched out into seal trips running primarily from Morston, but still launching from Blakeney on spring tides.

The fourth and smallest company was called Moreton's at the time. Tickets were sold on Blakeney Quay, but they launched from Morston in a white boat with a blue rim: *Ptarmigan*, which originally belonged to warden, Ted Eales. It was named after his favourite bird, although not a bird that has ever been recorded in Blakeney, which perhaps added a sense of humour to the boat's name. Indeed, customers on the boat needed a sense of humour on one occasion when the skipper, a little worse for wear after a few pints, ran it aground. Passengers were asked to get out and help him push the ferry into deeper water – or so I was told.

Even in August, Morston was relatively quiet at low tide, with the majority of visitors coming solely for the seal trips at high tide. The information centre only opened around high tide. So, over the course of a fortnight, opening times became progressively later until a split tide, when it would open both in the morning and evening. Throughout August, Graham, Chris and I would assist at Morston over the high-tide periods and carry out our warden duties across the reserve at low tide.

On a Monday morning, I would accompany Graham to the bank in Holt to pay in the cash from the weekend and previous week. Millie, Graham and Marilyn's beautiful and lovely natured black Labrador, rode with us in the Land Rover. She would lean against me as we turned the tighter corners along the 5-mile journey.

The money included cash from both the Blakeney and Morston car park machines, which we would count by hand and bag up ready for banking. Some of the cashiers would jokingly pretend to close their counters when they saw us, knowing we would be giving them lots of coins to weigh. At the time, neither car park machine took card payments and nor did Morston Information Centre, which only sold memberships, car parking, boat parking and three books: the Blakeney souvenir guidebook, an old book about Blakeney Point and Scolt Head Island and a *Flowers of the Norfolk Coast* guide. Postcards and keyrings could be bought from the café next door, who also only took cash.

Prior to 2010, the Morston car park did not have marked parking bays. So the Land Rover would be strategically parked to start a row of cars, using yellow traffic cones to mark the end of the row. It was impressive how invariably visitors would park beside it with others following in a row. We had to arrive in good time, otherwise an early car in the wrong place could mess up our pattern and reduce the number of car parking spaces. Every space could well be needed on a busy August day.

We would move the Land Rover forwards or backwards to start the next line. Just before the main car park became full, we put out arrow signs to direct cars over the flood bank into the overflow car park. If this ever became full, that left the lower quay, which we generally tried to keep free for disabled parking and the ferry operators.

On spring tides, the lower quay can be completely submerged, as can most of Blakeney Quay. Every year, there are cases of tourists who fail to appreciate that Blakeney Quay will flood as the tide comes in, often resulting in salt damage to their cars.

Although all of the ferry companies are completely independent, the nature reserve benefits from them in a number of ways. Principally, the trips enable thousands of visitors to have fantastic views of the seals and terns on the end of the Point without causing disturbance. The advantage of this cannot be underestimated. Additionally, the ferrymen are extra eyes, able to report any issues to the wardens, for example, if a private boat was to land on the tip. In fact, most ferry operators would not hesitate to enforce the no landing rules themselves.

The National Trust are a charity, dependent on funding from grants, legacies, car parks and membership. Pay-for-entry properties, such as mansions and gardens, offer a refund of the entry fee as an incentive to take out an annual membership. A bit of clever thinking by the Blakeney team enabled the cost of a seal trip to be refunded instead, regardless of the fact that the trips were not run by the trust. This proved immensely successful, combined with the feel-good factor of a wonderful wildlife experience.

Not having any interest or desire to be a salesman, I didn't think I would take to promoting membership. But, watching the team work, I felt a desire to join in. It was at the car park machine that we would engage with visitors, 'Have you come to feed our machine? It's £3 for a non-member, flat rate, until midnight if you so desire.' Note the friendliness, light-heartedness and subtle mention of membership. Quite often people would say, 'Oh, I am a member', in which case they did not need to pay and could enjoy the fact that their membership was helping us take care of this important nature reserve. Indeed, those paying for parking were also helping fund our nature conservation work, which we would always mention to those reluctant to part with their hard-earned cash. We felt it was good value, especially compared to the cost of most city car parks, which didn't offer seals or saltmarsh.

It wasn't a hard sell. If we could see someone was clearly in a rush to make their boat, we would help them get a ticket as quickly as possible and direct them to the right boat. We gave out little leaflets with the membership prices listed alongside how much we would refund for their seal trip. This gave people the chance to go away and consider membership. Obviously, it didn't appeal to everyone, but a good number of people were already tempted to join and we were able to show them the many benefits of membership. For a family freshly arrived on holiday in Norfolk, they could make back most of the cost of annual membership in a week by visiting the other local properties: Blickling Hall, Felbrigg Hall, Sheringham Park and Oxburgh Hall.

It was such a thrill the first time somebody I had spoken to came back to sign up. The membership forms were read by a machine, so had to be filled out correctly with black ink and block capitals, so we would always fill out the form for people. Sevens couldn't be crossed either, which was something I had done for years. Graham or Ray would look over my shoulder and whisper, 'Seven!' to make sure I didn't cross them. Within a week, I had stopped crossing my sevens and actually haven't ever crossed a single one since.

As well as parking cars, providing information, promoting membership and directing people to the toilet block, one of our Morston tasks was to check cars for parking noncompliance. If a car failed to show a valid ticket or membership sticker, we issued a notice asking them to purchase a ticket and attach it to the note so that we could cross their number plate off our list. This enabled the trust to gain a considerable amount of money towards caring for the reserve, which otherwise it would miss out on.

Naturally, not everyone would pay, and other times we would just not see their ticket if it had fallen into the footwell or been blown with the wind. On a couple of occasions, not knowing everyone's vehicles, I ticketed a ferry operator. This was usually met with good humour and even helped me build a friendship with the likes of Jason Bean, who would sometimes pop in to borrow a pair of binoculars.

John Bean was quite sociable too. I once bought a ticket for one of my visiting friends to go on his trip and he insisted on giving it for free. He was getting on in years and had a few health and mobility problems, so he would travel from his home in the village to the quay on his quad bike. There is a story that he was once running a bit late for a trip. He sped through the car park to the lower quay, churning up a cloud of dust. His passengers were stood in a line, waiting and watching as he crashed into a stack of lobster pots. He got up, dusted himself down, picked up his clipboard and started loading them onto the ferry as if nothing had happened.

I guess, just like us in the information centre, their jobs were almost like performances. You would arrive at work, step into character and provide the public with the persona and information they wanted. The true stars of the show were of course the seals, but Temple's skipper, Derek, became a bit of a tourist attraction himself, being so animated and entertaining when delivering his commentary and chatting to customers.

One of the ferrymen with Bean's Boats was Joe Reed. He had been warden on the Point for twenty years from the early 1980s and was promoted to property manager in the mid-1990s. Joe had managed Graham and later Dave, before retiring in 2003. He still leased the café next to the information centre. Joe's wife, Janet, had managed the tearoom in the Lifeboat House, just as Ted Eales' wife, Betty, Billy Eales' wife, May, and Bob Pinchen's wife, Alice, had all done since it opened in 1923. Eventually, running a tearoom on the Point ceased to be cost-effective and so it was moved to Morston Quay at the start of the new millennium. A decade on, it was surprising how many visitors still expected there to be a tearoom in the Lifeboat House.

Joe and Janet's younger son, Mike, ran the Morston café with various assistants. When they were growing up, Mike and his elder brother, Paul – who went on to become a butcher in nearby Holt – lived in the Lifeboat House with their parents during the summer months. As an assistant, one of Graham's jobs had been to take them across the harbour to get to school. Not many children go to school by boat.

There was a great camaraderie in the Morston Information Centre team, and it extended to the café team next door. At the end of a frantic high tide, we would sometimes chill out together with a well-deserved ice cream. There was a lot of banter between Graham and Ray, who was talking about retiring soon. Kim was also great company and it turned out she had been to the same university campus as me, Brackenhurst, now part of Nottingham Trent University. When she was there, it was still an independent college, so it was great to hear her memories.

Ray didn't really agree with people volunteering, essentially working for free. However, I knew that volunteering would benefit my future career and I enjoyed it. As well as giving me an advantage over my course-mates who weren't doing a placement year, it was a chance to really experience working on a nature reserve, to acquire skills and knowledge and also to make useful contacts. I wholeheartedly recommend conservation volunteering for those reasons.

When volunteering at a different property, I had been told by a warden how he missed his volunteer days and that I should make the most of them. I think he was alluding to the fact that, as an unpaid member of staff, there is less expectation. Everything I was doing to help at Morston, on the Point and on the Freshes enhanced what the paid team were doing, and they were grateful. It is lovely to be appreciated and valued. But there obviously comes a time when you need to earn a living.

I managed to pick up a few bits of part-time work locally. I washed pots in the Wiveton Bell during their busy periods and I also worked occasional shifts at Wiveton Hall fruit farm and café, next door to the reserve office at Friary Farm. This was great for local relations as the owner, Desmond McCarthy, also owned land on the Freshes. Blakeney's property manager, John – who had succeeded Joe Reed – had also worked for Desmond as a teenager.

Desmond was a real character with his thick eyebrows and eccentricity. A few years later, he became the subject of the fly-on-the-wall documentary *Normal for Norfolk*, which ran for two series on the BBC, following Desmond's life trying to make ends meet. The summer I worked there, he was taking part in a reality programme called *Farmer Wants a Wife*, which helped promote his café but did not provide him with a love interest.

Helping at Morston, on the reserve, and working part-time, my life was busy and eventful. I was starting to feel settled. The volunteer accommodation I was living in was certainly in a fantastic location and I enjoyed relaxing in the evenings, watching wildlife. I wrote about it in my diary:

Beautiful moments on Friary Hills, watching the sunset over the harbour and the mist forming over the Freshes as several Little Egrets came in to roost, with the church bells chiming in the distance behind. This peace and emotion does not exist in built-up, urban areas. This is an honour and a privilege to witness ... and it is completely free.

Stiffkey was becoming a favourite spot too, being that bit quieter than Blakeney, Cley and Morston. After the Morston shift ended one morning, Graham and I went to Stiffkey to remove some access restriction signs now that the bird breeding season had come to an end for the year. He knew a shortcut with the Land Rover, to save us carrying the signs too far. Graham rang up Aubrey Buxton, who he called 'Lord B', to ask for permission to drive on the edge of his land.

Aubrey lived in a house previously occupied by Henry Williamson, author of *Tarka the Otter*, and had created a private reserve at Stiffkey Fen, which often attracted spoonbills. Buxton's former gamekeeper, Barrie – who was now a contractor on Blakeney Freshes – had found a long-eared owl nest in an old wood pigeon nest there.

Lord B passed away not long after. Being a politician, writer and television executive, obituaries appeared in several newspapers. Aubrey had links with Blakeney and had worked with old warden Ted Eales at local events and meetings as well as on television series. Lord Buxton was director of Anglia Television for thirty years and was best known for creating the nature documentary series *Survival*, which Ted Eales had also been very involved with. Aubrey also wrote the foreword for Ted Eales' memoirs.

One Thursday in the middle of August, when the seal trips were at their peak, an unexpected sea mammal arrived on the shores of Blakeney Point. At 12.50, Richard Porter and Eddie were leading a guided walk when Jim Temple rang to say a party from a sailing yacht were helping a dolphin back into the water on the seaward side of Far Point. Along with assistant warden Richard, the three of them sped over with a seal rescue stretcher.

On arrival, they observed that it was in fact a whale as indicated by the smallness of its dorsal fin, which was set back along its body. Identification would have to wait, but Richard Porter took photographs while the wardens assisted the sailing party in their attempts to return it to the sea. The 140cm seal stretcher was about 40cm shorter than the whale, which weighed somewhere around half a ton. Needless to say, it took eight people considerable effort and frequent stops to move it 20m to the water. Once in the water, the whale tried to swim back ashore. Eventually, it swam out into the open sea and blew three times, met by applause from the spectating ferry passengers.

The next task was to identify the species from Richard's images. With assistance from others with more marine mammal experience, it was confirmed as being a juvenile Sowerby's beaked whale, a deep-water North Atlantic cetacean. This was only the second Norfolk record, the first being at Happisburgh in August 1952.

I had popped home for a few days and so missed the drama. I heard all about it on my return to the office, where there were newspaper clippings from the *Sunday Times*, *Daily Mail* and *Mirror*, as well as the local

Sowerby's beaked whale rescue, August 2009. (Richard Porter)

Eastern Daily Press, lovingly known as the *EDP*. All contained quotes from Richard Porter as well as his photographs.

Graham was pleased that the boys had managed to save the whale. He had vivid memories of a much sadder stranding along the coast at Brancaster, three years before. It was believed that up to twenty-five young male sperm whales became trapped in the relatively shallow waters of the North Sea after becoming disorientated on their journey to polar waters.

A 50ft carcass washed up on the end of Scolt Head Island. The following tide then washed it onto Brancaster beach. Law states that the landowner becomes responsible and therefore obliged to fund the removal of a health hazard.

Removing a heavy whale carcass from a beach is a considerable challenge. In order to remove the sperm whale, the carcass had to be cut up into several pieces. A photograph of this taking place would usually be included in Graham's illustrated talks, to highlight the breadth of work encompassed by his warden role. Those with a penchant for the macabre would raise a smile when he shared the fact that the man who had the grim job of chainsawing up the carcass was from a company called Peaceful Pets.

Back in Bob Pinchen's days as warden, in the early twentieth century, a 26ft whale had washed up on Far Point, one October. Unable to be successfully buried, the carcass attracted hundreds of rats and gulls through the winter. The following April, the rats switched their diet from the whale to tern eggs.

In May, Professor Oliver brought a party of UCL botany students to the Point and offered £5 to anyone who would 'dispose of the carcass'. Four men attempted to burn the whale, armed with petrol, paraffin and coal. With Pinchen's assistance, they 'started a good blaze', which persisted for three days until all of the combustible portion had been exhausted. It was then chopped into pieces with a boat hook and buried for good. However, a few year later, a large tide washed out the buried remains and a selection of bones were subsequently washed up on the shore.

The next Blakeney Point wildlife rescue of the summer was an injured seabird. I was in the office with Chris when the phone rang. At the end of the conversation, Chris said he had a job for me. I took the Land Rover to Cley beach, where Eddie pulled up on the quad bike with a large cardboard box. Inside it was a gannet he had rescued off the beach. These large seabirds look like majestic arrows when they dive into the sea to catch fish, folding their wings back the moment before they plunge underwater. On land, they can be dangerous with their strong, sharp bills, which they instinctively use to jab at the eyes of perceived predators. Indeed, people have been blinded by gannets.

An elastic band had carefully been put around this bird's bill, but we still agreed to put it in the back so that there was no way it could escape and attack me while I was driving it to East Winch RSPCA hospital. Over the coming year, I would make a few trips to East Winch with passengers ranging from seabirds to seals.

August ended with the bank holiday weekend, which I had been warned could be the peak of the 'silly season', as well as its end. It was regarded by many as the end of the summer and a chance for one last coastal blowout. Fortunately, all breeding birds have dispersed by this time, although large groups of waders – oystercatchers by the hundred – tend to congregate in roosts.

On this particular bank holiday weekend, it was the seals that were disturbed, over on the West Sands. With a split tide, a large group of people spent the day out there, pushing the seals off their usual haul-out area. The party, described as allegedly including just about every millionaire in Norfolk, had taken plastic palm trees out with them.

The sands are in fact part of Holkham National Nature Reserve, managed by Natural England. However, they do not have the resources to protect the seals on the foreshore. The Point wardens could only watch from the other side and hope that nobody ran into any trouble. The West Sands are accessible on foot at low tide, but inexperienced walkers can end up cut off by the tide. On occasions, wardens on the Point have spotted people about to get cut-off and have been able to contact the coastguard to rescue them before they end up in real danger.

5

Quieter Times

MY INVOLVEMENT WITH AND love for all things Blakeney grew immensely throughout August. As the holiday atmosphere evaporated and autumn arrived, it was a privilege to be able to stay on and develop a deeper connection with the place. September is a month of change, with the disappearance of summer swallows – including sea swallows – and the arrival of wintering wildfowl. Experiencing my first skeins of pink-footed geese flying in V-formation directly overhead was a splendid moment. Their calls are much softer than the harsh honks of greylag and Canada geese; they seem to almost say, 'pink feet, pink feet'.

I wrote in my diary on 3 September:

> It was so different at Morston today. The weather has changed immensely, from dry and balmy August, to windy and wet September, with only a fraction of the number of cars and visitors. Such a contrast to a week ago. As Graham says, it is as if someone has turned off the tap.

The pace of the warden's life changes with both the breeding bird and tourist seasons coming to an end. It is a chance to focus on different areas of work and also to fit in some annual leave. Graham went grouse shooting on the moors of North Yorkshire. In contrast, Eddie went to Malta to monitor the illegal hunting of wild birds on their autumn migration. Indeed, the two wardens I was to spend the winter working with were chalk and cheese ... but they had a great working relationship.

Seasonal warden Chris finished his Blakeney Freshes breeding bird report a few days before his contract ended. I had the pleasure of proof-reading it.

Eddie spent many, many hours working on the Blakeney Point report into the winter. He featured a systematic list of all the birds observed on the Point, breeding and migrant, as well as sections on invertebrates, mammals, disturbance monitoring and public engagement. It ended up being over fifty pages long.

I took on an interpretation project for the viewing room above Morston Information Centre. This was something I had heard mentioned lots throughout August: how some photographs might make it appear less bare and more interesting. Producing some posters with bite-size facts on the habitats and wildlife of the reserve was something I knew I could easily achieve and would show that I was reliable. It was a pleasure and also cemented my knowledge of the reserve.

From September until February, trees and hedges can be managed without fear of disturbance to breeding birds, although wood pigeons are known to nest into October. In fact, they have been recorded breeding in every month of the year in Great Britain. The management of Blakeney Point, however, largely involves leaving natural processes to shape the landscape without intervention. Across the wider Blakeney National Nature Reserve, there are a few trees to monitor during high winds.

On Friary Hills, the gorse provides habitat for nesting linnets and long-tailed tits. I had found a nest of the latter, intricately constructed to expand as the chicks grow. The Norfolk name for long-tailed tit is 'pudding poke', because their nest resembles a suet pudding bag. Although important nesting habitat, the sprawling mass of gorse tends to deprive wildflowers of sunlight, so we undertook a bit of scrub clearance to facilitate a greater diversity of wildlife, while leaving ample nesting habitat for linnets and tits to use the following spring.

Six miles inland lies Bullfer Grove, a small area of woodland just off the A148, near Gunthorpe, which was gifted to the National Trust and is managed by the Blakeney team. We spent a few days clearing laurels and thinning out trees to benefit bluebells.

As well as heading inland, I was sent both east and west along the coast to widen my experience. The trust's Norfolk coast property encompasses land 15 miles west of Blakeney at Brancaster and 40 miles to the east at Horsey Windpump and Heigham Holmes. One of my tasks involved assisting with a stock fencing project at Branodunum Roman fort, which is sheep-grazed by tenants.

I also had the pleasure of spending a bit of time at Heigham Holmes. I wrote in my diary:

> Heigham Holmes is a delightful place, enhanced immensely by seeing cranes for the first time – a great view of no less than 24 – by the chain ferry, which we used to cross the river onto the enclosed reserve. Heigham is similar to the Fens due to the flat landscape and many windmills. There were windpumps in every direction. The derelict ones, with bits of sails missing, had an element of romanticism and poignancy about them.

I was surprised to learn that the cranes were wild, having become extinct in Britain hundreds of years ago. There had, in fact, been ten nesting pairs in the Norfolk Broads that year. A pair from continental Europe had arrived at Horsey in 1979, settled and gone on to breed, rearing their first chick in the early 1980s. Under the protection of John Buxton, the population has been slowly growing ever since. Further continental birds had colonised the Fens in 2007, breeding successfully at Lakenheath Fen.

I had been given the opportunity to spend a day with a group of ecologists conducting a biological survey on Heigham Holmes. This involved sweep-netting and looking at invertebrate diversity in various ditches. Find of the day was a great silver water beetle, the largest water beetle found in the British Isles. A picture of it appeared in the *EDP*.

As October rapidly approached, it was suggested I might like to stay on the Point again, to see it at a different time of year, just before the team moved out of the Lifeboat House for the winter. Eddie was away in Malta, leaving Paul in charge, accompanied by Richard, whose contract had ended at the beginning of September but he had returned as a volunteer for a week to help monitor autumn bird migration. They were generous and welcoming as always. I caught a lift over on a seal ferry, then had 'a beautiful walk with the beach to myself. Slowly improving my wader identification.'

We had a television dinner, which was a treat for me as the volunteer accommodation didn't have the luxury of a television. Electricity was not available at the mere click of a switch in the Lifeboat House, however. Two wind turbines provided only enough power for the telephone. Power for the washing machine, internet and television came from a diesel generator, the use of which was limited to just a couple of hours per day. A diesel bowser would be filled and towed along the shingle ridge by tractor at the start of the season but could not be topped up easily until the shingle-nesting birds had finished nesting. The Lifeboat House cooker and lighting were powered by gas. Connection to the internet came via satellite link to the Friary Farm office on the mainland. The trees in front of the office had to be kept clear of the satellite so there was a clean line of sight to the Lifeboat House. On days with poor visibility, internet speed would be much reduced.

The following morning, which was 2 October, the three of us walked out along Far Point. It felt eerily quiet now that all of the terns and black-headed gulls had dispersed. On Middle Point, I spotted a wheatear, having become familiar with the species over the summer. This individual, they told me, would be passing through on its way south to its wintering grounds in Africa. In fact, this was the Point's last wheatear record of the year.

Also on Middle Point, my first snow bunting was pointed out. In contrast to the leaving wheatear, this was an arrival from the Arctic. As well as using their eyes, Paul and Richard were using their ears, focusing in on a call they thought was a Lapland bunting, an arrival from the high-altitude tundra of Scandinavia. Thirty snipe were recorded throughout the day, twenty grey partridges and ninety-four brent geese in the harbour at low water.

The brent was fast becoming my favourite goose, with its soft burbling calls and smart black-and-grey plumage punctuated by a white collar almost resembling a dinner jacket. They breed in Arctic Siberia, where predators include Arctic foxes and polar bears. I was told how brent geese have more productive breeding seasons when the lemming population is abundant, so that Arctic foxes feed predominantly on the lemmings rather than brent goose eggs. In years when lemmings are scarce, snowy owls can even predate adult brent geese from their nests. It was amazing to think that the number of brent geese we would see over the winter would be influenced by lemmings!

When the evening tide arrived, Richard launched the boat and dropped me off on Morston Quay. Four days later, I returned to the Lifeboat House, this time by Land Rover along the shingle ridge from Cley beach. I was given a quick training session on how to drive on the shingle, basically sticking in the tracks in a low gear and not rushing. If I did get stuck, I should just ring the office and ask for the tractor to come and pull me out. Obviously, getting stuck was best avoided.

I drove up and down three times in the course of the day and managed not to get stuck. I was helping Eddie move off for the winter. He would still be visiting the Point regularly throughout the winter and had the pleasure of the grey seal pupping season to look forward to.

6

Winter Wonder

THE BEGINNING OF NOVEMBER signals the start of the grey seal pupping season at Blakeney, which lasts just over two months. On the first Monday of the month, I went up the Point in the Land Rover with Eddie. I tried to go along with him whenever he went up. The place was slowly getting a hold of me, enhanced by his enthusiasm for which birds we would see. A low tide seal count recorded ninety grey and just a single common. This was normal, the common seals practically vacate the Point as the dominant grey seals come ashore to pup on the beach and in the dunes.

Common seals have been present on Blakeney Point longer than it has been a nature reserve. In autumn 1988, they suffered from the Phocine distemper virus when an epidemic spread through the north-western European populations. That summer, peak low tide counts on the Point had recorded around 300 common seals. The virus led to the death of over 200 on the Point. A digger was brought out to excavate a mass grave between Beach Way and the main dunes on the edge of Great Sandy Low. Whenever we walked over that part of the reserve, Graham would always comment on how we were walking on the graves of many seals. He remembered that grim autumn well.

Interestingly, that same year also marked a more positive seal news story: the very first grey seal pups to be born on the Point. Two were born, one of which was observed on the Landing Ridge. Seasonal warden 'Rambo' stayed on to help with the common seal burials and discovered two grey seal pups, which were a symbol of optimism among an otherwise depressing experience. Grey seals themselves were first recorded at Blakeney just three years previously, in 1985, when a group of five bulls arrived and had decided to stay around.

A third species of seal was recorded on the Point in 1988. Assistant warden John Walton recorded in his diary that a dead harp seal was reported on 2 April on Yankee Ridge. He did not find it until four days later, 'thanks to great black-backed gulls'. This was the first Norfolk record of a harp seal, an Arctic species found in the North Atlantic and Arctic oceans. John cleaned and kept the skull, taking it with him to Northumberland, where it sat on his office desk for the fifteen years he was manager of the Farne Islands, another reserve synonymous with terns and grey seals.

Blakeney seal data from the 1990s is sporadic. Frequent low-tide counts were conducted in 1991, which recorded a peak count of thirty-eight grey and 226 common seals. Clearly, the common seal population had recovered well from the virus and twenty-four pups were observed that year. The occasional grey seal pup was observed on the Point in the 1990s, but not every year. In early January 1998, Richard Porter recorded three pups on Far Point and in December 1999, he recorded five. Numbers were growing, and in 2001 a defined rookery established itself, with around twenty-five pups born.

The following year, Dave became Blakeney Point warden, Joe Reed's property manager role having taken him away from the Point with more mainland-based responsibilities. Dave recorded a peak of round 600 common seals in summer 2002, now much more numerous than they had been prior to the Phocine distemper virus outbreak. At the same time, however, the virus had returned to seals in the Netherlands. With seals travelling between British and Dutch shores, it was only a matter of time before it spread. Indeed, around 120 common seals died from the virus between August and October at Blakeney.

The Point's common seal population once again took a big knock. In contrast, the grey seal rookery doubled in size with the birth of around fifty pups. Two years later, this number had doubled again to about 100 and two years after that around 200 pups were born on the Point. Two years after that, in December 2008, numbers exceeded 400, with

Eddie's notes recording 433 births. He had introduced a more scientific pup recording methodology after liaising with other rookery managers, namely Donna Nook in Lincolnshire and the Farne Islands in Northumberland; England's other two grey seal rookeries.

Grey Seal pupping has been closely monitored in Pembrokeshire for many years. There, the pupping season begins in August. It then works its way clockwise around the British Isles to Scotland where Britain's largest rookeries are located. Pupping starts a little later, at the end of September on the Farne Islands, in late October at Donna Nook and then at Blakeney usually a few days after Donna Nook.

Learning this history of a rapidly growing rookery, I was looking forward to seeing my first pups. A few days into November, Eddie, Bee and I were on the Point again. We saw a peregrine on the beach as we drove up, plus two merlins and a flock of thirty snow buntings, the white on their wings flickering beautifully as they flew. We counted 108 adult grey seals and the first four pups of the year, aged between two hours and two days. Always cautious not to cause unnecessary disturbance to any form of wildlife, we kept our distance. I was assured that I would have better views in a few weeks' time.

The breeding seals were not widely publicised at that time. They were mentioned in our interpretation and leaflets, but nothing wider reaching. Publicity was generally minimised to prevent an increase in visitor pressure on the reserve, especially during the breeding bird season. However, I had helped to produce a downloadable walk for the website, which directed walkers along the Point to the Lifeboat House and back, with carefully worded information about avoiding sensitive areas. A dog-walking leaflet had been produced recently too, which explained the seasonal restrictions for dog walking during the breeding bird season, highlighting the areas dogs were welcome, as well as where they were excluded for four and a half months of the year.

To a large degree, nesting bird areas could be predicted with consistent zoning and fencing in place from year to year. With the seals, the rookery was still very new. Plus, walkers venturing up the Point in winter were few and far between. The winter was noticeably quiet compared to the summer. In my school geography lessons, I had learned about ghost towns like Blakeney, where a large number of properties are second homes, unused during the winter months. However, Blakeney was busy enough to maintain most local amenities year-round. There were even hints of growing winter tourism. The wintering wildfowl was a big draw to birdwatchers. Wiveton Hall Café, where I worked part-time, was staying open right through to Christmas for the first time.

A winter wildlife photography course was licensed to visit Blakeney Point one Saturday in early December, with a seal ferry landing the group for an hour or so. The condition was that Eddie would supervise access on the Point, to avoid any seal disturbance. The pup count stood at around the 450 mark at this stage, having just surpassed last year's total. I went along, jumping at any chance to visit what had become one of my favourite places.

This was a particularly memorable day. Eddie was accompanied by girlfriend Bee and her parents, who were visiting from Germany. My friend Rose was visiting and so came along too. With the photographers carefully briefed on staying at the gap – which at that time was the eastern limit of the rookery – Eddie, myself and our guests had a short walk along the dunes towards Far Point to view the scale of the rookery along the beach.

As well as the sight of all that blubber on the beach and the brilliant white fur of the pups, their cries were so atmospheric, sounding almost like human babies at times. Among the rookery of mothers, expectant cows and bulls holding harems and attempting to mate, we spotted a young female grey seal, not yet of breeding age. Something wasn't quite right. We noticed that she had some fishing net caught around her neck.

Sadly, this is not an uncommon occurrence. Seals come into contact with fishing nets quite regularly and if a young seal becomes caught up, the netting can cut into its neck as it grows. Not every seal is easily accessible, but being hauled out on the beach, we had a chance of helping it – *if* we could catch it before it reached the water and if we could safely hold it still for a couple of minutes to cut through the netting.

Bee had a sharp knife with a serrated edge and there was a seal-rescue stretcher at the Lifeboat House.

Having fetched the stretcher, we briskly approached the seal. Bee and I carefully pinned her down with the stretcher while Eddie cut through the netting. We covered her head with my coat to calm her down and keep her still enough to cut through the net. Within a very short time, she was free. We encouraged her into the sea so that the saltwater could help heal the wound. What a great feeling it was to have helped an animal in trouble. A couple of minutes of stress was worthwhile to prevent what was developing into a nasty wound. I felt a sense of adventure and a warm feeling of having made a difference.

Two days later, it was the monthly wetland bird count. I would help with the Blakeney Freshes count and each month aim to be better at identification. During July, I had learned to tell a female gadwall from a female mallard and now I could identify wigeon and teal, wintering ducks that I hadn't really encountered before. I felt a bit embarrassed at my limited knowledge among so many good birders. But the wardens and Richard Porter were very kind and taught me some useful tips.

Just from being on the Norfolk coast every day, I subconsciously developed the ability to separate brent, pink-footed and greylag geese by call. The whistling call of wigeon is very distinctive. Teal are much smaller and can almost jump straight out of the water and begin flying upwards. On my evening walks around Blakeney Freshes and Friary Hills, I learned to identify woodcock by their silhouette. Tawny owls could be heard most evenings and occasionally I would see one perched in a tree or even on a rooftop.

I was learning a lot about the natural world and also acquiring different skills. Like reversing a trailer, which is quite hard when you have never done it before. But having the time and chance to practise really pays off, especially when surrounded by supportive people.

Another great thing about spending time on an iconic nature reserve was meeting specialist recorders. During December, I was able to join fungi enthusiast Tony Leech on a trip up the Point.

Richard Porter had studied the plants of the Point in great detail, but fungi had been largely unrecorded, so Tony was excited to see what he could find. He pointed out some of the most distinctive species, such as dune waxcap, dune stinkhorn and the sand dune mushroom.

I didn't imagine the harsh environment of the Point in winter would harbour such a diversity of fungi. Tony was also surprised and excited to find a particular species, seemingly growing in association with sand sedge, which was something previously unrecorded. During what I described in my diary as 'a fascinating and enjoyable day', we observed eight plant species still in flower in December, including the yucca by the boardwalk.

One cold, frosty morning in mid-December, Eddie, Bee and I set off in the Land Rover to Heigham Holmes to help with some scrub clearance. Throughout the day, we saw at least 100 white-fronted geese on Heigham Holmes. After our day's work, we went to nearby Stubb Mill, near Hickling Broad. We drove right past my future brother-in-law's farm, although I didn't know it at the time. From the viewing area by Stubb Mill, we recorded over 8,000 pink-footed geese and more than fifty marsh harriers coming in to roost, along with two hen harriers. We also saw twenty-four cranes: the same number I had seen over Heigham Holmes two months earlier.

The following day, we took the Land Rover through the mist up the Point for a seal count. As we drove along the shingle ridge, we spotted six sea ducks sat on the water, common scoters, a new species to add to my wildfowl repertoire. One of them was clearly unwell, but still alive, a great black-backed gull was attempting to eat it. As we reached the headland, a female sparrowhawk caught and ate a female blackbird. Then, in the dunes, we found the remains of a woodcock recently killed by a peregrine. The harsh weather seemed to be driving the need for survival before our very eyes.

The oldest pups, born in early November, were weaned by this stage, so we were just counting newborn pups. I was given the area between Middle and Far Point to count. It looked so different to when I had been there at the start of October. I was still getting my eye in with regard to the ageing of pups. The youngest pups are quite easy to pick out because they are a yellow colour to start with and have an umbilical cord showing for the first few days. Moulted pups also stand out, many of them barrel-shaped, having been fed on their mother's rich milk for three weeks. Determining whether a pup is four or six days old takes a bit more practice.

In the evening, we went to the White Horse for a talk by Richard Porter about his conservation work in Iraq, which was fascinating. The following day brought a strong north-easterly wind with rain, sleet and snow. Amid a minor blizzard, I was out on the Freshes helping put in fence posts, which I described in my diary as 'great fun'.

Next morning, there was lovely, thick snow. We had the pleasure of another trip up the Point. An area of water on the edge of Cley Marshes hadn't frozen, being a stone's throw from the sea. One of very few substantial areas of unfrozen water in the area, it had attracted a number of waders, including a few dozen snipe. Due to the saltiness, not much snow had settled on the Point itself, but there were some areas in the dune lows with a thin, white dusting that was a pleasure to witness.

Inspecting the Lifeboat House for any damage, we spotted a barn owl in the adjacent shed. There was an opening to allow nesting swallows in during the summer, which was clearly now being used by the owl, the shed serving as a perfect roosting spot.

Over the course of the cold snap, we discovered a few birds that had perished, their depleting fat reserves not sufficient to keep them warm. We found two brent geese, a water rail and a woodcock. Because their plumage was in good condition, Norwich Castle Museum were interested in having them to update their stuffed bird collection. These specimens were sourced ethically, unlike their Victorian specimens, many of which had faded over the decades. We put the birds in a cardboard box, sealed it and took it to the village post office. The post-lady was blissfully unaware that the parcel contained four dead birds.

That evening, all of the Blakeney staff headed out in the snow to attend the ferryman's Christmas dinner at the Morston Anchor. This was the one time in the year that all of the ferry companies and reserve staff got together. In the morning, I carefully negotiated the icy roads back to south Lincolnshire for Christmas, sharing numerous Norfolk stories with my friends and family.

After seeing in the new decade with family and friends, I was excited to be on my way back to Blakeney for a further nine months. A few days working back at my local supermarket made me long to be back in a place where my work involved wildlife and adventure. It was an exciting journey back, driving in the dark with oncoming light snow flurries illuminated by the headlights. I must have been happy to be back because I wrote in my diary, 'How beautiful the coast, how lucky I am, how wonderful life is, how fantastically, amazingly brilliant.'

In January, I became involved in a bit more wildlife monitoring work. Little egrets were roosting in Desmond McCarthy's woodland strip next to Friary Farm. Sitting on the gate at the bottom of Friary Hills, I would count how many flew out of the roost, recording thirty-one, one morning. It was quite special to see a significant number of these birds fly overhead. Their numbers had increased over the previous few years, although a few had perished in December. We found a dead one and saw that, although long-legged, there is actually not that much to them at all.

Carrying out our warden tasks on Blakeney Freshes, there were several otter signs to be found. I got to learn what their footprints look like: quite round, with five toes, whereas foxes are more diamond-shaped with four toes. In fact, you can draw a cross between the pads of a fox print without touching them. I learned to identify otter spraints and collected some for diet analysis, it was clear they were feeding on fish from the scales contained within the spraints.

Richard Porter set up a coordinated woodcock roost survey, after Eddie and I had shared our sightings of double figures flying north to

Blakeney Freshes in the evenings. Richard organised a string of twelve observation spots between Salthouse and Blakeney.

I was stationed on Friary Hills. Counting them was quite simple, as they flew over one or two at a time. However, the coordinated brent goose roost survey was a bit more challenging. As the light fades, they fly into the harbour in a dense group. Block counting is the only option, counting a manageable chunk and then extrapolating to get an estimate of the total based on a sample.

Nobody could say the role of a warden isn't varied. One day Graham would be teaching me how to mix cement; the next, Eddie would be explaining the different calls of the water, rock and meadow pipit. All three were present on Blakeney Freshes in the winter, although only the meadow pipit breeds in Britain.

In February, I broadened my wardening experience further by spending a week at Runnymede in Surrey, very close to where I was born. There, I got involved in building a raised section of boardwalk and inspecting heritage trees.

Back at Blakeney, March involved preparation for the upcoming breeding bird season. One task was the annual beach clean, to make the Point as tidy as possible ahead of the terns and waders setting up territory. The local, independent station, North Norfolk Radio, were contacted to help promote our litter pick. I answered the office phone when breakfast show presenter Dick Hutchinson rang in response to our request.

This led to my first radio appearance, speaking live on his show. I was excited and very keen to do it. I remember waiting on the phone for KC and the Sunshine Band's 'Give It Up' to end and then I was on. My heart was pounding as the song played but the interview went well, and I was told that I spoke very clearly.

On the last Friday of March, a group of us headed out to the Lifeboat House ahead of the beach clean the following morning. Opening up the Lifeboat House for the new season felt like quite a moment. I wrote in my diary, 'It was atmospheric, it was special, it was like a scene out of a film. Against the backdrop of a stunning, orange sky, we arrived at the Lifeboat House and carried our belongings inside.'

The kitchen utensils had to all be washed because a mouse had moved into the cupboard over the winter. The mouse had chewed its way through some of Ted Eales' 1970s reports, which had been stored in a dresser drawer; a lesson to move all valuable literature off the Point over the winter. Supper that night was a vegetarian toad in the hole.

Our small team litter-picked eastwards down the Point while the main group headed westwards from Cley. The tractor, with trailer, and Land Rover zipped up and down the beach and ridge respectively, collecting rubbish bags that had been filled. There was a great turn-out, with lots of familiar faces and plenty of new ones who had heard about it and wanted to get involved. It is fantastic how many people a beach clean can attract and reassuring to know that so many people care about having litter-free beaches.

Of course, beach cleaning is a never-ending job due to the depressingly large amount of plastic in the sea, more of it washing up on every big tide. That March, the Point was particularly messy, with lots of large, plastic fish boxes having washed up. I remember seeing a washed-up doll's head lying on the beach, like a scene from a post-apocalyptic horror film, although it is the small pieces of plastic that pose the greatest threat to wildlife.

By midday, there was a sizable heap of rubbish bags at Cley beach car park. The Norfolk Wildlife Trust kindly let the rubbish lie there in a cordon until the council collection on Monday, which they did for free.

Feeling satisfied, a group of us lunched at the Watch House, where the two parties had met. As the Point's most frequent walker, Richard Porter would only miss the beach clean if he was abroad on business. I had learned that he collects interesting stones from the Point and displays them in his garden. For a while, I had been holding on to a stone resembling Edvard Munch's *The Scream*, which I had found on the Point. He was very appreciative when I donated it to his collection.

With the beach clean successfully completed ahead of time, I spent a Saturday afternoon watching birds and soaking up the signs of spring on the Point. There were two wheatears on the roof of one of the huts. Almost six months since I had seen the last one of autumn, it was a joy to see the first of these charismatic birds returning from their African winter. There was something quite playful about the way they flitted around, flashing the brilliant contrast of black and white on their tails. I took in the sandy and peachy pastel tones of their breasts as they caught the sunlight.

Alone, I wandered over to the Plantation. There was a single bird in there, small and dark grey. When it took flight, I knew from a brilliant flash of fiery orange that this was the black redstart I had been told to look out for. Black redstarts are a characteristic early spring migrant known for closely following the wheatear as one of the very first African migrants to reach the Norfolk coast at the end of March. I got equal pleasure from observing a skylark on the dune beside the Plantation, its crest raised. I studied its beautifully patterned feathers.

On Sunday, more avian delights were in store. We sat on Middle Point and watched the black-headed gulls, which were noisily occupying their territory on the end of Far Point. Among them were my first Mediterranean gulls, which can be picked out from the black-headed by their very different calls. The black-headed gulls are upstaged by the Mediterranean gulls' blacker heads, redder bills, redder legs and brilliant all-white underwings.

Near the gulls were the stars of the show: six displaying Sandwich terns. Four had flown past during the litter pick the day before, and were the first of the year. The terns' welcome presence on Far Point signalled the start of spring.

Spring Splendour

THE SAME WEEK AS my North Norfolk Radio appearance, I also had an interview of a different kind. It was for a part-time seasonal role at Morston Information Centre. On 1 April, I did my first paid shift at Morston. My contract worked out at around eighteen hours of work per week, fitting around the tides. I continued volunteer wardening, working about twenty hours per week, which enabled me to stay in the volunteer accommodation. It was brilliant to have my first paid role on a nature reserve.

With the abundance of washed-up fish boxes we had collected during the beach clean, I was tasked with making them into a storage unit by constructing a wooden frame into which they could slide and stack. It was satisfying to construct something practical from recycled materials, especially when it made it into the shed on the Point to be used for years to come.

Alongside volunteering on the mainland, paid work at Morston and a bit of temporary cleaning work at the Brancaster Activity Centre on a Friday morning, I tried to get out to the Point regularly to follow the progress of the breeding season. If I had Morston shifts on a Saturday and Sunday afternoon, I could walk out to the Point, stay the night, spend the morning there and then walk back to Morston for my next shift. I did this on the second weekend in April, helping put out the 'No further' and 'No landing' signs on Far Point.

All signs were taken down before the winter to prevent them being lost or damaged by winter storms. In fact, we once had to retrieve one of the signs from Sheringham beach. We also returned a sign to Holkham, which had washed up on the Point. Over winter, the seals had squashed some of the stake-and-string fencing. It is important that the tern colony area is fenced off and clearly signed, to deter anyone from landing and disturbing them. Digging into sand and shingle is not always that easy, as the sides cave in all too easily. The best technique is to dig as quickly as possible, put the signpost in, pack large pebbles around it to keep it straight and then knock it a little further in with a rubber mallet.

The following day, I joined the Blakeney Badminton Club. Later that week, I attended a Norfolk Wildlife Trust meeting at Cley village hall to see Martin Woodcock's talk on painting African birds. His illustrations have appeared in many bird identification guides, including *The Birds of Africa*. He was very likable and had a wonderful sense of humour. World renowned and well respected, when I saw him licking a stamp at Blakeney Post Office, it felt like I had spotted a celebrity. At his talk, I really felt I had become part of the community, bumping into various local naturalists I had got to know.

By now, I was getting to know a lot of local characters. As well as seeing Mike Reed in the Morston Café most days, I would see him at the Blakeney Royal British Legion. We both took part in the monthly quizzes and would often sink a pint or two of Guinness together. His father would occasionally pop in, as would Bernard Bishop, warden of next-door Cley Marshes Reserve. Bernard was an old friend of Graham, and the pair would often tease and compete against each other. Bernie would sometimes pop over to our office, especially if there was some news or a rumour in the village about something he thought we might know about.

I spent a lot of evenings watching the changing light, soaking up the atmosphere and listening to the sedge and reed warblers. One Tuesday evening, in late April, I wrote in my diary what a wonderful sunset there was as I listened to the many bird calls, 'Then a noise catches my attention. Surely it can't be. More or less every two minutes, my ears were treated to the wonderful sound of my first booming bittern. Stunning.'

Male bitterns use their booming call to attract a mate. The deep, low sound of their booming is able to travel more than a mile. The Norfolk name, 'bottle-bump', refers to the similarity between a bittern boom and the sound you get from blowing into a bottle. Their scientific name is the Latin for 'starry bull', their boom sounding a bit like a bull and their plumage having a starry pattern.

The following evening, Chris joined me to undertake a formal bittern survey. This was part of his Blakeney Freshes breeding bird monitoring. It was also part of a wider bittern monitoring programme coordinated by the RSPB. The bittern actually became extinct in Britain in 1886 due to loss of wetland habitat and persecution. They were a favoured target of both Victorian egg collectors and taxidermists. Bitterns returned to Norfolk in 1900 and began breeding again in 1911. In 1954, around eighty booming males were recorded. However, in 1997 there were just eleven.

The dramatic decline of the bittern in Britain led to the RSPB launching a research programme into their precise habitat requirements. Their findings resulted in clear management recommendations to attract them to breed at more sites. Blakeney Freshes is managed to conserve and enhance its reedbed and had hosted a successful breeding Bittern pair during Joe Reed's time as property manager. It was exciting to have a male back on territory. We kept our fingers crossed that it would attract a female and breed successfully.

Just a few hundred metres to the north, on the shingle ridge, a completely different bird species was also holding a territory. During April, a cock pheasant had begun defending a stretch of the Point between Cley and the Watch House, known as the Marrams. So fiercely was it defending its territory that it would literally attack poor, unsuspecting visitors. The pheasant would chase the quad bike and even ride on it. I wrote about my encounter in my diary:

Walking up the Point, a pheasant comes bobbing over and follows me. Runs by my side. Blocks my way. Follows me back. Follows me forwards. Gets very close. Starts pecking my leg. I go in the sea. It follows and continues to peck me. Sheer craziness.

After a few weeks, it seemingly realised it was not going to attract a female and so abandoned its territory. At least, that is what we assumed. However, a short while later, a dead cock pheasant washed up on the beach further up the Point, which may well have been the same bird.

I spent the second weekend of May out on the Point. Sheltering in the Plantation was my first nightingale. They could be heard singing a couple of miles inland at Salthouse Heath. On adjacent Kelling Heath, there were nightjars. I had a wonderful evening listening to them churring there. Walking through the brambles behind the Lifeboat House, looking for any other migrant birds that had dropped in overnight, I got a shock when a mallard shot off her nest just a couple of feet in front of me. She was incubating a clutch of ten eggs and had sat tight on them until the very last minute.

As usual, I walked off to Morston for my shift in the visitor centre. Towards the end of the shift, Dave came off a boat and handed me a cardboard box. Inside it was an injured Sandwich tern that had been blinded in one eye. I drove it to the RSPCA animal rescue centre at East Winch. They did their best to help it, but unfortunately it didn't make it.

It was well into the evening by the time I got back from East Winch to Friary Farm. As I parked the Land Rover, Graham drew up hurriedly in his car. He took the keys, mentioned something about needing to drive the police up the Point and sped off to Cley beach. It turned out that a drunk middle-aged man had been spotted staggering along Yankee Ridge. When approached, he spurted verbal abuse, so the wardens left him alone but kept an eye on him from the lookout tower.

The man waded through Pinchen's Creek and headed to Clarke's Hut. He broke inside and passed out on a bed. The man was known to the police and regarded as dangerous. The story would go on to feature in all of the illustrated talks Graham gave the rest of that year – in the 'Tales of the Unexpected' section towards the end.

I met Andrew, owner of the hut, on Morston Quay the next morning. He was heading out there to repair the damage from the break-in. He disposed of the bedding that the intruder had passed out on and inspected his hut for any signs of theft. All that had been taken was the contents of a tin of baked beans.

I met another local gentleman at Morston, four days later. It was Merlin Waterson, former regional director of the National Trust. He and two photographers were going out to the Point by boat to capture some library images for future interpretation. They photographed the swallows nesting under the eaves of the information centre, above the car park machine. It was great to have swallows breeding on the building, which they had done for a number of years. I was amazed at how many people seemed completely oblivious when parent birds skimmed right over their heads.

One of the photographers took a picture of me in front of the information centre, a staged pose pretending to be engaging with a visitor. This photograph made it into the following year's handbook and went on to appear on countless subsequent posters, leaflets and adverts for several years to come. It became a bit of joke because it was staggering just how often the image was used over several years. Being of mixed race, I evidently ticked the diversity box.

That spring, Graham was booked for a talk in Hunstanton to a holidaying group of pensioners with a natural history interest. Graham had arranged for me to come along so that I could dine with them and talk for a couple of minutes towards the end. Having seen him give a talk at least once before, this time we thought it would be good for me to contribute.

So, I spoke about bitterns for two minutes and about how excited I was to hear one on the Freshes. Having had an action-packed day and a three-course dinner, the group were quite tired by the time I spoke, and I noticed that many of them had in fact nodded off. Years later, I would actually have someone faint during a talk.

I mentioned how we were not sure whether the bittern had attracted a female or not and that we were looking for signs of young. As time went on, no indication of young was found and no feeding flights were observed. This highlighted that a booming male does not necessarily guarantee a breeding pair but having a bittern in the reedbed was still something positive and such a thrill for me to hear. It was also a good lesson: that you can't count your chickens – or your bitterns.

A marvellous opportunity presented itself on the penultimate Sunday in May. Chris invited me out to Scolt Head Island in his fishing boat. He had mussel lays in Brancaster Harbour and earned a living as a fisherman during the winter months. He had to check on his mussels and give the boat a run, so kindly offered to land me on the island for an hour. It was a hot day with a clear blue sky, and it felt Mediterranean. There were obviously lots of similarities to the Point, but it also felt quite different to me. It seemed that bit further from the mainland and slightly more remote. I didn't see a single other person there. Unlike the Point, there were no seal ferries because no seals haul out on Scolt Head. That year, there were 2,500 pairs of nesting Sandwich terns recorded on the Point and 480 on Scolt.

Scolt Head Island had been bought by the National Trust in 1923 for £500, following the death of its previous owner, the Lord of Brancaster. The first watcher was ornithologist and bird photographer Emma Turner. In 1953, the Nature Conservancy Council took over management of Scolt Head, on a ninety-nine-year lease from the National Trust. By this time, the warden was Bob Chestney, who, like Ted Eales, had succeeded his father as warden.

In 1991, the Nature Conservancy Council became English Nature, which became Natural England in 2006. Chris, like many of his generation, still referred to them as English Nature, as that is what they were called when he worked for them in the early 1990s, succeeding Bob Chestney.

The day after my visit to Scolt Head, Ray Mears visited Blakeney Point. He was filming the 'Shingle Shore' episode of his *Wild Britain* series. Dave gave a wonderfully honest interview, speaking about the pressures that terns and ringed plovers face on the Point.

I didn't get to meet Ray because I had to make another trip to East Winch, this time with an injured guillemot. However, the following day, I was able to briefly meet Chris Packham and Kate Humble. They had come to board a ferry from Morston Quay to film a VT for *Springwatch*, which was being broadcast live from Pensthorpe, just up the road near Fakenham. The next time I was to see Chris Packham and Kate Humble together would be when I appeared alongside them on the *Curious Creatures* television quiz show seven years later – not that I could ever have imagined that back then.

Some evenings, as I looked through my binoculars from Friary Hills out to the Point, I would long to be out there. But Friary Farm had a number of nesting bird species not found on the Point. Tawny owls were a wonderful soundtrack to my winter evenings. I had been told to listen out for the high-pitched squeaky calls of the chicks, knowing that they would be breeding among the trees surrounding the caravan site.

One early evening in May, I heard what I was sure were young tawny owls. I followed the sound and managed to locate them. Thrilled with my discovery and eager to share the moment, I knocked on the door of a nearby caravan, owned by a couple I had got to know, Pat and Alan. They grabbed their binoculars, put on their wax jackets and hurried over to share the moment. The same belt of trees – between the caravan park and Wiveton Hall farm – was also home to a much larger breeding bird that I was soon to discover.

During the half-term week, the spare room of the volunteer accommodation was occupied by Sam, a sixth-form student from Cambridge on a three-week placement. Chris suggested that Sam and I should investigate the heronry.

I was fascinated with herons as a young child, having been amazed at how much bigger they are than the ducks and small garden birds I was familiar with. Now, aged 20, I was excited to see my first heron nests. They took a bit of searching. Eventually, we spotted an adult flying in and followed it to see where it landed. We heard a noisy sort of gargling sound, which was the chicks being fed on regurgitated fish.

Looking several metres up into the top of a Scots pine, it was hard to see the nest. Although, being quite large by this stage, we were able to pick out the heads and bills of two hungry juveniles the next time an adult flew in with food. In the course of our couple of hours observing, it also became apparent that there was a second nest in the tree immediately next to it.

Later in the summer, I spotted juvenile grey herons on the nearby Freshes and wondered whether these were the same birds I had seen in the nest. A Norfolk name for grey heron is 'harnser'; another is 'Old Frank' – perhaps because their harsh call almost sounds like 'Frank!'.

8

Rare Birds and Impressionable Youngsters

OUT ON BLAKENEY POINT, the third warden that year was Joe, from Somerset. Like Richard the year before, Joe had been a seasonal assistant on the Farne Islands. There, Joe had worked alongside Jason, who had been an assistant on the Point the summer before Richard. Jason had told Joe all about his time on the Point, including the legendary 31 May 2008 when a first for Norfolk turned up.

Strong winds from the north-east had combined with mist, four days before, bringing numerous migrants to ground on the Point. The weather had cleared on the 31st and so Eddie, Paul and Jason were busily conducting breeding wader surveys into the evening. As they walked along the track beside Beach Way, heading back to the Lifeboat House, conversation turned to what they would have for tea, as Paul reported in the 2008 *Norfolk Bird and Mammal Report*: 'It was then that Jason drew our attention to a finch sitting on the top of a Suaeda bush. As I focused on the bird, my words were – in a Norfolk accent – "Thass a Trumpeter Finch, bor". Tea was going to have to wait.' This was a tale often recounted.

Exactly two years later, Paul's first words to Joe in the morning were, 'You know what day it is today, bor? Trumpeter Finch Day!' Joe was a bit frustrated that six weeks of hard fieldwork had produced none of the rare birds the Point is legendary for. So, imagine his excitement and disbelief when a pink-rumped passerine flitted past the Lifeboat House window. He was on the phone at the time but promptly hung up to confirm if history was repeating itself. It was. Exactly two years after the first, Joe had spotted Norfolk's second trumpeter finch, just a few metres from where the first had been found. Like the first, this was also a male.

Early in the afternoon, the bird was relocated further down the point at Cley's east bank. News inevitably spread fast that this desert species from North Africa to southern Asia was showing well at one of England's most well-known birding spots. With the tide out and my Morston shift completed, Sam and I were encouraged to go and take a look, being such a rare vagrant and in such an accessible location. So, we took the HiLux to Walsey Hills and walked along the east bank to the shingle ridge, where a large crowd of people with binoculars, telescopes and cameras had congregated.

We enjoyed fantastic views of the bird. Although fairly small, its chunky bill and the candy-floss-coloured tinge to its rump made for an impressive sight. It was so exciting to know just how unusual a find it was. Often, vagrant birds that are so far off course go on to perish through starvation and exhaustion. But we wondered whether, being another male, it could possibly have been the same bird from two years ago, following the same migration detour on the same day, having survived the first time.

Three days later, Sam and I caught the tide and headed out to the Point. News had reached the Point that we had successfully 'twitched' the trumpeter finch and we were asked how we found the experience.

Mass twitches were not always that pleasant. There are numerous stories of twitches involving people – almost exclusively men – so desperate to tick off a new rarity on their list that they behave quite irrationally and selfishly. We only had positive things to say about our experience at east bank. People were being respectful to the bird by giving it space. A kind lady even let Sam and I view the finch through her telescope.

We went along on a breeding wader survey. The birds we observed included a particularly protective oystercatcher in Great Sandy Low. She flew noisily towards us and started dive-bombing. Contact wasn't actually made with our heads, but it was enough to make us duck and beat a hasty retreat. Her technique successfully moved us on from where she didn't want us to be.

Graham had told me about an oystercatcher that nested on the landing ridge for many years. Nicknamed Evil Edna, she would dive-bomb anyone who came too near her nest. In fact, she would actually give a clonk on the head. Edna was a hit with the many schoolchildren who met her because their teachers would be the ones to get struck, being taller than the children.

With the tide out and the sun shining, we crossed the harbour to get back to Friary Farm, having been carefully instructed which route to take. It was easiest to take shoes and socks off and walk barefoot through the thick, black mud. There were areas of firm sand as well as shingly spots.

Waders probed in the mud, searching for worms and crustaceans. Occasional terns flew overhead, calling. A truly special landscape and a wonderful soundscape. The warm sun on our backs and the cool water up to our knees, it felt like the perfect summer holiday as we waded along New Cut to Blakeney Quay. There the atmosphere changed, as bird calls were drowned out by people – it felt like a different world.

On the first weekend in June, with a few days off from Morston, I headed out to the Point to stay for the first time in a month. Eddie had gone with Graham to Northumberland to visit the Farne Islands. Back on the Point, with the breeding season still in full swing, I helped make up numbers and assist with tasks. This included a 4 a.m. start to keep watch for potential egg thieves. Although no longer as common an issue as it once was, there was still the chance of egg theft: an obsessive collector might target the Point in search of tern eggs. My dawn patrol was grey and rainy; I didn't see a soul.

The rain showers and easterly winds brought in a subalpine warbler. Another first for me, and exactly the kind of migrant Joe had been expecting to turn up in May. At the beginning of the century, it became one of only four national rarities to amass over ten records on the Point. Subalpine warblers tend to occur on the Point when they overshoot the Mediterranean during warm south-easterly conditions. We toasted the occasion with a shot of whisky in the evening. In the absence of suitable glasses, metal eggcups were the usual method of serving a wee dram in the Lifeboat House.

Next morning, I felt nervous about what lay ahead. A bit like the feeling you get before an exam. And just like preparing for an exam, I was writing up notes and revising facts.

A large school party were landing for an hour's guided walk. The group was to be split into three, with me leading one of the groups; my very first experience of a guided walk with primary schoolchildren. I've still got the tattered notes I made, with key facts about the shingle, saltmarsh and sand dunes. We sneakily prepared an area of beach with 'treasures of the tideline' so that the children could do a ten-minute scavenge and collect items for us to identify.

High tide came and the ferries headed out, but no school parties landed. It turned out that the guided walk had been written on the wrong page of the diary. It was actually scheduled for the following day. Having geared up for it, I stayed an extra day on the Point.

Sure enough, twenty-four hours later, the school arrived on a grey and drizzly Blakeney Point. I did my introduction on the landing ridge and then led my group of fifteen towards the Lifeboat House to my designated oystercatcher nest.

It was as we gathered around the cordoned-off nest that the magic happened. I explained about how their camouflaged eggs blended in with the shingle to protect them from predators but made them vulnerable to accidental trampling. We gazed at the eggs for a moment. In front of our eyes, one of them was visibly hatching. A small, wet chick poked out of the shell. It was a very special moment, and the children were captivated. We watched for a short while before moving on to leave it in peace and explore the next habitat.

I was buzzing as we waved the children off on their boat trip back to Morston. My research had sufficiently prepared me and seeing a hatching chick was a fantastic bonus. This filled me with confidence, and I felt a hunger to deliver more guided walks, having found it easier and more enjoyable than I thought it would be.

A few days later, back at Morston Information Centre, I met a visiting primary school teacher and her husband. They were doing a recce for a primary school trip a couple of weeks later. I spoke enthusiastically about how brilliant a guided tour on the Point would be for the children. She then contacted Marilyn in the office and booked a guided walk for her school group. The small cost of the tour would directly fund conservation work on the reserve. Again, I helped lead the tour and was pleased to learn that they would be returning the following year.

To further develop my experience working with schoolchildren, I helped with the Guardianship Project. This involved engaging with Blakeney Primary School throughout the year. In the winter, we had done a session on owls. Pellets were collected from the shed on the Point for the children to dissect. My group included ferryman Jim Temple's granddaughter. We identified field voles, bank voles, common shrews, a pygmy shrew and also the skull of a small bird, possibly a wren. In spring, we did a session on trees and flowers on Friary Hills and in summer we took them across the harbour at low tide.

Giving the local children a positive experience and connecting them with the nature reserve on their doorstep is so important. It was surprising how many of the class had never been to the Point before. We trudged across the harbour at low tide, as groups from Aylmerton Field Studies Centre did regularly. In fact, they had kindly advised me the best route to take. Accompanying parents lifted the children up when we crossed the channel near the Watch House. On the shingle ridge, we did a beach clean and recorded the different forms of litter we found, submitting our data to the Marine Conservation Society.

I would sometimes go birdwatching on Cley Marshes in the evenings. On the evening of 20 June, I watched a grey heron swallow two mallard chicks, one by one, on the north scrape. But there was more drama on Simmond's Scrape – a pair of Chilean flamingos!

They were obviously not truly wild vagrants, but feral birds, possibly from a northern European population. The pair had been in the area for a couple of days and had been seen on the Point that morning. Surprisingly, this was not the first Chilean flamingo record on the Point; a bird had previously been recorded in July 1967.

9

Strange Goings-on

A SURPRISING AND SOMEWHAT sinister turn of events took place on Blakeney Point in July. As early as the previous Boxing Day, Graham had found a grey seal washed up by the Lifeboat House with distinctive cut marks around its body. A few subsequent seals were discovered early in 2010. In June, two common seals washed up on the landing ridge showing the same sort of spiral cuts. Then, from 12 July, carcasses with identical injuries washed up almost daily for the remainder of the month.

The Point team bagged a total of thirteen fresh common seal carcasses, which were sent to the police, who had launched an investigation. The Norfolk Police wildlife crime officer drove the seals to RSPCA East Winch for post-mortem investigations.

Naturally, there was a lot of speculation among locals. One theory was that a local fisherman was responsible, inflicting the injuries with a knife after catching the seals in his nets at sea.

A more popular theory was connected with the Sheringham Shoal offshore windfarm, which was in its construction phase. The bases of eighty-eight wind turbines were being pile-driven into the seabed using vessels with ducted propellers. Initial research by the Sea Mammal Research Unit and the University of St Andrew's later 'revealed a number of features that show the injuries are entirely consistent with the animals being sucked through large ducted propellers'. They had used scaled simulations with wax model seals.

Ray, our senior visitor reception assistant at Morston, retired in mid-July and we had a fish-and-chip supper in Morston village hall to mark the occasion. Alongside property staff, attendees included former Point warden, Joe Reed, and ferryman John Bean, who had actually been winter warden on the Point during the 1960s and '70s.

Inevitably, conversation turned to the mysterious seal injuries. Everyone had an opinion. It was very much like the scene in *Jaws*, leading up to fingers being scraped on the blackboard.

The crescendo of our evening at Morston village hall was Ray's retirement speech, which affectionately teased everyone he had worked with. I suppose we needed a good laugh amid the darkness of the grim seal deaths.

None more so than the boys on the Point. They had vivid stories of having to bag up these gruesome carcasses for post-mortem. In struggling to bag up a particularly large seal, Joe had been spattered with 'blood sand', a spec or two landing on his lips. He allegedly rushed back to the Lifeboat House to wash out his mouth with water followed by whisky to take away the taste.

If you've ever encountered raw seal flesh, you will know it has a strong and unpleasant odour. Dog walkers will discover this when their pets roll around in a rotting seal carcass. Graham had a story about calling on a Morston resident to warn him about a washed-up dead seal on the marsh near his house. As soon as their front door was opened, the smell of seal reached Graham's nostrils – clearly, it was too late, the dog had already found the carcass!

Attempts were made to keep the story out of the media at first. However, in August, it was decided to put out a proactive statement as it was generating attention and news was spreading. I had gone to stay with my grandparents for a few days in Burwell, Cambridgeshire. We were watching the evening news when, sure enough, Blakeney appeared. The report showed Norfolk Constabulary going out in a police boat to collect carcasses from the Point. An image 'that some viewers may find distressing' was shown and the trust's national media consultant was filmed outside Friary Farm talking about how it was upsetting and distressing for the team on the Point.

Sure, it wasn't at all pleasant seeing wild animals you are trying to protect washing up in such a state, but the Point team were very resilient. They joked about being mentally scarred but actually took it in their stride and were very professional. I obviously heard a lot about the seals but wasn't involved in handling any of the bodies.

But that's not to say that life on the mainland side of the reserve was not without its dramas. One weekend in July, a couple of local lads decided to go and see the seals. They headed out from the Stiffkey Freshes at low tide. The only thing was, they were in a Land Rover. Unsurprisingly, they didn't get very far before it sank into the soft mud. By the time news reached us, the tide was flowing. There was no chance of retrieving it until the following day.

Graham took a photograph of the top of it sticking out from the water, which made it into the 'Tales of the Unexpected' section of his future illustrated talks. Using the tractor and a strop, we towed it back to terra firma. The two lads were quite embarrassed as they really should have known better.

The following morning, Graham pulled up outside the volunteer accommodation and told me that Morston was on fire. I jumped in the vehicle straight away. When we arrived at the quay, the fire engine had

Flooded Land Rover, July 2010. (Graham Lubbock)

finished extinguishing the blaze, which had initially been spotted from the Lifeboat House. Among charred gorse bushes and singed grass, was a disposable barbecue. Some sailors had cooked themselves a hot breakfast before catching the tide. Having not extinguished it properly, the dry summer grass had ignited, and the fire had spread into the scrub. A couple of nearby dinghies were damaged by the fire. This clearly demonstrated why there is a 'no fires' bylaw on the National Nature Reserve.

'Quite a crazy weekend at Morston: fire and water,' I wrote in my diary. 'But the day ended peacefully with a couple of pints at the Legion whilst watching Spain vs. the Netherlands in the World Cup final.'

Although England didn't do too well in the World Cup, the summer certainly had some highs. One of these was a very special event out on the Point: a charity lobster supper in aid of the Blakeney Twelve.

The Blakeney Twelve are a group of twelve businessmen who raise funds to benefit those in need in the village and surrounding district. They were founded in the 1960s and have supported a range of local causes helping the old, disabled and hospitalised.

Charity suppers on a sensitive nature reserve such as the Point are generally not possible, but this was a local cause, with the ferrymen providing transport for free. After careful discussions, the event was given the go ahead for a Tuesday evening after the oystercatchers had finished breeding on the landing ridge.

Graham and I helped load tables and chairs onto fisherman Willie Weston's boat, which he carefully steered through the harbour, mooring directly in front of the Lifeboat House at the top of the spring tide. There, the Point team waded into the water to help with the offloading. They set up the tables and chairs on the shingle beside the Lifeboat House the following evening. While the donors were out on a dusk seal trip, I helped transport the food. Willie's boat was so loaded up with food, drink and helpers that it rocked from side to side with the weight.

We made it ashore, loaded up the quad bike trailer and helped line up plates and cutlery inside the visitor centre section of the Lifeboat House. The organisers were so grateful for permission and the help of the wardens that Willie made sure we all had a good plateful of food and plenty to drink. We devoured the crab, lobster and salad in the Lifeboat House kitchen, joined by some of the ferrymen. Joe Reed even poked his head in to see how his old home was being looked after.

Before long, everyone was being rounded up to board the ferries for the return trip, now in darkness. Of course, the Beans and Temples were so familiar with the harbour that darkness was not a problem, however, they did need sufficient water depth to get safely back without fear of running aground. So, it was important to get everyone aboard in good time.

It was a bit like herding cats, some folks having consumed rather a lot of champagne and one or two struggling to walk in a straight line. But we all made it safely back to Morston.

I think the wardens on the Point were relieved to see everyone go. Although the breeding season was almost over, it was still stressful to have such a large group of people on the Point, but it was for a good cause and, as a bonus, they ended up with a fridge full of leftovers, much to the delight of Eddie, known for his healthy appetite and dislike of seeing any food go to waste.

My twenty-first birthday was a few days later. I arrived at my desk to find a cake with a lit candle on it. On to Morston and the visitor centre had been decorated with a 'Happy 21st birthday' banner and balloons. On the counter was another cake, iced by my fellow seasonal Morston team member, Sally.

My birthday also happened to be on the last day of the summer that a spiral cut seal was found. For the rest of August and beyond, no more washed up, which was a big relief. There was a rumour that, with the finger being pointed at them, the windfarm construction vessels had fitted guards over all of their ducted propellers to prevent any more seals being sucked in and killed. However, the windfarm company was adamant all along that their vessels were definitely not responsible for the seal deaths.

Now well into the summer holidays, there were numerous family-focused events taking place along the Norfolk coast. The Norfolk Wildlife Trust asked if I was interested in representing Blakeney at their Cley Marine Day. Sally from Morston kindly helped me deliver an engaging activity for children. She was also a volunteer at Sheringham Park, where they had lots of great educational activities for children.

Sally brought along a magnetic fishing game, which went down very well. There were various laminated pictures of creatures you would want to find in the sea, along with litter you would not. Each had a paperclip attached to the back. With a fishing rod that had a magnet on the end, the children could fish for items, and we would discuss each one they caught, raising awareness about litter and the harm it does to the marine environment.

In the evening, Sally and I went to watch the annual Blakeney rural sports day on the village playing field. This is part of Blakeney Regatta, the best-known event of which is the greasy pole contest. This dates back to 1873 when the prize was a hog. Each year, a horizontal pole is erected over Agar Creek opposite the Blakeney Hotel. The object is to walk along the heavily greased pole and make it to the end, although in recent years contestants have tended to slide, rather than walk. Highly entertaining to watch, the event draws a big crowd.

I went along to watch with Mike and Laney from Morston Café. We sat on the railings with pints of cider from the King's Arms, or the 'KA', as locals refer to it. I couldn't believe how many people there were spectating, it felt more like a city than a village. Graham's brother, Chris, took part. He had allegedly practised in his garden on a drain-pipe greased with Fairy Liquid. But, like the majority of contestants, he slipped off into the creek before reaching the end.

As August came to an end, the autumn bird migration started getting under way. With an influx of birders on holiday coming to the coast over the bank holiday weekend, there are usually plenty of sightings. On this particular Bank Holiday Monday, a red-backed shrike had been spotted at Salthouse, just off the coast road. By the late afternoon, most tourists were heading back home, so it was quiet when I arrived. The red-backed shrike is known as the 'butcher bird' because it catches bees and impales them on thorns to feed on later. Their colourful and highly variable eggs were prized by egg collectors and as they became rarer, throughout the twentieth century, so their eggs became more sought after. This, combined with destruction of hedgerows, led to their extinction as a British breeder, although they have since made a very small comeback.

Over on the Point that day, the first Lapland bunting of the autumn was seen and so was a barred warbler. I was on the Point the following day and enjoyed good views of the latter in the Plantation.

Although less rare, I was particularly keen to find the wryneck that had been reported at the Hood. It was one of the British birds I longed to see. Accompanying Richard Porter, we looked in vain.

Desperate to see one, I returned to the Hood in the evening. There were three other young birders also searching for the bird. Before almost giving up, we found it, and I had a couple of great views through a telescope. It was smaller than I had expected but its intricate plumage did not disappoint. A truly gorgeous creature.

I was on a real high as I walked back to the Lifeboat House, having successfully seen a bird I had dreamed of seeing. Walking over the dunes in the evening light, I thought of the many evenings I had viewed them from Friary Hills. In fact, the pleasure of just walking over the golden dunes was almost equal to that of seeing my first wryneck. Around the dinner table that evening, Eddie, Paul and Joe all shared their excitement that September was just one sleep away, the month that birders most look forward to.

10

Farewell for Now

THE FIRST SATURDAY OF September marked the beginning of the end of the summer, with the end-of-season dinner in the Lifeboat House. Hut owners Andrew and Kay kindly cooked dinner for the Point wardens plus Bee, myself and visiting former seasonal warden Richard. Graham Bean kindly ran me over on his ferry after I finished my Morston shift. I wrote in my diary, 'As we wound along the creek into the harbour, I felt a sense of belonging. I felt like we were in the opening scene from a film. A moment of happiness.'

It was great to see Richard again after almost a year. I had obviously grown in experience and he told me he was proud of what I had achieved over the past year. Andrew served up some sea bass he had freshly caught off the beach.

Towards the end of the evening, Kay asked the wardens why they were so obsessed with birds, how it started and what their parents thought. Richard replied, saying that, as a teenager, birds could reach him in a way that his parents could not, which was quite profound. He explained that his obsession was rather a keen interest, a fascination, an appreciation and something healthy, alluding to it being beneficial for mental health, which is something that is now widely recognised, although at that time the term mindful birdwatching hadn't yet been conceived.

With the end of my placement at Blakeney fast approaching, I was really taking in the atmosphere of the Point with added fondness. I wrote a short piece inspired by Eric Ennion's last walk around Adventurers' Fen:

Sat amongst the Marram grass on a dune bathed in morning sun. Headed to the sea hide, its wood very much weathered and flaking away in many places. From here we watched Arctic and great skuas fly above the choppy sea in straight lines. By afternoon, the sky had turned a deep grey, but we proceeded to venture along Far Point. The calm atmosphere was refreshed by a vibrant, heavy rain shower. Amongst the Suaeda, a Lapland bunting and a chiffchaff were flushed, the latter lit beautifully as the sun shone after the rain, resembling a watercolour painting.

There was a succession of goodbye meals. Laney, from the café, did a dinner party with some of the Morston crowd. Friary Farm caravan owners Pat and Alan had me over for a buffet. We watched a couple of BBC programmes featuring Blakeney, which they had recorded over the years.

One was called *A Wild Winter's Day*, which I recognised because I had watched it at the time that I was applying for nature reserve placements. It was this programme that had prompted me to get in touch, inquiring if there was a possibility of me volunteering at Blakeney for a year. So, it brought things nicely full circle. Many of the people interviewed in the programme I had since got to know, such as Jason Bean and Bernard Bishop.

Savouring my last week on the Norfolk coast, my sensitivity seemed heightened to the wildlife around. An hour at Cley beach one sunny morning felt particularly magical. Out to sea, there were three harbour porpoises. A Sandwich tern flew by, being chased by an Arctic skua. Then a hobby caught a dragonfly. On the edge of the Point there was a great spotted woodpecker and a couple of blue tits, both species being relatively rare sightings on the Point, 'The sea and sky looked such a brilliant blue, with a slight haze separating them.'

My final Morston shift was an evening tide. Towards the end, there was such a calm atmosphere, so still and quiet. Bee popped in to say goodbye before walking down to the quay and literally disappearing into the sunset. I spent the following day with Chris, who was also coming to the end of his seasonal contract. We had to do some jobs out

Brancaster way, which was a good chance to give the new Land Rover Defender a good spin.

We called in at Brancaster Activity Centre so I could say goodbye to the team there. They reminded me that their placement student was also returning to Brackenhurst in October. Chris and I then headed to Morston Quay:

> As evening began to fall, the still water was so tranquil. Having loaded up the boat, I steered us across the pit to Pinchen's Creek. It was getting dark, but I had to go for a swim. I jogged along the boardwalk and walked in, gradually getting used to the temperature. Floating in a calm dark blue state of relaxation with an almost full moon reflected in the water, it was perfect. I was joined by an inquisitive seal.
>
> Back in the Lifeboat House, after darkness had fallen, lit by candles and with Classic FM playing, it felt so homely and comfortable. My last night on the Point ended beautifully. Looking out of an upstairs bedroom window I saw the distant lights of Blakeney and Morston. So still, so quiet, so beautiful.

It was grey and drizzly crossing the harbour back to Morston. Back at the office, a cake appeared, and John made a speech, saying I had surpassed all previous volunteers. I was given a card and a copy of *The Birds of Blakeney Point* signed by the authors and my colleagues. Graham and Marilyn kindly gave me National Trust gift membership as a thank you for helping over the last fifteen months.

Setting off home to Market Deeping, I drove via Morston for a quick look out from the viewing platform above the visitor centre. There were gale-force northerly winds, and it was so grey that I couldn't see the Point. I hopped back in the car and headed home.

Meanwhile, Eddie, Paul and James McCallum were trying to identify a vagrant American flycatcher that had dropped into the Plantation. It was identified and later accepted as the second-ever British record of an alder flycatcher, some 3,000 miles off course. The first had been found in Cornwall, two years earlier. Naturally, it attracted hundreds of birders and twitchers, especially as there was some speculation that it could be a yellow-bellied flycatcher, which would have been a first for not only Europe but the Middle East and north Africa, too.

It was undoubtedly bird of the year on Blakeney Point. Joe was absolutely gutted that he had left nine days before it arrived. He wrote a post on his blog expressing respect and admiration for the lads for finding it 'with only a smidgen of the bitterest jealousy'.

Over the previous fifteen months, I had made such a wealth of memories and developed a deep love for the north Norfolk coast. It was quite a wrench having to tear myself away and return to my old life. I felt deflated. It was incredibly hard to communicate what my year in Blakeney had meant to me and how down I felt about the fact it had come to an end.

Before returning to university for the final year of my degree, I managed to squeeze in a short trip to stay in Finland with a friend. While over there, Graham sent me an email. As well as mentioning the flycatcher twitch on the Point, he mentioned a Channel 5 documentary called *Nature Shock: The Seal Ripper* – which, he jokingly said, suggested that the unlikely culprit of the summer's seal deaths was the Greenland shark.

I later watched the documentary, which featured Sable Island in the Atlantic Ocean. Over 100 miles off the coast of Nova Scotia, the island has a population exceeding 400,000 grey seals. Eight years of research had been conducted on 'corkscrew' seal injuries, the same kind of spiral lacerations that we had seen in Norfolk. Their theory was that Greenland sharks were causing the seal deaths on Sable Island. However, the Sea Mammal Research Unit ruled out the possibility of the Norfolk and Scottish seal deaths being caused by any shark species, still favouring the boat theory.

I didn't, for one minute, think sharks were to blame, but one part of the documentary did really grab my attention. It explained that the collagen fibres within seal tissue form a diagonal pattern around the body. This means that, once a piece of seal tissue is torn, if it continues to be pulled, it tears off in a spiral-shape naturally; the tear running along the line of least resistance.

Following on from the media attention surrounding the corkscrew seal deaths, it was thought that Blakeney should put out a good news story. Slowly, the tide was turning as Blakeney was no longer being kept a secret. In mid-October, an article appeared in the *EDP* titled 'It's a bumper year at the Point as migrant birds flock in to rest'. Dave was quoted as saying it was one of the best years for bird migration during the decade he had worked on the reserve, as well as sharing the important message that 'it was important visitors took care not to disturb the birds'.

Back in Nottinghamshire, I was immersed in student life. Norfolk soon seemed like a distant dream, but the experience had genuinely changed me as a person. Once or twice, I listened to North Norfolk Radio online, but it's really not the same when you're not in the county.

When term ended for the Christmas break, I headed back to north Norfolk for the National Trust Christmas party. At Friary Farm, it felt like nothing had really changed. Soon, I was in Graham and Marilyn's Citroën Berlingo on the way to Blickling for a tour of the house and then lunch in the pub opposite.

In the evening, it started snowing as I stood by the church to meet Eddie. He was 'overwintering' in Cley at respected conservationist Simon Aspinall's house. We went to the King's Arms, the Blakeney Hotel and then on to the Legion, where various familiar local residents were dotted about.

The following evening was completely different with the rare opportunity to stay overnight on the Point, 'There was an almost full moon and stillness similar to my last night over here, only it was *so* much colder.' There was no heating and no running water either. According to my diary, 'It was a bit cold, in fact probably my coldest night ever, but I managed to sleep quite well.' In the morning, I helped with the penultimate grey seal pup count of the year, recording forty-nine pups under a week old. Throughout the whole day, we didn't see another person on the Point.

April Fool's Day marked a year since my first paid shift at Morston. A year on, I found myself at Morston Quay once again, on my way to the barn to meet Eddie and Bee. They were heading out to the Lifeboat House for the start of the next new season and I had come along to help on the annual beach clean.

It was so great to be back as we headed along the Point on the quad bike and trailer. Dinner was Friary Farm rabbit curry, which was delicious. Like the previous year, we met the rest of the litter-pickers at the Watch House for lunch and I spent another afternoon pleasantly wandering around the Point. I also helped pluck a roadkill pheasant for our dinner. Bee had found it in the road a few days earlier, it having just been hit by a car. She was predominantly vegetarian, but would occasionally eat meat that was ethically sourced. While being run down by a car may not be most people's definition of ethically sourced, it had had a good life up until the end and at least it wasn't wasted, nor should there be any shot in it, plus the food miles were as low as the rabbit we had eaten the night before.

Sated from our roast pheasant and content we had done a good job cleaning up the beach, we slept well ... until 2.30 a.m. when the fire alarms went off briefly. Then again, a little later ... and again!

The alarms had only recently been installed and something clearly wasn't right:

> We resorted to getting out a stepladder and removing all six, unable to deactivate them. Stacked together on the kitchen table, they went off and went on and on. So we then resorted to putting them in the tractor and driving it a short distance away from the building, because they just would not seem to turn off. A truly sitcom moment.

On the morning tide, the Norfolk National Trust volunteers arrived by ferry to help with some demolition. Half of the group helped take down an old shed in the garden, while my group dismantled the old sea hide. The dune it was situated on was gradually eroding and the hide, already somewhat dilapidated, was now at risk of dropping into the sea. The regular birders were to mourn the loss of their sea-watching hide but appreciated the reason for its demolition.

A few days later, there was an article in the *EDP* about the wardens moving out to the Point for the start of the season, titled 'Away from it all with the birds'. It contained an amusing quote from Eddie, who:

> ... realises that successive evenings spent chatting to fellow wardens, or reading, would have little appeal to night-clubbers or computer addicts. As national frenzy mounts with the approaching royal wedding, does he plan to fire up the generator and watch it on the wardens' rarely used TV? 'What royal wedding?' he asked.

For me, it was back to Brackenhurst for my final weeks of university, finishing at the start of June. Being too late in the summer for any seasonal posts relating to breeding birds, a cycle hire assistant role at Wicken Fen proved ideal. As I was able to volunteer on the reserve alongside, it seemed like an opportunity to gently slide into a career in conservation. Some of my course mates were struggling to find a job relating to their degree, but at least I could be based on the edge of one of the country's prime nature reserves, somewhere with which I already had a strong connection.

I also accompanied the bird-ringing group on a few occasions. None more memorable than on my birthday, when I helped mist netting hirundines at dusk in the reedbed. It had rained in the afternoon and become quite humid by evening. At the end of the ringing session, my hands were covered with mosquito bites. But it was a truly magical experience and I imagined this was what it would have been like living in the undrained Fens of centuries past.

At the start of July, I took a trip along Blakeney Point. As I walked along the spit from Cley beach, I saw more little terns than I had remembered ever seeing before. During my visit, I met the newest Blakeney volunteer, Al; a cheerful chap who was incredibly passionate about little terns and clearly enjoyed being involved in their protection during what was an outstanding year for the Point's population.

The previous year, eighty-one pairs of little terns had bred across the reserve with just fifteen young successfully fledging. This year, by mid-June there were over 100 incubating birds in the beach colony alone. In fact, a minimum of 160 pairs nested on the Point and Stiffkey Meals combined, with breeding success a very healthy 0.875 per pair.

When the nation's little tern data was collated later in the year, it became clear that the Blakeney population contained 8 per cent of the nation's breeding little terns and had the highest productivity of any colony that year. Sandwich terns also had a great year, suggesting a healthy food supply in the nearby waters as well as very low levels of predation.

Naturally, the team were in very good spirits as I joined them watching the tern colony. In the garden, I was shown a meadow pipit nest with chicks. There were a small number of honeybees showing an interest in the wood of the Old Lifeboat House, and we wondered whether they would take up residence there, imagining how marketable Blakeney Point honey could be.

As the light faded outside, the gas lights were turned on in the kitchen. Their soft light gently lit the wooden panelling. A candle in a bottle flickered in the centre of the table. There was a warm glow and the analogue radio crackled slightly. It felt like we were on a boat, in a faraway land and in a long-ago time. We were listening to 'Smooth Classics' on Classic FM and Ralph Vaughan Williams' 'The Lark Ascending' created the perfect atmosphere.

It was a special moment. Soon the gas lights would become redundant, candles would be banned for fire safety and the old, crackly radio would be replaced with a digital one. Maybe this was an echo of past times on the Point, how it might have been back in the 1920s. In some ways, this would be the end of an era: in just a few weeks' time, solar panels would be installed on the Point. This would be the last season with the electrical power limited to just two hours per day. Another step into the twenty-first century.

Back in Cambridgeshire, I was having a fantastic summer. A local outdoor sports company were operating stand-up paddle boarding at Wicken Fen, and I was asked to help out so I could chat to people about the wildlife of the fens and help them identify the creatures spotted on their paddle-board safaris.

My two fellow cycle hire assistants had become my good friends. I managed to spark a genuine interest in the nature reserve in them both, especially Pete. He was between his second and last years of a degree in economics, but his growing interest in Wicken Fen and nature conservation prompted a career change, with him eventually going on to become a ranger in the Lake District.

At the start of October, I was asked to open up cycle hire for a workshop centred around conservation grazing, which Wicken is renowned for. One of the attendees was Blakeney's head warden, Dave. His big news was that he was leaving Norfolk to become site manager for the RSPB on the Isle of Islay. The following week, I went to Blakeney for Dave's leaving do: dinner at the King's Arms and then drinks at the Legion. All the core Blakeney team were there. There was such a feeling of warmth and familiarity.

I absolutely loved being at Wicken Fen, had a great social life, great housemates and was extremely content. However, deep down, I had a nagging feeling that, as a graduate, I should be trying to get a paid role in nature conservation. So, throughout the winter, I applied for a wide variety of seasonal and permanent roles across the British Isles.

I was invited to an interview at Aigas Field Centre, up near Inverness, where BBC *Winterwatch* were based the following year. Considering I had never been to Scotland before, I did well to get an interview. I managed to get full marks on my identification test, including a capercaillie tail feather. I didn't quite make the cut to become one of their seasonal rangers and was told that being a bit older would benefit me. I suppose at least you don't have to do anything to get older, it just happens.

Before dawn on Valentine's Day, I found myself setting off for Morston Quay. Shortly after I arrived, Chris drew up in his van, hoping to return to the Freshes for a fourth season. Paul then arrived a few minutes later, followed by Joe: the three of us were all applying to work on the Point and there were only two positions. Knowing I was the least qualified of the three, after my interview, I returned home, convinced I wouldn't be given a job.

Two days later, a call came through from Blakeney offering me 'an annualised 22-week contract'. However, I would only be paid for three days a week but would get free accommodation on both the Point and mainland. I weighed up the advantages and disadvantages. I had been told that I could stay on at Wicken for another season of cycle hire, which was now going to include boat trips too. It was like being torn between two mistresses: Lady Blakeney and Lady Wicken.

Although the boat and cycle job would enable me to earn more money for a longer period of time, Blakeney would provide more relevant experience – that sought-after first paid post in nature conservation. Surely the chance of a season on Blakeney Point should not be missed?

Part 2

Point-Based –
A Season on
the Shoreline

1

April: Anticipation

ON EASTER MONDAY, I arrived at Friary Farm. It felt like only yesterday I had last been there. Graham and Chris helped me load my supplies, bedding and guitar into a trailer, carefully wrapping everything to keep the sand and fine shingle dust off while being towed up the Point by tractor. The usual banter ensued as I helped them tidy the workshop while we waited for Joe to arrive from Somerset.

Like me, Joe had accepted a twenty-two-week, three-day-week ranger contract. The chance to spend another season on the Point and hopefully 'see some rares' outweighed the reduced pay.

Eddie was relieved that he did not have to let one of his friends down, which so often has to happen in the competitive world of nature conservation. So, everyone was more or less happy and Blakeney Point had four rangers for the price of three. Technically, three rangers and a warden, in fact, with all new contracts adopting the new role title, but Eddie's full-time contract remaining 'warden' until the official ranger launch in the autumn.

Around mid-afternoon, the tractor pulled up outside the Lifeboat House. Joe and I were given the two smallest bedrooms because they were equal in size, so it didn't look like one of us was being favoured. My room looked out over the garden, which now contained an array of shiny solar panels.

After a bit of unpacking, we paired off and went for a short walk in the drizzle and mild south-westerly breeze. Eddie and Joe headed out to Middle Point, where they found the first nest of the season: a mallard's, containing fifteen eggs covered with down and dead grass.

The Lifeboat House during the 2012 season. (Ajay Tegala)

Paul and I crossed Pinchen's Creek, as the tide was out, heading along Yankee Ridge. Despite seeing no noteworthy birds, it felt special because it was my first walk on Blakeney Point as a paid ranger. This was the start of the season. Five months of adventure lay ahead.

During the week before, in anticipation of a summer by the shoreline, I had written my first song on guitar, fondly remembering what I loved about Blakeney and imagining what lay ahead:

At the end of the Point, there's a reason
Four miles of shingle away
On the edge of the land, there's an answer
And we're living it right here today

Out here with the terns and the plovers
Out here each and every day
Living close to the seals and the swallows
Feeling more than four miles away.

Eddie had organised a cake and ale meeting to kick the season off. It was a cleverly informal way of outlining his targets and expectations for the season. Lists of daily, weekly, monthly and ongoing jobs were then pinned up on the wall.

Also pinned up was a black-and-white photograph of a serial egg thief. Jokingly captioned 'enemy number one', he had been imprisoned for egg collecting three times. The thief had been caught stealing eggs in Scotland the previous June and a police raid of his home had unearthed a collection of 700 eggs, including avocet, osprey and golden eagle. He had recently been given an ASBO (antisocial behaviour order), which banned him from Scotland during the breeding bird season for ten years.

As we ate cake and discussed everything from our working patterns to bird migration patterns, Bee cooked us a delicious dinner. She made her specialty Käse Spätzle, a homemade German pasta dish with black olives, grated carrot and cheese.

After the oven had cooled down, a super-sour gas heater had to be brought out because April can still feel like winter in the Lifeboat House. It takes a few weeks to properly warm up in the spring. Some years later, I met a former seasonal warden, Tracey, who told me how she and the two other assistants had huddled together on the sofa under a duvet to keep warm in April. Now, with the addition of solar energy for the first time, we could give our bedrooms a blast of hot air from a fan heater each evening, being careful not to use too much power on grey days.

After a cup of tea and breakfast, the Blakeney Point day starts with checking the bushes to see what migrant birds have dropped in overnight. This involves following a set route that takes in the garden – also known as the Lupins after the large number of this non-native species that had been planted there before such introductions were considered inappropriate – the Plantation and the large tamarisk behind the UCL laboratory. The birds present are a consequence of weather conditions and an indication of both migration routes and population size of a whole variety of species with varying conservation statuses.

For the Blakeney Point ranger, this is a fascinating insight into what birds are both leaving and arriving in the country. It is quite exciting waking up in the morning and not knowing exactly what birds you will find in your garden.

This is an important part of the job, not just for scientific monitoring, contributing to long-term data sets, but also for visitor management. If something significant turns up, you can expect greater visitor numbers, which means greater potential pressure on vulnerable nesting birds. After a round of the bushes, the morning's sightings are chalked on the blackboard in the visitor centre. Any interesting shells, feathers or skulls found on the beach are labelled and put on display as interpretation for visitors. Grey seal skulls were fairly numerous, but commons were harder to find. I resorted to burying a common seal carcass near the Lifeboat House with the intention of digging up the skull years later ... but I'm pretty sure it's still there.

The centre floor is swept daily, as is the house. Sand is forever finding its way into the building, so sweeping is essential. The public toilets also need to be cleaned each morning. These domestic jobs are divided up between the team, so that the day's visitors can arrive to find clean toilets and a tidy visitor centre with bang up-to-date information on what birds are around. The tide then dictates the rest of the day.

A day when low tide is somewhere between midday and early evening will be ideal for seal counting. After the second Phocine distemper virus outbreak in 2002, more effort was put into gathering consistent seal population data. By their nature, seals are quite hard to count when diving and swimming, hence low tide being the best time to see the greatest number on land, when they are relatively simple to count. A telescope is essential as the majority are usually hauled out on the opposite side of the channel: the West Sands. Use of a telescope enables each individual seal to be inspected sufficiently to identify it as either common or grey.

Low tide is defined as a four-hour window opening two hours before dead low water and closing two hours afterwards. With a minimum of one count per fortnight between the start of April and the end of September, there was now almost a decade of historic data, which enabled the analysis of population trends throughout each year and from one to the next.

Evening high tides in April are a time to conduct Sandwich tern roost counts. These are done as often as possible to take stock of how many terns have arrived on territory and what the general mood of the settling colony is like. High tide is ideal because it reduces the available roosting area to the tip of the Point. With the harbour and much of the beach submerged, the terns are bunched into a more manageable area to count.

Sitting opposite, on Middle Point, watching the developing colony on Far Point from early to mid-April is a wonderful spectacle. Seeing the terns returning after their winter in Africa, hearing their distinctive calls alongside the noisy black-headed gulls and picking out occasional Mediterranean gulls in the sound mix, it is a feast for the senses. Brent geese may also be heard softly gurgling in the harbour, their numbers decreasing as they migrate north to their breeding grounds in Siberia.

Like our domestic duties, seal and tern counts would be shared between us. Often, one of us would cook the evening meal while the others were out watching the terns. We took it in turns to cook. On my second evening, I offered to cook my first Point meal. I had found a recipe for vegetable lasagne, which was well received and went on to become my signature vegetarian dish.

Vegetable peelings went into a compost bin tucked behind one of the sheds. It had limited success due to underlying sand rather than soil, but nonetheless reduced the amount of rubbish sent back to the mainland. Each week, our filled bin liners were taken to Cley in the quad trailer and then on to the wheelie bins at Friary Farm. We tied blue baler twine around bags of recycling so these could be distinguished and put in the appropriate bins. Up until just a year or two before, rubbish was burned in a metal drum in the evening when all visitors had gone. Before the turn of the century, rubbish had been buried in the dunes, until it was eventually considered inappropriate on such a scientifically important site.

The third day brought with it new birds. Cold weather meant a rather slow arrival of summer migrants, so it was a delight when, on the morning round of the bushes, we observed the first willow warblers of the year along with a chiffchaff.

Telling these two species of warbler apart can be difficult without a good look at their leg colour. The chiffchaff's tendency to constantly flick their tails is a clue, as well as its song differing from the willow warblers. The name chiffchaff comes from its two-note call, much like its German name of *Zilpzalp*.

Combining our counts on the headland with Richard Porter's along the main shingle ridge, we estimated there were easily over twenty-five wheatears on the Point that day. Out to sea, 120 common scoter and fourteen swallows flew west, as well as the first 'sea swallow' of the year: a common tern.

The first Sandwich terns arrive a few weeks before the common terns. Indeed, that year the first Sandwich tern of the season was seen on 16 March at Cley. Paul and Eddie had moved out on the 30th to conduct the annual beach clean, get the Lifeboat House ready for the season, start erecting the breeding bird fencing and also to get to grips with the new solar panels and storage battery system. As the season progressed, one of our weekly tasks was to manually cut the grass around the panels, using a pair of garden shears, to stop any shadows reducing their efficiency. They would also be wiped weekly using rainwater and a soft sponge, removing the accumulation of meadow pipit droppings.

A week before Joe and I started, a dramatic chase had been witnessed when a merlin flew in pursuit of a skylark. Both birds found themselves inside the Lifeboat House kitchen. The merlin flew into a windowpane and promptly dropped behind the bin. All windows were frantically opened and a few minutes later, it flew out of an open window on the opposite side of the room, landing in the garden to recover. When moving an armchair to watch the merlin through the window, the skylark flew out from behind it. Its tactic of flying inside a building may have been accidental, but had saved its life.

After just two nights on the Point, I was heading inland with Eddie to promote the reserve at the Spring Fling event held at Norwich Showground. We had taken sand, shingle, shells, skulls, feathers and fish-egg cases to make a mock-up beach display as a way of engaging with visiting families. We may have looked the least polished and professional stall there, but visitors seemed to love it.

This was a good revision tool for me, ahead of upcoming school groups. I was impressed at how many children and adults were more than happy to handle the gull wings we had included in our beach display.

Bee was also there on the Norfolk Wildlife Trust stall. She told me that she didn't think it was fair that the Point should have two rangers for the price of one, which a few people had also said to me. I explained that the reason I accepted the half-job was because I needed paid experience on my CV, as well as really wanting to be on the Point for a season. I think some people wanted Joe because he was the stronger, more experienced candidate, and others wanted to give me the opportunity, having volunteered for over a year. In recent years, consistency had been maintained by trying to employ one experienced assistant alongside someone else less experienced, to give them that valuable first step along their way into a career in conservation. This was my valuable stepping stone.

After a successful day at the Spring Fling, we were happy to be returning to the Point, where a black redstart had arrived and the first seven whimbrel of the year had been seen; an appropriate number for a bird known as the 'seven-note whistler'. With their down-curved bills, they resemble a smaller curlew. The breeding range of the whimbrel extends from Iceland to Russia and includes a small Scottish population. They winter in west Africa and birds are observed in Norfolk on passage in spring and autumn.

As I drove the HiLux between Norwich and Holt, Eddie called the Point to catch up with what had been happening over the past twenty-four hours. There was big news. It wasn't just a black redstart that had landed on the Point.

Part of our disturbance monitoring work includes noting the registrations of any low-flying aircraft and recording the impact they have on the wildlife. Joe was near the Lifeboat House when he spotted a helicopter, with the registration G-JKAY, flying worryingly low over the main dunes. He ran over and found, much to his disbelief, that it had actually landed in Great Sandy Low.

Joe spoke to the pilot, explaining that this was an important nature reserve with sensitive ground-nesting birds, where aircraft are only permitted to fly over at a minimum height of 1,000ft. It turned out the pilot thought he was at Brancaster, which incidentally also has the same flying restrictions in place. The passengers were polite and apologetic, promptly taking off. Wracking his brain afterwards, because the passenger looked familiar, Joe put two and two together with the helicopter's G-JKAY registration. It was Jay Kay from the 1990s pop group Jamiroquai.

A letter was sent explaining our concerns and I believe a phone-call apology was received, although our suggestion to make a donation towards the conservation of Blakeney Point was not followed through. We were advised not to alert the media, although news inevitably spread around the local community.

Thankfully, the incident happened early enough in the breeding season not to have an impact on any nesting birds and the helicopter did not leave a footprint. If it had landed on the end of Far Point, it could have resulted in the gulls and terns abandoning. I reflected on their fragility as I trudged westwards along the shingle ridge on my 4-mile trek home. The sun was setting behind the Lifeboat House where I was given a welcome plate of chilli on arrival.

Each evening, we had two diaries to fill in, which we usually did after dinner. All disturbance incidents were logged, from low-flying aircraft in the air to loose dogs on the ground, scoring the impact between one and five depending on how the birds reacted. The other log listed the birds themselves. Migrants were listed in taxonomical order – from wildfowl to finches – on the left side of the page and notable breeding behaviour was listed on the right. Any insects and mammals of interest were noted at the bottom of the page.

We had two Blakeney Point bird bibles, which were always to hand, usually laid out on the kitchen table. The *Collins Bird Guide* is essential for checking identification notes on lesser-encountered migrants.

The other book is *The Birds of Blakeney Point*, authored by regular Point birders Andy Stoddart and Steve Joyner. Their book contains a systematic list of all known bird sightings on the Point up to 2004. We would often flick through the 'weather and migration' chapter to see what we might expect at a particular time of the spring and in particular conditions.

As well as a lot of data that the pair had painstakingly compiled, they had referred to two historic annotated checklists of the birds of Blakeney Point: Rowan's from 1917 and Doctor White's from 1967, updated in 1981. These two checklists give a fascinating insight into what the Point's bird life was like at two interesting snapshots in history. So, for example, at the end of my first week, when two goldfinches appeared, we were able to quickly find out that Rowan never recorded them, and White recorded them as 'occasional'. Since then, Goldfinches had become a common spring migrant on the Point. The two we saw were probably British birds moving north from European or north African wintering grounds. Knowing this context and history deepens one's understanding and appreciation.

Later on that mid-April Friday, we headed down to Middle Point. Roosting Sandwich tern numbers had reached around 1,800. Migration was rather slow due to cold weather and the linnets that had started nest-building at the beginning of the month had stopped due to the weather. We discovered that the mallard nest had been predated, all fifteen eggs having gone with no sign of any shell fragments or yoke. This suggested that a stoat had presumably rolled the eggs away. The first mallard nest on the Point was recorded in 1953 near the Watch House and the first brood of ducklings were recorded in the main dunes in 1964. Since then, one to three nests have been found most years. There was still ample time for this bird to lay another clutch.

Walking over the crest of a dune, I flushed a short-eared owl, which had been sat hidden in the grass just a few feet in front of me. I could hardly get the words out to tell the others, surprised and delighted to see it so close. Over the winter, I had seen them regularly on Burwell Fen, where we had a wintering population reaching double figures, but I had never seen one so close. These impressive and beautiful birds are in fact on the list of tern predators. During Ted Eales' time as warden, he noted that owls breeding on the nearby mainland had taken many tern chicks and occasionally even sitting adults. As majestic as these birds are, their presence at a tern colony is not particularly welcome.

My second week on the Point began with just Paul and myself on duty. The other two were on days off. On the midday high tide, Graham brought over *EDP* journalist Steve Downes and a photographer. Various photographs were taken of Paul and I with our telescopes and one of Graham leaning on the information board at the gap. In the Lifeboat House, Paul and I were interviewed about our roles for a story about the National Trust's centenary as owners and protectors of the Point.

I wrote in my diary, 'It puts into perspective what a unique job and lifestyle we have out here' and noted that 'since coming here last week, every night I have had clear dreams that I have remembered in the morning. Not sure if it's the sea air, but normally I would only recall about half as much or less.' The relentless Norfolk coast winds, some of them blowing straight from the Arctic, can really sap your energy when you're out walking in them for any length of time. Clearly, I was sleeping well in my new home.

The following morning started with strong westerly winds and heavy showers. Two new migrants had arrived in the bushes: a female blackcap and a male common whitethroat. *The Birds of Blakeney Point* states that spring whitethroats appear on the Point from the third week of April. This bird was bang on time.

With the bushes checked, toilets cleaned and floors swept, our next job was to put out yoghurt pots and saucepans to collect raindrops – because there were a lot of leaks upstairs in the Lifeboat House. In fact, my room was the only one without a leak. Rushing around together to catch all of the water, I noted that 'there was a definite feeling of "being part" today'.

In the afternoon, the clouds cleared, the wind dropped and the temperature rose, treating us to a still and bright few hours. A couple of swallows flew west and a male hen harrier put in a distant appearance near Beach Way.

On Wednesday, there were more rain showers, heavy at times. Our bird of the day was a rough-legged buzzard. This Scandinavian breeder is a rarity on the Point.

The rain had eased by the evening when we headed out to monitor the colony. Nestled into the Middle Point dunes with our telescopes, we scanned across to Far Point and noted the first two Arctic terns of the year along with fifteen common terns on territory. Roosting Sandwich tern numbers had also increased to over 3,000 birds.

To our left, a red-throated diver was sat on the edge of the shingle, not usual behaviour for this bird, which led us to suspect illness or injury. We made the decision to leave it in peace overnight and intervene in the morning, if need be. On the Middle Point dunes behind us, a lone rabbit was spotted, which was in fact a notable sighting.

At times in the previous century, rabbits had been prolific on the Point. However, they have also been exterminated by myxomatosis on two occasions, the first being in 1954.

The early wardens would supplement their income by shooting rabbits and selling them to the local butcher. Original warden Bob Pinchen had, in fact, been a butcher, as well as a farm labourer and wildfowler, prior to becoming warden. There was a great photograph of Ted Eales in the visitor centre, taken in the 1930s or 40s, showing him with eight to ten freshly shot rabbits tied to a stick balanced on his shoulder.

Numbers bounced back after the 1954 extinction and by the 1980s literally dozens of rabbits could be seen around the huts. However, they were struck by myxomatosis a second time in the 1990s and soon became extinct again. Sightings since then had been very rare. The disappearance of rabbits had led to a significant increase in flowering plants in the dunes, with plants such as sea holly, sea bindweed and cat's-ear thriving now that they were no longer being grazed. As a consequence, insect life had also improved, thanks to a greater abundance of nectar sources and food plants.

Numbers of hares on the Point also seemed to increase following the disappearance of rabbits. Although some of the hares seen on the Point are from nearby mainland populations, there are a number that breed in the main dunes and are seen throughout the year.

The Middle Point rabbit had made a burrow into the dune, but appeared to be a lone individual. Being non-native and having had such a negative impact on the Point's native flora, we were happy not to see rabbits make too much of a comeback but were content to let this individual be.

On my second Friday, Graham had a guided walk on Blakeney Freshes scheduled. With all four of us Point staff on duty that day, I was happy to head to the mainland and assist Graham with his walk. We followed the classic formula of setting the scene on Friary Hills, heading along Desmond's permissive path towards Cley and picking up the coast path from the River Glaven back around to Friary Hills. Graham led and I brought up the rear, chatting to walkers along the way. At the closest part of the coast path to the Watch House, I spoke to the group about terns and life on the Point.

By the weekend, the weather had brightened up a little and a pair of pied wagtails were seen around the Lifeboat House with nesting material. On Saturday afternoon, the Far Point colony was distinctly unsettled, with birds up in the air and not settling back on the ground. Their behaviour indicated that something on the ground was causing upset.

The birds' state of panic not showing any signs of settling down, we had to resort to something usually avoided in the second half of April: entering the colony. We soon found out what had been bothering the gulls and terns: a short-eared owl was sat on the ground. We hoped that scaring it off would be enough for it not to return. During the maximum two minutes we were in the colony, we also flushed a mallard that was incubating ten eggs right in the middle of the gulls. We wished it luck in such a risky location, surrounded by potential predators.

Sunday brought a small number of migrants over the Point: twenty swallows, three house martins, a sand martin, two yellow wagtails and an osprey. The latter naturally caused the most excitement when Andy Stoddart phoned it through to us. We literally ran outside in our slippers to look for it. Andy was walking up from Cley with Richard Porter.

They would always let us know if they encountered anything of interest or concern on their frequent walks up the Point.

That afternoon, we proved we were all-round naturalists by spending some time appreciating and investigating the plants of the sand dunes. Having mapped and classified all species on the Point, Richard always kept a keen eye on any noticeable changes in plant distribution and abundance. In the dunes between Glaux Low and Great Sandy Low, there was an abundance of spring vetch interspersed with tiny early forget-me-not and occasional heath dog-violet. With a hand lens, we examined the striking colours of these small flowers. One of the most widespread plants across the Point, which is in bloom in April, is Danish scurvy-grass. Its small, white flowers can be seen growing along high tide lines.

Following the previous day's short-eared owl disturbance, we walked up to the colony again in the afternoon to make sure it had settled. We were pleased to see that all was calm. However, a couple of walkers were heading along the beach in the direction of the colony. It turned out to be a couple I had met on Graham's guided walk. Having enjoyed hearing me talk about the Point, they were keen to walk up and see it for themselves, which was great, but it highlighted the fact that it was time to start gap duty for the season. The signs alone were not enough to keep walkers far enough away from the terns at low tide and the colony was now in the vulnerable settlement phase. During this phase, the terns are deciding whether to nest and can choose to abandon if there is too much disturbance, be it from people, short-eared owls or a whole host of other predators and disruptions.

I was to be the only member of staff on the Point on Monday, so volunteer and little tern enthusiast Al had kindly agreed to join me for the day. I had met him on a walk up the Point the previous summer and he remembered me. He kindly walked up from Cley to help me cover the gap throughout the day. First, we checked the bushes, discovering a male and female ring ouzel, traditional spring migrants. Al was keeping a keen eye out for the first of his beloved little terns of the year, which were due any day. He had counted oystercatchers along the ridge on his walk up: along with my observations on the headland, we estimated a minimum of seventy territories across the Point. The first little terns were seen the following day.

That evening marked another Blakeney Point first, when we uploaded our very first blog post. Creating a Blakeney Point blog was on the to-do list. Joe was an experienced blogger so had technical expertise and I was excited about the possibilities. Our aim was to create something very much in the vein of the hugely successful Farne Islands blog, with a running narrative throughout the season, enabling readers to follow the progress of the breeding and migrant birds. It would also be a method of reinforcing our anti-disturbance guidelines. This was something that, although there had been some nervousness in the past, we were all very excited about.

It was quite late into the night when the post went live, by which time only Eddie and myself were left at the laptop. We toasted the momentous occasion with a shot of whisky, served in the traditional Blakeney Point method: a metal eggcup. We wondered how successful our blog would be. Some Norfolk birding blogs had huge followings and one of our favourites was Penny's Hot Birding and Life. Penny would occasionally walk out to the Point, searching for rarities, mentioning the rangers she met if we were lucky.

The following day was not conducive to securing nice photographs for the next blog post. Heavy rain persisted throughout the day. The thought of venturing out to Far Point didn't feel particularly inviting in the heavy rain. However, we were all glad we had made the effort when we spotted a young grey seal tangled in thick netting on the beach.

Paul rushed off to fetch the seal stretcher while I kept an eye on the seal. My task was to prevent it getting to the water and swimming off before we could free it. In the time Paul took to return, the seal gradually moved closer to the sea. I had to resort to physically holding the seal still to stop it escaping – being cruel to be kind. It was a great relief when the quad bike finally came into view. The act of cutting the seal free took about sixty seconds. Fortunately, the net hadn't cut too deeply into the young seal's neck. However, it was pretty tight and would only have dug tighter into its flesh as the seal grew larger over the coming months. We could now return to the Lifeboat House with big smiles, despite being soaked through.

The last Thursday in April brought the first swift sighting of the year, in line with the expected first returning date of these African-wintering acrobatic birds. There is a lovely record from August 1935 of them roosting inside the Lifeboat House overnight. Being one of many birds showing declining numbers in Britain, action had been taking place to encourage them to nest. Nest boxes had been erected on Blakeney Church tower and swift calls were played to attract passing birds to nest in them.

Eddie and Bee were keen to attract swifts to nest on the Lifeboat House lookout tower. They had made some nest boxes over the winter and attached them to the tower. With the first birds seen, we began playing a recorded loop of their calls every day. This method works best in areas where swifts are already nesting in the vicinity. The Point is obviously quite isolated, with no other nesting swifts close by, but it was worth a try. Research suggested it could take a number of years.

A summer of events themed around Blakeney Point's centenary kicked off at Blakeney village hall on the last Saturday of the month, with a talk on the geomorphology of the spit. It was hosted by the Blakeney Area Historical Society, who had also reprinted copies of a paper on the subject by Professor Oliver, from the early days of the reserve. I attended the talk with a few colleagues, and we all found it very interesting.

We went on to the Legion afterwards for a drink. It felt as if we had entered another world when we arrived in the middle of a stag do, complete with a stripper. Somewhat unexpected in Blakeney, especially after a scientific talk!

Being off the Point that Saturday meant I unfortunately missed one of the birds I had been hoping to see. The only British owl species I hadn't yet seen alive in the country was the long-eared owl and I had hoped I would get to see one during the season. Although very rare in spring, one had chased a robin over the colony, disturbing the gulls and terns. Such is the risk of leaving the Point during migration time, even for a few hours – you can miss out.

After the short-eared, the long-eared is the second most frequently recorded owl species on the Point. Although there had been some night sightings of hunting barn owls at the Cley end, the one recently roosting in the shed during winter had been the first daylight record on the headland. There were six records of little owls on the Point over the latter half of the twentieth century, although Bob Pinchen described them as 'the most destructive of the raptorial birds' during his time as warden in the early years of the reserve, having observed one decapitate an incubating tern. This behaviour is, in fact, also typical of short-eared owls.

There has only been one record of a tawny owl on Blakeney Point. However, it did not find its way there completely on its own. In the early 1980s, a birdwatcher picked up what he thought was a dead tawny owl from the road between Attleborough and Dereham. When his car arrived at Morston Quay, the boot was opened and the owl flew out. The following day, a tawny owl was flushed from Yankee Ridge, undoubtedly the same bird, having most likely been sheltering in the Suaeda in its disorientated state.

April ended with a day of sunshine, warmth and a south-easterly wind, which brought in a number of migrant warblers. With records from the regular birders, we recorded a total of sixty-eight willow warblers and around eighty wheatears across the Point. These were the sort of migration days I had heard about and had longed to experience – losing count of bird numbers.

The fine conditions were ideal for a butterfly transect, one of our weekly jobs. A formal butterfly transect was set up on the Point in 2008 with the help of Norfolk's county butterfly recorder. A circular route of ten sections was established, running from the landing ridge, through the garden, along the boardwalk, through the dunes to the lab and past the Plantation to the Old Lifeboat House. It is walked once a week from the beginning of April to the end of September, recording all butterflies observed along the way.

This was the fifth transect of the year and the first to actually record any butterflies: a single small copper and a single small tortoiseshell. The first butterfly of the year had been recorded ten days earlier; a peacock, not on a transect. Richard Porter had started his own informal butterfly transect along the ridge from Cley beach to the Hood back in 2002. Also taking advantage of the weather, he walked his transect on the same day and had also recorded a single small copper as well as a small white.

We watched little terns displaying over Far Point and near the Lifeboat House. The first passerine eggs of the spring were also discovered that day. At last, one of the linnet nests in the garden contained an egg. On Yankee Ridge, a reed bunting nest containing four eggs was uncovered and two meadow pipit nests, both with four eggs, were spotted in the dunes when adults were seen flying off suspiciously from among tussocks of grass.

The discovery of these four nests was a fitting prelude to May. We would soon find ourselves monitoring as many nests as we could manage.

2

May: Migration

NORMALLY, 1 MAY WOULD be a celebration of lush greenery. But, out on the Point, it didn't feel like May at all to me; it didn't even feel like England. The harsh environment means that the trees in the Plantation are not only stunted but also do not come into leaf until a good couple of weeks later than the same species on the mainland. The plants of the saltmarsh, shingle and sand dunes also tend to lack fragrance. You don't tend to smell blossom on the Point. The exception being sea campion, which has a very subtle and delicate scent of honey.

The second day of May brought a bit of extra colour to the shingle ridge when a blue-headed yellow wagtail landed briefly. A continental subspecies of yellow wagtail and an uncommon, but regular, spring visitor to eastern England.

The afternoon produced an adult red-breasted flycatcher in the Plantation, living up to its name. The Point is known for its afternoon arrivals of migrants. An afternoon check of the bushes can sometimes prove more fruitful than the morning, as was the case on this occasion. The flycatcher stayed for four days. By now, common redstarts were turning up in the bushes, having started to appear at the end of April. Whinchats follow the same pattern.

May sees another morning task added to the list of daily jobs. With the discovery of the first oystercatcher egg on the last day of April, a check of the landing ridge is required prior to the arrival of the first visitors each day, especially if there is a morning tide. An area of such high footfall may at first seem a strange place for so many pairs of oystercatchers to choose to nest. However, humans tend to deter gulls and other aerial predators.

Sometimes, a morning check of the landing ridge results in the discovery of uncovered eggs, the parent bird already having slipped off inconspicuously. On other occasions, an incubating bird will be spotted running away from her nest so as not to draw attention to it. Recognising this behaviour and making a mental note of the spot often leads to the discovery of a nest, so this behaviour is looked for. Multiple scrapes will be created prior to laying, so making a mental note of their locations gives a good place to start a search.

It is then a case of nipping back to the Lifeboat House to collect four metal road pins, a lump hammer and some baler twine. A large stone can be used to drive in the road pins if there isn't a hammer to hand. The road pins form the four corners of the small enclosure. Some years before, it was discovered that small, square fence lines were actually more of a help than a hindrance to gulls, who soon learned that each had a meal in the centre. Varying the shape and size and not necessarily having the nest in the dead centre is enough to outwit these clever predators.

The day after the first oystercatcher egg had been laid on the landing ridge, the first ringed plover egg was laid on the shingle beach behind the Lifeboat House garden. Up to 100 pairs of ringed plover bred on the Point until the mid-1990s when numbers began falling significantly. A key factor was common gull predation, so a method of extra nest protection was devised.

The Norfolk name for ringed plover is 'stone runner', because they usually nest on shingle and always run off their nests when startled, rather than flying. This behaviour means that a shopping-basket-sized cage can be put over the eggs. Gaps on all four sides, large enough for the birds to fit through, enable them to run off their nest as normal whenever they wish. But the mesh prevents gulls from reaching the eggs. We waited until a second egg had been laid and then proceeded to cage the nest.

On the same day, we found a nest of the Point's third breeding wader species: the redshank. The adult will sit tight on their eggs, which are usually laid in grass. The brown-grey plumage of the redshank blends in remarkably and can easily be missed. But if you happen to be walking too close, the bird will lose its nerve and fly off erratically. This happened on Middle Point, alerting us to the nest's location. A quick and careful inspection revealed four eggs, a full clutch.

A large pebble was found and placed a few metres from the nest. Not so close that it could be a clue to a gull or mammal, but close enough for us to recognise it. This year we were to begin nest monitoring for the BTO (British Trust for Ornithology) Nest Recording Scheme. The scheme was started in 1939, to collect information on incubation and fledging periods, making it the longest-running scheme of its kind in the world. In fact, I attended a seventy-fifth anniversary conference a couple of years later, held at the trust's headquarters in Thetford.

Always keen to collect useful ornithological data, Eddie set us the task of each monitoring ten nests from the nest-building stage through to the young hopefully fledging. Naturally, this became a bit competitive to see who could find the most nests and the most different species.

Nests would be visited every four days, so that they were not disturbed too often, and they would not be checked during poor weather. Collectively, we recorded 171 nests of seventeen species between April and September. This did not include any gulls or terns, due to them nesting in dense colonies. Nor did it include shelduck, because of their tendency to nest down old rabbit holes. The majority of our monitored nests were oystercatcher – an impressive eighty-two nests – meadow pipit, ringed plover, linnet, redshank and mallard. A number of nests were re-lays after failed first clutches.

As well as the excitement of being able to follow the progress of individual nests, it was motivating that our findings were contributing to a national database, forwarding our knowledge of bird nesting habits. The data would also give a clearer picture of nest productivity and any trends in causes of failure. At that time, there had been relatively few meadow pipit nest records submitted, so our nineteen records were a valuable boost for the scheme.

After a few welcome days of spring-like weather, suddenly we were back to biting northerly winds and rain. This didn't deter twenty-five little terns from feeding offshore. A meadow pipit with a beak full of flies indicated it was feeding chicks.

Migration trickled on with a stunning hobby fly-by. These migratory falcons spend winter in sub-Saharan Africa, returning to Europe once their prey of large flying insects becomes plentiful, so we kept our fingers crossed that the weather wouldn't restrict its food supply too much. Migration is primarily driven by food availability, with the British climate suiting many African species.

Down at Pinchen's Creek, the bright white plumage of a spoonbill shone out from the grey weather. After a 300-year gap, they bred in Britain in 2010, just a few miles west at Holkham National Nature Reserve.

The May Bank Holiday weekend got off to a flying start in terms of raptor species. It was a famed four-falcon day, with merlin, peregrine falcon, hobby and kestrel all observed. It was also a double harrier day too. Marsh harriers are recorded most days, when nearby breeding birds come out to the Point to hunt. Early May can still produce hen harriers, but that day, an even more special harrier put in an appearance: a pallid harrier, passing west. They are a rare visitor to Great Britain from Eastern Europe, the first for Norfolk having only been recorded a decade previously.

Later that day, there was a big tide. Combined with winds from the north-east, it came quite high up the beach. By now there were numerous occupied oystercatcher nests along the landing ridge, all of which were high enough to stay dry. But the same could not be said for the ringed plover behind the garden. High water reached the eggs and started to float them. So, we carefully moved the eggs about a metre higher up the beach to safety. Care was taken to also move some of the more distinctive stones and shells surrounding the nest. This way the adult birds would not get confused and would still be able to find their nest. Moving a nest too far can lead to abandonment, but these precious few centimetres were enough to save the eggs from being washed away.

On Sunday, we were treated to the appearance of a migrant bird synonymous with Blakeney Point, a bird I had dreamed of seeing.

Since Victorian times, birdwatchers and naturalists have come to the Point to look for this passage migrant. Now relatively rare and also quite elusive, we were all excited when a message came through from James McCallum, which read, 'Bluethroat near the Hood'. We were fortunate to enjoy clear views of this well-marked male under the shelter of a Suaeda bush, its red spot prominent within its blue throat. It was absolutely gorgeous to behold.

Our monthly wetland bird count coincided with Bank Holiday Monday. A high tide in the morning produced the ideal conditions to record waders and wildfowl across the coast. With Richard Porter surveying the main ridge between Cley beach and the Hood, we divided the headland between the four of us, recording sanderling, common sandpiper, whimbrel and curlew alongside our breeding wader species. There were still double figures of brent geese in the harbour. A male eider was also recorded, this individual having been seen most days since early April. He finally moved on at the end of May.

It was a tradition to follow the wetland bird count with a fry-up. However, our toast had to be briefly abandoned while we ran outside to watch a pair of cranes flying west over the harbour.

When the next tide came in that evening, we headed down to the colony to monitor numbers. Little terns now exceeded 100, we estimated up to 3,000 apparently incubating Sandwich terns and around 1,700 black-headed gulls. With Sandwich terns now on eggs, we had added another task to our daily job list: dawn patrol.

From the start of May to the middle of June, we took it in turns to rise at 4 in the morning to essentially make sure the birds were free from human disturbance. Our motivation being the very real chance of egg theft. While this was fortunately declining, there was still a risk that the Point could be targeted. The few remaining egg thieves tended to be obsessive and in pursuit of rare species to complete their collection, for example, stone-curlews in the Breckland. A species like the Mediterranean gull, for example, could be desirable as it is only a relatively recent breeder in England.

If anyone was to enter the tern and gull colony on Far Point in search of Mediterranean gull eggs, thousands of birds would go up and make a racket. However, if we were all asleep in the Lifeboat House, there was a possibility that none of us would notice, the building being almost a mile from the colony. This is partly why the wardens of old lived in houseboats. They could be moored beside the colony. By being out and about from dawn, we would soon pick up on any disturbances. Dawn patrols on the Point usually started off with a check of the colony through a telescope and then involved walking to the Long Hills to scan along the beach and main ridge to the Watch House area.

It was the little tern colony near the Watch House that had been targeted in the most recent case of egg theft. This had occurred in June 2004, when ten nests were raided. At the exact location of a loose cluster of five nests, a large smiley face had been carved into the shingle, which made the theft even more infuriating. The previous case had been in 2001 and resulted in two convictions. However, the 2004 thief – or thieves – sadly got away with their crime.

Partnership working is key to preventing egg theft. Operation Compass is an initiative run by the RSPB and Norfolk Police to target active egg collectors. Information and suspicious vehicle registrations are shared between more than 100 nature reserve staff and police across Norfolk, Cambridgeshire, Lincolnshire and Suffolk.

In fact, the efficiency of Operation Compass was demonstrated that May when local birdwatchers in the Breckland noticed two men behaving suspiciously. Operation Compass was alerted and the following day, the same men and vehicle were also spotted at two other stone-curlew nesting locations in the area. Police investigated the vehicle and visited the house it was registered to, whereupon a number of eggs were discovered, including little tern and marsh harrier. Justice was delivered.

Back in the 1980s, communication between sites wasn't so easy and egg theft was more common, as Graham well remembers. Occasionally, I would go along with Graham to visit Cley Marshes warden, Bernard Bishop and his wife, Shirley, at their home overlooking the marshes. They would often reminisce about how they had to be vigilant and creative to catch egg collectors.

Shirley would help her husband, once posing as a holiday-maker on Cley beach with a bottle of water as a last-minute prop.

Keeping watch, she alerted Bernard of the suspect's location when it was safe to do so discreetly, and the police were able to catch the thief with eggs in their possession.

That was the hard thing about our dawn patrols. If we did see someone taking eggs – which I am pleased to say I never did – rather than intervening, we would have to let them take them. We would have to fight our instincts and stay hidden from view, calling 101 and quoting Operation Compass, stating that we were witnessing a crime in progress. If the thieves suspected they were being watched, they could dispose of the eggs and there would be no evidence. In order to be prosecuted, they had to be caught with eggs in their possession. This is why recording vehicle registrations is also important.

Back in August 1903, the *Norwich Mercury* reported how warden Bob Pinchen had helped to prosecute the guilty parties of two separate bird crimes. A Cley resident was charged with taking eight tern's eggs in early June. Also, two Blakeney residents were charged for shooting a ringed plover and a dunlin on the Point in early August.

Immersed in a haven of nesting birds, I was fast developing an eye for finding meadow pipit nests in the dunes, but pinpointing the exact location of a ringed plover nest could be quite a challenge, even when a definite territory was apparent. One morning, on the landing ridge, I found a clutch of five passerine eggs that did not belong to a meadow pipit. I knew it was a reed bunting nest because the eggs matched the ones I had been shown on Yankee Ridge. Their Norfolk name is 'scribble lark', because the eggs look as if they have been scribbled on with ink. A wonderfully descriptive name.

One week into May, we enjoyed a day of warm weather and impressive passage migration. Out at the gap, there was a constant stream of swallows passing through in a westerly direction. We counted numbers with finger clicker counters as we kept watch on the beach. An estimated 3,000 swallows were recorded throughout the day along with around 100 house martins and sand martins and about 200 swifts.

The latter flew very close over the sand dunes, the sound of their beating wings clearly audible as they zoomed by. Almost batlike, swifts are the fastest bird in self-propelled flight. The peregrine falcon has flown at higher speeds, but while diving with gravity on its side.

A record from exactly eighteen years earlier, to the day, estimated an exceptional swallow passage of 2,500 per hour. Between one and five pairs of swallows have nested on the Point most years since 1929. During the previous summer, a pair had raised a brood inside the men's toilets. With the door being kept closed this year, we put up shelves inside our new garden sheds and the newly refurbished old tern hide on Near Point.

On Near Point, we also created a rock pile in an attempt to attract wheatears to breed. Rowan's 1917 annotated checklist records two to three pairs of nesting wheatears each year. They stopped breeding on the Point soon after the Second World War. However, Ted Eales did record a pair in 1956, but it is unclear whether they actually reached the egg-laying stage.

A pair had held a territory in a rabbit burrow during May 1999, with the male in song. Again, in May 2003, a female held a territory in a rabbit burrow on Near Point. With this in mind, we thought Near Point might be a suitable place to create a rock pile because wheatears are known for nesting among the safety of piles of rocks. Our nearest breeding birds were on Orford Ness, in Suffolk, where they nested between cracks in old concrete.

I made the most of a sunny evening. At high tide, I took *Albifrons* down Pinchen's Creek to the *Yankee* wreck and back. *Albifrons* was the name of our rowing boat, which had been recently restored by Chris. Our Bonwitco motorboat was kept on a mooring in Pinchen's Creek, reached by rowing a few metres out to it.

On a rising tide, the water flows up Pinchen's Creek with terrific speed. I wanted to maximise my rowing abilities to prevent ever being swept unwillingly up the creek. 'The sun was going down, the sky orange, all was calm, a perfect time to be on the water.'

The next day was rainy, but the morning after was warm and sunny, with more birds flying west: over 6,000 swifts, 2,000 swallows, 1,000 house martins and 200 sand martins as well as eighty-three linnets and ten goldfinches. The fine weather early in the morning was conducive to a breeding bird survey. As well as mapping individual wader territories, we conduct breeding bird surveys across the Point to monitor breeding passerines; the dunes supporting significant numbers of breeding skylarks and meadow pipits along with linnets and reed buntings, plus small numbers of dunnocks and wrens.

Spaced out in a line, the four of us would walk in a straight line across the dunes and points, pivoting at the end and returning back and forth until we had surveyed the whole area. This was done over multiple visits. We would shout out everything we saw to Eddie with his clipboard and photocopied maps.

'Meadow pipit with food!' was called out a lot, often truncated to 'Mipit with food!' During these surveys, we were able to find several 'Mipit' nests, as adults emerged suspiciously from under tussocks of marram and couch grass. On this particular morning, we joyfully watched a meadow pipit feeding a successfully fledged chick.

Three days later, a sunny Sunday morning meant another breeding bird survey, this time on Middle Point. As well as the expected bird species, we encountered a muntjac and were able to get within 5m before it noticed and fled. The gulls and terns were not comfortable with this dog-sized deer so close to their nests and showed their frustration by mobbing and dive-bombing it on the beach.

Although deer feed mostly on vegetation, they have also been known to eat eggs and young birds. With a roe deer seen five days earlier and red deer in the harbour at the end of March, we had recorded three deer species on the Point. Chinese water deer are often seen nearby on the mainland, but there had been no records of them making it out to the Point.

The second Monday of May brought a cuckoo to the Point, spotted flying over the dunes. This was the first of the season. There are two records of cuckoo chicks being reared in skylark nests on the Point during the 1960s. Seeing one in spring did make us wonder whether history could be repeating itself. However, it was clearly only passing through and not hanging around. We hadn't actually managed to find any skylark nests, despite mapping numerous territories.

Multiple hours of watching could be needed to locate a skylark nest. However, we were busy managing many other species, namely the little terns near the Watch House. In recent years, little terns had been following a trend of settling in two separate areas on the shingle ridge; to the east and west of the Watch House. However, the precise spots in which they settle tend to vary from year to year. Therefore, we were waiting to see where precisely the birds would settle before fencing them off for protection, not just from human footfall but from human presence too close by.

When an incubating little tern sees a person too close to their nest, they will take flight for safety. However, this leaves the eggs vulnerable to chilling or overheating, not to mention predation. Fences must be erected swiftly so that we do not present them with too high a level of disturbance.

We would attend en mass, often with the assistance of Richard Porter and Al, in order to make the operation as slick as possible. Many hands not only make light but quick work. Because we needed to use the quad bike and trailer to transport the metal fence posts, little tern fencing had to take place in the low-tide window. This meant that the gap would be left unattended for an hour or so, and therefore early mornings were best. Our journey to the Watch House would act as a recce along the beach to see if there were any early walkers heading up. Once erected, these fenced enclosures also benefit oystercatchers and ringed plovers.

As we headed into the second half of May, we had some more feathered visitors to the Lifeboat House. Warming temperatures had promoted the opening of windows and, within minutes, a couple of swallows were flying around upstairs. We had even taken off a shed door to try to encourage them to nest in there, but they seemed determined to nest in the Lifeboat House. We managed to keep them out of the visitor centre by putting up a noisy bead curtain, which would also alert us whenever visitors were about.

Doing the washing up at the kitchen sink and looking out of the window towards the landing ridge, I spotted two familiar faces. It was my parents' neighbours from Market Deeping, my former driving instructor and his wife. They were excited to see me and accepted my offer of a cup of tea and access to the lookout tower. Inside the tower, a swallow was circling. My visitors were surprised that, not only was I looking after birds, I also appeared to be living with them too.

Another example of birds coming into close contact with humans was an awkwardly located oystercatcher nest found the same day. It had laid an egg in a scrape right in the middle of the path by the landing stage. We quickly erected a large fence and put out a warning on our blog for all seal trippers to have a quick look but then pass by quickly so as not to disturb the nest for prolonged periods of time.

By this stage in the season, the number of oystercatcher nests on the landing ridge prompts the need for high-tide patrols. These are an opportunity to engage with visitors, encouraging greater appreciation of the reserve while at the same time ensuring dogs are kept on leads and no barbecues are lit. It is understandable that, to the average visitor, staying outside of the fenced areas seems enough. However, if an hour-long picnic takes places too close to a nest, the parent birds will not return in that time, which can lead to eggs failing if this happens too frequently.

As well as one of us patrolling the landing ridge at high tide, someone would be based in the lookout tower. From here, an eye could be kept on visitors heading along the boardwalk and into the dunes. As well as surveying a greater area for potential loose dogs, tents and barbecues, an eye was kept out for people damaging fragile dunes.

We sometimes came across as killjoys, but we always tried hard to make people understand we didn't take pleasure in dampening their fun; rather, we took even less pleasure in seeing vulnerable wildlife accidentally disturbed.

If there was an evening tide and the weather was good, we would need to keep watch. Needless to say, we always kept our uniforms on in the evenings, just in case. If we were on the Point, we were always on duty. That was the reason for us being there, ever ready to respond to anything that could arise.

Shelduck over the Point. (Ian Ward)

On the second Thursday of May, we saw our first linnet chicks of the season. In the garden, under a lupin bush, a fledged dunnock was being fed. Butterfly numbers were slowly starting to pick up, after what had been a rather slow start. Spring was now in full swing and the next morning we had a coordinated shelduck count in the diary.

We were all up bright and early on Friday for the survey. Each of us had an assigned area to head to. Shelduck congregate in the dune slacks early in the morning, making it relatively simple to count the numbers present and therefore estimate the breeding population. I headed out first because my area was furthest from the Lifeboat House: the Hood and Long Hills. Paul was counting Great Sandy Low, knowing that to get an accurate count, he would have to get close enough to them, which would prompt them to take flight. So, he made sure I was in position before getting too close, to ensure that some of 'his' birds did not fly into my sector or Eddie's and get counted twice.

These striking black-and-white birds are as much goose as they are duck. A closer look at their plumage reveals glossy green and chestnut-brown colours and a bright red bill. They nest in the safety of old rabbit holes, where they are hidden from avian predators. For that reason, we were unable to monitor any individual nests, but occupied holes could be identified by their footprints in the sandy entrances.

One Saturday evening, a sudden change in the wind led to a small boat getting into considerable difficulty. It became swamped and lost power before it could reach the safety of the harbour. The three men on board managed to escape safely to the Point. Watching from the look-out tower, we were able to meet the three wet and cold men, providing them with towels, dry clothes and a restorative whisky. Once recovered, we took them to the mainland in our boat.

Their stranded boat was left anchored on the beach. It was battered by pummelling waves overnight. Sunday morning, when the tide had gone down, we bailed out the water and sand that had accumulated inside overnight. Jim Temple and Graham came up at low tide by trac-tor to pull the boat out of the sand, into which it had sunk deep. It was then dragged to the water's edge ready to re-float on the evening tide and be towed back to Morston for repair work. Being the first on the scene in such incidents meant that Blakeney Point rangers had to be part-coastguard, a responsibility we took seriously.

The second half of May brought migrant spotted and pied flycatch-ers, garden warblers and a second bluethroat, this time a young female at the Long Hills, there had been an impressive arrival along the east coast in recent days. A different female was spotted on Middle Point the following day and a male common rosefinch turned up on Yankee Ridge in the evening. Other sightings that day included a purple sand-piper, two siskins and a fully fledged young skylark. The first redshank chicks were also noted in one of the nests we were monitoring. Like ducklings and goslings, young wader chicks are downy and down-right adorable.

Entering the last week of May, we took stock of oystercatcher nests, having found at least one new nest each day throughout the month. Excluding a few that were predated, there were at least thirty-five active nests on the Point. The textbooks state that oystercatchers usually lay two to four eggs. We found that most first clutches on the Point had four eggs, with subsequent re-lays of lower numbers. We even found a nest containing five eggs.

Monitoring was assisted by a dissertation student from the University of East Anglia in Norwich. Kieren enjoyed his time on the

Point and the banter. He took a bit of teasing for bringing his own saucepans with him to the Lifeboat House.

The weather didn't really settle all month. By mid-morning, one Thursday, a thick sea mist had formed. Out on the beach, visibility was so low it was hard to look for visitors and we didn't even attempt any nest monitoring for bird welfare reasons. Early in the evening, the mist started to clear, before rolling back in again and creating an eerie atmosphere. I took some photographs and reported on our blog, 'Due to the poor visibility, we have resorted to staying inside and drinking Norfolk ales this evening.' We tried to give our blog a personal feel without it being more about our personalities than the reserve itself – wildlife was the clear focus.

We had many great nights enhanced by Norfolk ales and Scotch. But I have to say that, had alcohol been banned on the Point, my experiences there would not have been any less special. What makes the Blakeney Point life so unique are the natural surroundings, the landscape, weather and wildlife, the Lifeboat House, the local characters, history and atmosphere. I once met someone who said they had stayed overnight in the Lifeboat House when visiting a friend who was an assistant, one year. When I asked them about the birds and the reserve, they said all they remembered was staying in and drinking, which I thought was a real shame in such a special place. The true spirit of Blakeney Point does not come in a bottle.

The night before our Sandwich tern nest count, I didn't drink a drop. I wanted to be completely focused on what was a very delicate operation. Being inside the colony is obviously a disturbance, so the key is to be as quick but as cautious as possible. The conditions were ideal: early mornings tend to be quiet for visitors, dry and warm weather prevents eggs from chilling and at low tide birds can land on the adjacent saltmarsh. We were prepared ... with bags of pasta.

Counting over 3,000 densely packed nests is near impossible, even with four people. Being able to physically mark a nest avoids both double counting and missing nests. That is where macaroni was ideal. Something biodegradable, harmless, light, not too large and not too tiny. We counted, double-checked and then triple-checked four bags

Sandwich tern chick resting on egg. (Graham Lubbock)

of 1,000 pieces of macaroni. When we entered the colony, all we had to do was watch every step and mark every nest. The number of macaroni pieces left would be counted and subtracted from 4,000 to reveal our total number of Sandwich tern nests.

As we approached the colony, the terns and gulls went up in the air. The noise was incredible. So was the strong smell of guano. It was as if we had entered their world – we were privileged but also intruding. First, we passed the black-headed gull nests in the Suaeda bushes. Then we started to spot the black-and-white Sandwich tern eggs on the ground. Sandwich terns don't leave the nest to defecate, merely spraying guano around the edge of the nest. This gave the nesting area a very distinctive look and smell.

Counting had to be focused and methodical because there were so many nests in a dense area. Some were tucked under Suaeda bushes. You lose all concept of time with all attention put into finding each nest and not accidentally treading on any eggs.

Because of the exact shape of the colony, which we did not know until we entered it, some areas had more nests than others. I had ended up in one of the denser patches, whereas Eddie was in a sparser patch, so he helped me finish my area when he had finished his.

Then the moment came when we realised that all nests had been counted. We left, heading back via the Middle Point dunes. From there, we could see that the birds had returned to their nests in the short time it had taken us to walk away. It was a relief to see them back on their nests without any problems. Satisfied that all was well, we hurried back to the Lifeboat House to find out what the number of nests was. It was good – 3,735, which was just over a third of the Great British breeding population.

Still reeling from the buzz of being in the colony, the morning rolled on and the tide rolled in, bringing the Stiffkey Cockle Club with it. They had been granted permission to use the Lifeboat House kitchen to cook bacon sandwiches for all of the sailors. We were very helpful and accommodating but were left with the washing up rather than a bacon sandwich – and Blakeney Point wardens are known for their appetites.

That evening, we had a couple of guests staying with us. I found that chatting to them highlighted how fantastic a responsibility and pleasure the job is. Something to be savoured and not taken for granted, especially as time seemed to be passing by so fast. After dinner, we looked at the moon through one of our telescopes. The day had started with one spectacle and ended with another.

Towards the end of the month, four children from Blakeney Primary School came to stay for a night in the Watch House with their teacher. We involved them in our daily tasks to make them feel like young rangers, while teaching them about the habitats, history and wildlife along the way. We tasked them with fencing around a newly laid oystercatcher nest and showed them the moth trap we had put out overnight.

Walking along the Long Hills, we saw fledged wrens zipping around in the Suaeda. There was also another bluethroat at the Long Hills, the fourth of the season.

We knew, from our nest monitoring, that the first oystercatcher nest was due to start hatching, following twenty-eight days of incubation. An evening walk along the landing ridge revealed our first oystercatcher chicks of the year were indeed hatching. This was an added bonus for the schoolchildren. It was encouraging to hear that they enjoyed moth trapping too.

We were very keen to support the school visit because the experience of staying in the Watch House and going 'back to basics' is another world to so many children. Having twenty-four hours on the Point enabled us to really give them a flavour of how important and special it is, and we hoped they would share this with their parents and friends.

3

June: Hatching

DURING EARLY JUNE, MIGRATION is still evident. Three days into the month, there were still ringed plovers migrating north. Some roosted near the Lifeboat House at high tide one evening. They chose a spot right by one of our nesting ringed plovers. This didn't impress the incubating female, who ran down and attempted to chase them away from her territory. We watched the unhappy interaction through telescopes from the Lifeboat House steps. It was interesting to observe how our British *hiaticula* race are noticeably larger and paler than the passing *tundrae* birds of northern Europe.

The warden focus in June is almost entirely on breeding birds, with numerous chicks as well as eggs to protect. We knew that the most recent egg theft on the Point had happened in early June, so we didn't let our guard down and continued the dawn patrols well into the month. With young oystercatchers learning to walk and feed, we afforded a greater area of protection to them and spent more time encouraging visitors to be mindful of what was happening on the landing ridge and around the Lifeboat House.

Out on the beach, a survey at the very start of the month recorded seventy-eight apparently incubating little terns alongside fifty-one apparently incubating common terns. This colony was a few hundred metres east of the main Sandwich tern colony. Fifteen pairs of little terns and at least twelve common tern pairs also bred by the Sandwich terns, along with a pair of Arctic terns. Meanwhile, towards Cley there were twelve little tern pairs west of the Watch House and four to the east.

About half a mile further towards Cley beach, to our surprise and delight, an avocet colony appeared to be forming. Birds had been seen on the shingle in late May and two nests were found on 2 June. We rushed down to erect a sizable fence around them. This was very exciting, being the first avocets ever to nest on Blakeney Point. When we started nest recording just a few weeks earlier, we had no idea we would be monitoring avocet nests on the Point. We were licensed to monitor this Schedule 1 species due to their presence on the wider reserve, namely Blakeney Freshes. These birds may well have been displaced from the Freshes or Cley Marshes.

Each day, we took turns to have a presence at the avocets, walking the 3 miles from the Lifeboat House to get there. They were on a part of the Point where dogs were permitted, so we made sure all dog walkers kept their animals on short leads and ensured all visitors gave the avocets sufficient space.

It was fascinating to observe their behaviour, the avocets were quite bold and would give black-headed gulls a good seeing off if they came too close to their nests. The two breeding pairs attracted more and we had to keep extending our enclosure until a total of nine pairs were cordoned off. These included a colour-ringed female, who had been ringed in 1993 as a nestling at Holme in west Norfolk. This made it nineteen years old. We presumed these birds were failed breeders from Cley Marshes and Blakeney Freshes, although some laid full clutches of four eggs.

Busily protecting growing colonies of various rare birds across almost 5 miles of Blakeney Point, we had to shrug and smile when an oystercatcher was seen taking a little tern egg near the Watch House. Little tern, avocet and Mediterranean gull are all Schedule 1 protected species under the Wildlife and Countryside Act, making them the most protected of Britain's breeding species. Mediterranean gulls are also known to predate little tern eggs: one Schedule 1 species predating another Schedule 1 species.

Another factor out of our control was the weather. Unfortunately, the spring tides of early June coincided with northerly winds, creating a perfect storm. This resulted in at least three ringed plover nests being washed away plus an estimated ten common tern nests and an unknown number of little terns'. This bad news – although it is just nature, 'good' and 'bad' are human emotions – was balanced by seeing many oystercatcher eggs hatch and meadow pipit chicks fledge, which we observed as part of our nest monitoring work.

The same day as the flooding, we recorded four broods of oyster-catcher chicks finding their feet and being fed by their parents on the edge of the saltmarsh. A hunting kestrel ate two of the chicks two days later, but for every negative there seemed to be a positive elsewhere on the Point, such as a displaying little ringed plover near the avocets, another Schedule 1 species.

My diary entry for the first Wednesday of June reads, 'Another misad-venture. Typically, we were running late ...'.

Eddie was steering the boat to collect Al, who was to join us on our Stiffkey Meals survey. 'Meals' is an old word, deriving from the old Norse topographical name *melr*, which means sand hills. In the past, they would have been sand dunes, although years of tidal action have reduced them to a small amount of sand and shingle, which is good habitat for nesting little terns, oystercatchers and ringed plovers plus an occasional redshank in the grassier areas. In the twentieth century, significant numbers of little, common and Sandwich terns had nested there some years. There had actually been a little tern watcher at Stiffkey as early as 1890, when the Holkham Estate employed a game-keeper to guard beach-nesting shorebirds between Stiffkey and Wells: one of the very first conservation efforts on the Norfolk coast.

When the boat had been launched at the end of winter, one of Eddie's first jobs was to drop off bundles of road pins at Stiffkey Meals, ready for Graham and Chris to use to erect breeding bird fencing. On foot, Graham and Chris would cross saltmarsh to get to the Meals, which are impossible to reach by terrestrial vehicle due to a network of tidal creeks. It made sense to travel by boat to survey the little terns there.

We arrived at the top of the tide, anchored the boat and set off in search of nests. Treading carefully, we recorded a single little tern nest as well as two alarm-calling redshanks – suggesting they had young hidden in the grass – a ringed plover nest and three oystercatcher nests. We also saw a barn owl in the vicinity.

We were so absorbed in exploring Stiffkey Meals that we ended up taking just a bit longer than we should have done. 'It was inevitable that we would not have sufficient water to get back into the harbour. We tried punting, then pushing, but there was no hope, it was too late. So we anchored the boat and walked ashore.'

Joe and Kieren were in the lookout tower and could see us, so they were sending mocking text messages to us. There was now no way we would make it back for the sausages Joe was preparing for second breakfast. Graham collected us in the Land Rover and stopped off at Blakeney Quay so we could buy a breakfast bap instead. I was then dropped off at Cley beach to walk up the Point, arriving three hours later than had we been able to return by boat.

Not planning to go back to the mainland, but suddenly being there was an interesting sensation. The greenness really stood out, as did the number of people. Eddie spent the rest of the day on the mainland, returning to the boat ahead of the evening tide to successfully bring it back to Pinchen's Creek.

Two days later, there was more drama. Eddie rang the Lifeboat House, requesting the seal stretcher and as many knives as we could find. My diary entry reveals what happened next:

Quadded to the beach where Eddie was with the seal. He cut through the fishing cable that was tightly bound around its neck and right flipper. The cuts were deep and there was quite a lot of blood. We managed to get it bound up in the stretcher, put it in the trailer and set off carefully down the beach to Cley. About two thirds of the way there, Joe noticed it was escaping. We struggled to get it back into the stretcher and re-tie it. It came close to biting me twice. At Cley, we carried it up the beach to the Land Rover for Graham to drive it straight to the RSPCA. Luckily, it didn't get out of the stretcher whilst in the back of the Land Rover. This was the most graphic seal injury I had seen – other than the dead ones from two years ago – and the most involved I had been in the rescue. We did well, but the cut around the neck was deep and the skin had been severed all of the way around.

Sadly, this did not turn out to be a rescue success story we could share on the blog. The poor seal had to be put down because the injuries were so serious, with fishing hooks deeply embedded. In some ways, it would actually have been a good story to share in order to emphasise the seriousness of leaving discarded fishing hooks on the beach. As well as the potential of being swallowed by birds, they are obviously a serious hazard to mammals.

As the long days of June rolled on, life was seldom short of surprises. An exhausted racing pigeon rested by the Lifeboat House one day, which wasn't unusual. Although it decided to roost on my windowsill for three nights in a row. One day, it ventured into the bathroom, inspiring a blog post titled 'Pigeon in the Privie', continuing our liking for alliteration.

A less amusing surprise was the discovery of a decapitated little tern near the Watch House. This could well have been the work of a short-eared owl. Indeed, one had been recorded most days in the first half of the month. The same day, we saw a kestrel in the Plantation feasting on an oystercatcher chick.

A day later, we greeted the arrival of an icterine warbler. A scarce but regular Point migrant, they are more commonly observed in autumn than spring, with the small number of spring sightings usually in the last week of May and first week of June. This one had turned up on the 11th, which happened to be the first of my four days off, the longest I had been away since moving in two months before. I had gone to Somerset, travelling by train and bicycle.

Cycling across central London from Liverpool Street station to Paddington felt like I was a million miles from Blakeney Point. As did going to a nightclub on student night, with pints for £1. I felt closer to home when I noticed several herring gulls nesting on Bath's rooftops.

We spent a day cycling through the Somerset Levels and saw Britain's first breeding great white egrets, as well as fantastic views of bitterns.

Back on the Point, after a few days away, I was keen to catch up with the nests I was monitoring. At last, the ringed plovers nesting near the Lifeboat House had hatched two chicks. With so many oystercatcher chicks hatching, it became very difficult to keep tabs on them as they generally leave the nest within a few hours. Redshank chicks are escorted onto the saltmarsh as soon as they are able to walk, but some oyster-catcher families could be seen on the beach near the gap, day after day, enabling us to watch the chicks growing in both size and confidence.

The Point was not just busier with chicks, but students too. UCL were in residence. In the course of our daily duties, we would see them counting yellow horned-poppy seed pods or observing ringed plover, oystercatcher and seal behaviour.

Students would spend four nights sleeping in bunk beds in the lab. With no showers available to them, they would have to make do with flannels or wet wipes. Part of their daily routine involved cleaning the public toilets for us. The lecturers would stay up to two weeks, so we would offer them the use of our downstairs shower in the Lifeboat House. In return, we'd be invited for dinner on their last night.

Janet was a wonderful cook, able to cater for hungry students and rangers alike. She would be assisted by a returning student from the previous year. When she left, pairs of returning students would handle the catering. We would kindly be given their leftover ingredients at the end of their stay. This particular season's offering included a rather large quantity of lemons.

The middle of June saw the first black-headed gull fledglings in full flight. We also saw young grey partridges and watched a brood of six mallard ducklings being led past the Plantation to the saltmarsh early one morning.

At just four days old, we noticed the two ringed plover chicks by the Lifeboat House were able to feed themselves. Things were moving fast, already the first shelduck flocks were seen heading north-east at dusk. The majority of British breeding shelduck migrate across the North Sea twice annually, flying to a moulting site in Heligoland, Germany, leaving the young of that year behind in large crèches with a small number of adults to look after them.

Where Middle Point branches off from Far Point there is a gap in the dunes. This would have been created when a storm tide punched through it, much like what had happened to the Long Hills in 1953. Consequently, the Middle Point dunes become an island during the biggest tides. The shingly, low area between Middle and Far Point had a ridge of Suaeda, which supported a sub-colony of black-headed gulls.

By the third week of June, there were at least fifty young here, while the adjacent four pairs of Arctic terns were still sitting tight on their eggs. We were still experiencing some rough weather. I remember being down at the avocets and wearing a thick coat to keep warm during what was supposed to be summer.

Tucked among marram grass on the Middle Point dunes, we flushed a female gadwall from a nest, which contained eighteen eggs of two distinctly different sizes. Seven were gadwall eggs and were hatching. In the nest with them were eleven smaller eggs that had been laid by a grey partridge. We had uncovered a curious case of inter-species egg dumping.

Sometimes, two female grey partridges will lay eggs in the same nest. Other gamebirds, such as pheasants, have displayed the same cuckoo-like behaviour, with one female laying in another's nest and then playing no part in egg incubation or chick provisioning.

On the Point, there have been cases of two female oystercatchers sharing a scrape and both contributing towards egg incubation. There had also been a lone female oystercatcher who would incubate stones instead of eggs. One year, some abandoned oystercatcher eggs were found and so, to prevent them from failing, they were put in place of the stones the lone female had been sitting on. She incubated them and they hatched successfully. The bird, presumably barren, now had the opportunity to raise her first chicks and did a fine job of looking after them.

In the case of the grey partridge laying eggs in a gadwall nest, we speculated that perhaps she had misidentified the nest she was laying in. The day after we had discovered the gadwall eggs hatching, we returned with interest and saw seven incredibly cute chicks.

The weather was warming up and there was a south-easterly wind, which produced two notable migrants: a male stonechat and a male red-backed shrike.

A day later, another visit was made to the shared nest. We were not surprised to see that the gadwall chicks had been led away from the nest. This meant that the eleven partridge eggs were no longer being incubated by the gadwall and were therefore getting cold. The warm weather was apparently sufficient to keep the eggs warm, however, as a couple of eggs were actually beginning to hatch. Our soap opera suspense continued.

A few metres away, one of the Arctic tern eggs had just hatched. There lay a damp, newly hatched chick, looking so small and vulnerable. I couldn't help but be amazed by the fact that, in just a few weeks, this helpless-looking creature would be flying all the way to southern Africa. We kept our fingers crossed for it as the weather had once again turned cold and wet.

This did not bode well for our un-incubated grey partridge eggs. Despite the initial optimism when they began hatching in warm weather, the cold and rain prevented the chicks from successfully hatching out. In the absence of devoted parents, they were fighting against the odds. Thus, a natural conclusion was brought to our wildlife drama.

As ever, there were signs of success elsewhere on the Point. On the Summer Solstice, the first two little tern chicks were observed in the beach colony. A cuckoo put in an appearance and a noisy group of at least 200 resident starlings from the nearby mainland flocked together near the Watch House.

The same day, some of us headed west to Snettisham for a little tern partnership meeting. Over the course of the spring, I had learned that little terns were rarer and more vulnerable than I had initially appreciated. With the UK's breeding numbers in decline, the Little Tern Working Group had been set up. Just chatting to rangers from other sites is important, allowing us to see that other rangers face the same challenges as us; some worse. It appeared that we were the safest site from foxes that year. We had seen signs of foxes earlier in the season, but we hadn't experienced the predation that some other sites were suffering from.

Other sites represented at the meeting included Winterton in east Norfolk and Scolt Head, our Sandwich tern sister site. That year, Scolt had about a tenth of Norfolk's breeding Sandwich terns and we had most of the rest. The previous year, Scolt hadn't had any Sandwich terns nesting at all, so this year was an improvement for them. Interestingly, the total Norfolk population appeared to be about 500 greater than the last year, which was encouraging. Little tern numbers in the British Isles unfortunately seemed to be going in the opposite direction.

The following day, I dropped in at Cley to have a look at the Pacific golden plover there. Many a Blakeney Point assistant has walked to Cley to see a rare bird since the days of Ted Eales. In fact, I had heard that Ted didn't like his assistants spending too much time searching for rarities. But what more appropriate reward is there for the hours spent protecting nesting birds than the pleasure of seeing rare migrants? Not all of Ted's assistants had the happiest of experiences during his later years as warden. In fact, 1974 saw both of his seasonal staff do a moonlight flit in late July.

While on the mainland, I also relished the opportunity to visit a field behind Blakeney Garage. Not to see a bird, but an impressive abundance of bee orchids in bloom. There were estimated to be between 1,000 and 4,000 flowering spikes.

Interestingly, orchids are a real rarity on the Point, despite many other sand dunes supporting good numbers of them. Richard Porter's Blakeney Point plant atlas records a single marsh helleborine found in 2008, two southern marsh-orchids found in 2009, occasional pyramidal orchids on five occasions, plus a single common spotted-orchid in the dunes in 2007. This year, he was excited when we discovered a second common spotted-orchid at a new location in the dunes.

Alpine swift over Blakeney Point, June 2012. (Joe Cockram)

As we entered the last week of June, with day length beginning to shorten slightly, an early sign of autumn appeared. Over the course of the 25th, over 200 curlews were observed passing westwards. Females and failed breeders are among the first returning waders from the Continent.

But summer was far from over, indicated by the discovery of a new meadow pipit nest – a second clutch. Meadow pipits usually produce two broods per season and occasionally three.

Our nest monitoring data showed that meadow pipits were having high hatching and fledging success, whereas other birds were battling against various predators. During daily gap duty, we watched a ringed plover nest decrease by an egg a day until all had gone. Two common gulls were seen suspiciously each side of the nest cage. It seemed that these cunning gulls had worked out a way to get their heads inside the nest cage to reach the eggs, being that much smaller than herring gulls.

Later that day, Paul arrived at gap to take over from a student who had been volunteering for a day a week with us. A grey heron was sat in the middle of the beach colony being mobbed by little terns. Learning that this had been going on for twenty minutes, Paul walked straight over to the colony and flushed the heron out. At the same time, three ringed plover chicks were observed, having managed to escape common gulls and the heron.

As June reached its end, the first fledged Sandwich tern chick was seen away from the colony. A happy moment for us, as was the hatching of Blakeney Point's very first avocet chicks.

The last day of the month produced another reason to smile when an alpine swift zoomed over the Plantation. Joe pointed his camera at it and captured the moment, before it powered low towards the mainland.

This was only the second alpine swift to be recorded on the Point. The first bird had been recorded over the Hood forty years previously. Alpine swifts breed mostly in the mountainous areas of Europe, as their name suggests. Their long migration from southern Africa sometimes leads to birds 'overshooting', making them a regular vagrant to the British Isles. Having one fly right over our heads made for a happy ending to a dramatic month.

4

July: Fledging

THE FIRST WEEK OF July was unique in the history of Blakeney Point. As part of the centenary celebrations, a writer in residence stayed with us in the Lifeboat House from Monday to Friday. The original aspiration had been to get Bill Bryson. In the end, the residence was taken by Norwich-based *EDP* columnist, Steve Downes, who had visited in April. Steve fitted in well and was keen to get involved with every aspect of our work. As well as being writer in residence, he was to be a ranger for the week.

His first challenge was a trip to Budgens in Holt to stock up on all the food he would need, within a budget that matched what we normally spent. He would join in our evening meal rota, cooking for us all on his last night.

The next task was the walk from Cley beach to the Lifeboat House. This was really the perfect way to start a week on the Point: walking its length to really appreciate the remote location. I was tasked with accompanying Steve on the walk up and introducing him to the characteristic flora and fauna of the shingle ridge.

Avocets and oystercatchers were the ideal first two bird species to identify, both large and with distinctive appearances. We looked in the old Glaven channel for avocet chicks, the first ones having been seen three days earlier.

Soon after hatching, the parent birds would lead their young off the shingle onto the safety of the saltmarsh, its vegetation providing cover from predators. Cley Marshes assistant warden and car park attendant Carl had watched a pair of the Point's avocets usher three small chicks across Beach Road in front of the Norfolk Wildlife Trust car park. He stopped cars so that the family could cross safely.

Having survived the road, sadly one chick succumbed to black-headed gull predation. The rest of the group took up residence on the Eye Pool at Cley Marshes until they, too, were predated. We hoped that the birds hidden on the saltmarsh were faring better, although Steve and I couldn't spot any. But we did spot a shelduck crèche.

Venturing further westwards, I showed Steve ringed plovers and little terns, camouflaged among the shingle, plus Sandwich and common terns flying past. It obviously takes a bit of time to get your head around the differences in size, bill colour and behaviour of the four tern species, especially separating common and Arctic terns from a distance. Indeed, our bird log sometimes had 'Comic Tern' listed where separation was not possible.

It was then that the rain came, as if the walk wasn't initiation enough. Eventually reaching the main dunes, the sun returned, and the yellow cat's-ear flowers caught the light. The Point's spring flowers are dominated by the white sea campion and Danish scurvy-grass. By summer, yellow flowers take centre stage, of which the yellow horned-poppy steals the limelight. Its seedpods are the largest of any British plant. Their flowers drop off after about a day. Along with curled dock, the seeds go on to provide valuable winter food for finches.

Within thirty minutes of our arrival at the Lifeboat House, all of the birds in the harbour went up. We explained that this meant either a low-flying aircraft or a bird of prey. An osprey came into view, being pursued by a group of noisy oystercatchers.

The commotion settled and we headed to the beach for some important survey work. In addition to the standard breeding bird monitoring work, this year we were taking part in a Natural England survey of little tern foraging areas. This involved recording the number of birds and dives within our sector during a coordinated time period. Steve Downes was our scribe. The data would be important evidence of little tern foraging areas to aid their conservation.

Day two as writer in residence and honorary ranger involved the inevitable gap duty. No summer volunteer on the Point can escape the important task of helping to keep the precious tern colony free from human disturbance.

The tide rose throughout the afternoon and a scan from the Long Hills revealed all the walkers had gone home. This was our green light to head to the Middle Point dunes and perform one of the landmark moments of the season. Five and a half weeks after the Sandwich tern nest count, it was time for the chick count.

With the tide covering the marsh, all chicks were pushed into a concentrated area, forming a large group. Through our telescopes, we counted, double-counted and conferred, reaching a conservative figure of 2,200 chicks. We always erred on the side of caution. This equated to a respectable 0.59 productivity per pair. It was a happy moment, to see that the birds we had worked hard to safeguard had raised their young and would soon be migrating to Africa.

However, the breeding season was by no means over. A stone's throw from the Sandwich terns, there were still common and little terns incubating eggs. It would be another month before the last little terns were fledged (fledging being defined as capable of flight rather than completely independent of their parents).

We were determined to ensure our writer in residence was introduced to as many forms of wildlife as possible. By this stage in the summer, two of the Point's distinctive butterfly species were on the wing: the grayling and the dark green fritillary. The former could be seen throughout the headland, with considerable variability in size and blending in well with its sandy and shingly surroundings. The latter is more elusive, although larger and more distinctive. Its upper wings are orange with black markings and its underwings have bright white spots. The area around Glaux Low is a favoured spot. It also produced a red-veined darter, a rare migrant dragonfly from southern Europe.

Grayling butterfly nectaring on common sea-lavender. (Richard Porter)

Moth trapping was a must. On the Wednesday night, the Robinson trap was set up in the garden. There was a full moon, reflected perfectly in the harbour. As well as setting up the moth trap, we set up a telescope and pointed it to the full moon. Inspecting the lunar craters for the first time was a memorable moment for our writer in residence.

So was encountering a shrew in the Lifeboat House. Throughout the season, there was many a time when it would scuttle across the kitchen floor and disappear under the oven. We would shout 'shrew!' in an exaggerated Norfolk accent to herald its presence whenever it appeared. This amused Steve, unlike the many flies that enter the Lifeboat House in summer. The coldness of early April seems a distant memory three months on, with spirals of fly paper hanging from the low ceiling.

He was, however, impressed with the hawk-moths we introduced him to. In fact, they were more of a highlight than the seals. Six years later, he penned an article titled, 'What's so great about seals anyway? They're just boring lumps of blubber'. The elephant hawk-moth and the privet hawk-moth were a big hit, with their colourful markings and impressive size.

After we had tucked into his signature chili dish, darkness fell, and we released the moths. Letting them go during daylight would result in a massive feast for our neighbouring swallows and pied wagtails, so waiting until nightfall is much kinder to the moths.

Kindness had, however, strayed into mild mickey-taking as we pulled Steve's leg when discussing Norfolk bird names. He could understand why the ringed plover behaved like a 'stone runner', the avocet resembled a 'shoehorn', the lapwing called like a 'peewit', the swift like a 'devlin screamer' and the bittern like a 'bog bumper', but he didn't buy 'rainbow bird' for Arctic tern, nor the fictitious 'wibbly-piggy' and 'globby dobbin'.

Joking aside, in his fifth and final 'Point Break' column in the *EDP*, Steve described the experience as five of the best days of his life. He really got into the spirit of things, made the most of the opportunity and – much to our satisfaction – really grasped why the work we did was so important, helping to bring this to a wider audience. In return, we gained a greater appreciation for the everyday privileges we were enjoying as coastal residents. A marsh harrier may be a daily sighting but is an impressive bird to watch hunting over the dunes and is, in fact, rarer in the UK as a whole than the golden eagle.

As we rushed out onto the shingle to show Steve four spoonbills flying over, Eddie wondered what he was missing out on as he was stuck to the landline, touching base with the office. 'Only spoonbills,' I reported, inferring it wasn't a rare enough migrant to justify aborting his phone call. Mr Downes exclaimed that they may be 'only' spoonbills to those for whom they are old hat, but it was an exciting moment for him. We had done it – he had become a bird lover. A few days on Blakeney Point is all it takes.

There were a couple of things that weren't published in the newspaper. Namely, how much whisky four Blakeney Point rangers consumed in a week. Also, the fact that we had a fifth housemate, Nikki, a master's degree student from UCL. She was collecting data for her research project, looking into the feeding ecology of Sandwich terns and their interactions with black-headed gulls. Her research was of great interest to us, so she was welcome to stay with us to secure the data she needed, which we hoped would aid our conservation efforts.

Aerial view along Blakeney Point from Stiffkey West Sands, January 2016. (Ian Ward)

Common seals and Sandwich terns on the tip of Far Point, August 2016. (Ian Ward)

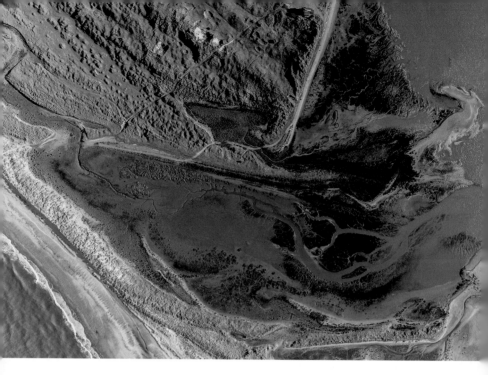

Aerial view of gap, boardwalk, Near Point and Middle Point, January 2016. (Ian Ward)

The main dunes, August 2016. (Ian Ward)

Morston Creek on an evening high tide, September 2012. (Ajay Tegala)

Common sea-lavender and samphire on the saltmarsh, July 2016. (Ajay Tegala)

Happy to be on the Point for first season as lead, April 2013. (Pete Stevens)

With Graham and Eddie, Blakeney, Christmas 2012. (Marilyn Lubbock)

Sandwich tern colony on Far Point during annual nest count, May 2012. (Ajay Tegala)

Little tern courtship on the beach with lesser sand eel, May 2019. (Richard Porter)

Common tern pair nesting on the shingle, May 2020. (Richard Porter)

Arctic tern on a buoy in Blakeney Harbour, May 2020. (Richard Porter)

Oystercatcher in flight over Blakeney Point. (Richard Porter)

Ringed plover by its nest. (Graham Lubbock)

Particularly showy male bluethroat, May 2015. (Richard Porter)

Wryneck in suaeda. (Richard Porter)

Grey seal rookery west of the gap, November 2017. (Ajay Tegala)

Day-old grey seal pup, November 2017. (Ajay Tegala)

Moulted, melanistic grey seal pup, January 2015. (Ajay Tegala)

Moulted and weaned grey seal pup, January 2018. (Ajay Tegala)

Puss moth caterpillar on white poplar in the Plantation. (Graham Lubbock)

Dark-green fritillary nectaring on bramble, June 2017. (Richard Porter)

Hare in the snow, January 2013. (Graham Lubbock)

Wreck of the *Yankee*, October 2017. (Ajay Tegala)

Lifeboat House shortly after renovation, May 2013. (Ajay Tegala)

Watch House, April 2012. (Ajay Tegala)

Boardwalk displaced by the tidal surge, December 2013. (Graham Lubbock)

Floodwater and displaced seals following the tidal surge, December 2013. (Graham Lubbock)

Breaches in Blakeney's sea wall caused by the December 2013 tidal surge. (Graham Lubbock)

Rangers and hut owners end-of-season dinner, September 2015. (Ajay Tegala)

Sunrise over the sea, captured during a dawn patrol, May 2012. (Ajay Tegala)

Setting sun, captured on an evening walk along the Point, April 2010. (Ajay Tegala)

After a briefing on where to locate herself for her observations without disturbing any breeding birds, she spent many hours observing terns flying into the colony, recording the prey type and size they were feeding their young and whether or not the feeding attempts were successful. She observed lots of sand eels and clupeids – young herring – being brought in, alongside the occasional squid, crustaceans and invertebrates.

Dinnertime conversation would generally centre around her observations as we were all keen to hear what she had seen. Terns avoiding gulls could land as many as fifteen times before actually feeding their chick. Her data showed that the likelihood of kleptoparasitism – gulls stealing fish – increased with the size of the fish, clupeids being the riskiest because they are highly reflective and so draw more gull attention. Away from the colony, terns have Arctic skuas to contend with, which also attempt to steal their fish.

As well as some horror stories, Nikki had tales of terns fighting back and shielding chicks with their wings. She also saw an oystercatcher attack a black-headed gull that was attacking a tern chick. We enjoyed these tern tales, not having the time available to see as much of this behaviour ourselves.

We also enjoyed the excellent pies Nikki made for us, always a hit with hungry rangers. It is often said that the way to win a man's heart is with a good pie ... so it was perhaps no surprise that one of the team – not me – asked for her hand in marriage over dinner. She declined.

Her last night coincided with the Blakeney Twelve annual charity lobster supper, soon to become biennial. Excitement built in the early evening as we laid out tables and chairs in front of the Lifeboat House. We then took the quad bike down to the landing ridge to meet Willie Weston's boat and transport the cool boxes of food to the Lifeboat House. His jolly assistants were Jim Temple's daughters, Louise and Diddly. The latter was full of praise for the wonderful time her daughter had had staying in the Watch House with Blakeney Primary School and being an honorary young ranger with us for a day. That had earned us a few complimentary drinks, not to mention lobster and crab.

Scarcely two hours after they had arrived, the boatloads of champagne-swigging, seafood-munching charity supporters disappeared and the whole event seemed like it had been just a dream – although one look in the fridge at the leftovers revealed it certainly had been real. Getting a taste for crab, when an intact pot washed up one day, we decided to put some bacon inside and attach it to the *Hjordis* wreck, as we could walk out to it at low tide. It seemed genius but didn't catch us any crabs ...

A weekend of chick sightings followed. We were woken up on Saturday morning by two juvenile starlings inside the Lifeboat House. A flock of around 200 had roosted on the roof with a couple flying in through the open windows of the lookout tower, then through the hatch and around the landing. On Sunday morning, five starlings had entered the building. One was digging at the soil of a potted basil we had by the telephone at the bottom of the stairs. They hadn't hatched on the Point itself, but on the nearby mainland. The juvenile pied wagtail that had flown through my bedroom window at 5 in the morning, however, had hatched just a few metres away.

That Sunday, four swallows fledged from the nest inside the old tern hide on Near Point. The swallow nest under the eaves of the Lifeboat House was a few days behind. While tidying up around the building in the morning, we noticed part of the nest had collapsed, leaving two, somewhat shaken, small chicks on the ground beneath it. We fetched a ladder and returned the chicks to the ledge on which the nest had been built. We wrote about the incident on our blog, titling it 'Larks ascending ... swallows descending'.

Our good deed for the day was rewarded with the sighting of a vagrant from southern Europe: Blakeney Point's fifteenth short-toed lark. Its arrival was most unexpected in the second week of June, when very little migration is taking place.

A trip to observe the Far Point colony revealed that the number of juveniles had dropped by about 700, showing that several had already left the colony. At the front were twenty-six Mediterranean gull chicks, which had increased to forty the following day. From around twelve pairs, this was very high productivity.

On Far Point, three day-old grey partridge chicks were observed. The brood would have been much larger than this, but the many hungry gulls would undoubtedly have accounted for the loss of a number of them. A brood by the Lifeboat House had fared slightly better, with five chicks.

So much drama could be witnessed on Far Point. We watched a pair of herring gulls eating a black-headed gull chick alive in the morning and then a Sandwich tern chick in the afternoon, probably the same pair. Meanwhile, over near the Hood, two flying juvenile little terns were observed and at least one more on the shingle, sheltering behind a small branch. Throughout the second week of July, we watched numbers of flying Little Terns near the Watch House increasing, day by day.

Between trips to the Watch House to monitor the little terns, we had a visit from the BBC *Countryfile* team. They were filming their summer special in north Norfolk and featuring Blakeney Point in the programme.

Returning to the Point after a day off, I waited on Morston Quay alongside the crew and almost the entire Blakeney office team, all jostling for positions. I just wanted to get my weekly supplies into the fridge, which I eventually did while the obligatory seal shots were filmed in the harbour. Over lunch, we met John Craven ahead of our sequence, having a cup of tea and chatting to him on the Lifeboat House front steps. The original plan had been to film it inside the kitchen, but it was felt that having the iconic blue building behind us would look better. On camera, I mentioned how part of our role involved dawn patrols to prevent egg theft. However, when the episode aired on August Bank Holiday, my speaking part had been cut.

After the hustle and bustle of the filming had evaporated and we were left alone on the Point, I headed to the Watch House, passing the short-toed lark on my way. It was such a calm, still evening. In my quiet solitude, I counted ten little tern chicks as well as two broods of ringed plovers alongside five oystercatcher chicks of varying ages. Evenings such as this were gold dust, a chance to soak up the coast with not a soul in sight.

Returning to the Lifeboat House for supper, I passed the Plantation, which was alive with white satin moths fluttering around the white poplars. Their movements and clean white colour alongside the silvery-white of the poplars was quite magical. As the sun sunk below the horizon, the sky turned orange and a marsh harrier flew low over the dunes.

The white satin moths in the Plantation attracted an adult male cuckoo to spend a few days feeding up on them. We were surprised to spot a juvenile cuckoo alongside it, as cuckoos do not raise their own young. However, they are known to form loose groups at rich feeding grounds on migration. The Plantation was indeed providing rich feeding.

On a site boasting rare seabirds, it may have seemed strange that we should be excited to see a female pheasant with a young chick in the Plantation. This was the first confirmed breeding record on the Point. Although abundant on the nearby mainland, the first record of a pheasant on the Point was not made until 2003. Since then, there had been a few records of wandering males and indeed the aggressive individual that had held a territory in 2010. But this was confirmation of a new breeding species. Prior to this season, the Point's breeding bird list consisted of forty-three confirmed species. It could now be upped to forty-five with the addition of the avocets and pheasant.

As mid-July became late July, we continued to keep a close eye on our nesting little terns across the Point. In the daytime, we were able to see small numbers of fledged birds. However, these numbers were lower than we had hoped. Having spotted small mammal prints heading towards the beach colony, we deployed a couple of camera traps in the dunes, kindly on loan to us from Natural England.

The cameras captured a hedgehog, which was a bit of a surprise to us, not expecting it to make it all of the way out to Far Point from the mainland. However, a look at the Point's historic mammal data revealed that hedgehogs had been recorded on the Point twice in the 1960s and three times in the 1970s, predating a redshank nest as well as tern eggs and chicks. A series of images captured at three o' clock one morning showed a short-eared owl by one of the cameras: another little tern predator. In fact, within a couple of days the little terns had given up and abandoned the main beach colony.

There was little we could do about this. Being so late in the season, the terns simply did not have time to lay again. We took solace in the fact that little terns are long-lived birds. They had had a highly productive season on the Point the previous year and would do again. Still, we couldn't help feeling a bit disappointed.

The next day was the warmest of the season and made us all feel grateful to be living and working in such a beautiful place. The sand looked stunning against a brilliant blue sky and the sea was inviting. Autumn passerine migration started with two juvenile willow warblers in the garden and twelve yellow wagtails flying over.

Autumn was the last thing on the minds of the boat owners whose vessels were now filling up the harbour. Sunny summer days afloat were ever popular, with new moorings being put in each year. One of the newest arrivals was, in fact, the oldest boat in the harbour; a former lifeboat from Winterton, named *Mary*, which had been converted into a houseboat with the clever addition of a shed.

The five beach huts on the Point were the envy of many. The owners pay rent and are not allowed to extend their huts beyond the foundations, which were put in before the Point became a nature reserve. Now such a protected site, no more huts are allowed to be built and the existing ones get passed down the generations of the families who have historically owned them. *Mary* the 'shed-boat' was, in fact, a clever way of having a hut on the Point. Although in the harbour and afloat at high tide, it was just a short walk to the toilet block at low tide.

The last few days of July brought more migrants. Seabirds on passage included red-throated diver, common scoter, tufted duck, red-breasted merganser and pomarine skua, waders included purple sandpiper and curlew sandpiper and passerines included wheatear and common whitethroat. A juvenile stonechat at the Hood had colour rings and turned out to be a bird ringed as a nestling at Gramborough Hill, Salthouse, on 1 June. Clearly it had followed the spit westwards.

Our last job of July was to enter the now vacant Sandwich tern colony to conduct a census of dead chicks. We recorded just shy of 100, which is a very low number from well over 3,000 pairs. Seeing this area so empty felt strange, being used to seeing it bustling with squawking gulls and terns. It felt like the party was over. However, for the hundreds of holidaymakers heading to the coast on their summer holidays, the party had only just begun.

5

August:
Autumn Arrives

AUGUST WAS TO BE a month of celebration on Blakeney Point, being its 100th birthday as a nature reserve. An intricately carved wooden sign had been commissioned. The artist had never visited the Point before but produced a wonderful three-dimensional carving of its contours using maps and aerial photographs. Graham and the visitor services manager, Iain, brought it up to the Lifeboat House at the start of the month and we dug a trench to install it. We covered it with an old curtain to keep it hidden until its unveiling a few days later.

The first Sunday of August was to be a Point Sunday, lovingly resurrected for the centenary celebrations. Jim Temple and Jason Bean ferried over an assortment of people associated with the Point's history. A wonderful Lifeboat House cake, made by countryside manager Victoria, was put on a table and a crowd gathered around the carved wooden sign for property manager John's speech, followed by the unveiling, which was done by Graham and Marilyn together, having worked at Blakeney for almost forty years between them.

The cake was cut and fizz was sipped as former assistant warden Henry performed his song 'Watch Tower Blues'. He had composed it in the lookout tower during his season working on the Point in 2001. We then led guided walks for the few who had chosen to stay on the Point until the evening tide.

The relaxed atmosphere and beautiful warm weather was enjoyed by all who attended. It was a fitting celebration for a wonderful reserve. Our guided walks were also a success, rewarded with a hobby chasing starlings and swallows. A handsome pied flycatcher also put in an appearance.

By the second week of August, juvenile Sandwich terns were fishing proficiently all around the Point. The harbour was filling up with whimbrel, grey plover and turnstone. One morning, we watched four juvenile marsh harriers fly clumsily over Far Point, having recently fledged from either Blakeney Freshes or Cley Marshes.

Among the groups of westward-passing swallows, we spotted a ghostly white leucistic bird. The garden was alive with young linnets, rattling the dried lupin seed pods as they flew from the bushes. On the brambles were several emperor moth caterpillars, large and bright green.

I tore myself away from the Point for a day to help along the coast at Branodunum Roman Fort. *Time Team* were excavating the fort to look for Roman remains. It was all very exciting, and I had offered to assist with crowd control in exchange for views of some of the fort walls that lay beneath the ground. I also enjoyed a hearty lunch from the crew's catering van.

Another mainland-based day was spent in Blakeney village hall helping at the Tidal Lands Exhibition. We had prepared a number of information boards about the history and wildlife of the Point. I had created a soundscape, which mixed together the sound of breaking waves, footsteps crunching on shingle and the distinctive calls of oystercatchers, ringed plovers and Sandwich terns.

The exhibition had been organised with Blakeney Area Historical Society including John Peake, who had worked alongside Ted Eales on the Point in 1955. John had a very old photograph in the exhibition that had clearly been taken before 1898 because it showed just one Lifeboat House. It was absolutely fascinating to see the Old Lifeboat House without the 'blue building' in front of it.

After a day in the village hall, it was great to get back to the Point. My return coincided with the removal of the seasonal dog restriction signs on the ridge, symbolising the end of the breeding bird season.

From the second weekend of the month, autumn migration started to pick up. Birds moving south from Scandinavia towards African wintering grounds were drifted across the North Sea by easterly winds. This brought an icterine warbler and a red-backed shrike to the Point, along with a dozen pied flycatchers and a few whinchats.

Further easterly winds brought more special birds from the Continent: honey buzzards, wood sandpipers, black terns, a little gull, tree pipits and wrynecks. The bank holiday weekend produced dotterel and a greenish warbler.

The Point has a reputation as one of the country's top sites to see the greenish warbler. This bird was the twenty-fourth record for the Point and the eighth in as many years.

The greenish warbler attracted lots of birdwatchers, with news spreading via pagers and social media. They flocked around an isolated bramble bush near the boardwalk to glimpse this warbler, which breeds east of the Baltic and winters in India. Lots of birders head to the Norfolk coast over the August Bank Holiday weekend in the hope of finding autumn migrants such as this. Many trudge along the Point in the hope of finding something special in the Plantation, often only to be disappointed. On multiple occasions, people visiting from afar have misidentified relatively common birds in their belief that the Point *must* surely produce a rarity without fail.

As much as I appreciated seeing the greenish warbler, it did seem a bit nuts watching so many people crowding around a bush. We were on hand to control the crowd, to ensure nobody went too close to the bush and unnecessarily flushed the bird. As well as irritating the other birders, this would cause unwelcome disturbance to the already exhausted bird and could also lead to unwanted trampling of the dunes.

Scanning the harbour in the evening, excitement built that we may have found a rare gull. It turned out to be a leucistic herring gull, although it was interesting, nonetheless.

Before calling it a day, we set some Longworth traps, baited with mealworms, to survey what small mammals were around the Lifeboat House. We knew we had a shrew because we saw it inside most days.

The traps revealed that we also had wood mice around the building. They are largely nocturnal creatures with beautiful, large eyes.

Seals overtake breeding birds in their need for protection during the second half of August. While we no longer needed to worry about dogs disturbing breeding avocets at the Cley end or picnickers disturbing nesting oystercatchers on the landing ridge, we still needed to have a presence at the gap to ensure that no walkers went too close to the hauled-out seals. Indeed, our highest low-tide seal count of the season was made on Bank Holiday Monday. I observed 924 grey and 386 common seals spread across the West Sands and the end of Far Point.

Our series of centenary celebrations concluded with an overnight visit from *Guardian* journalist and natural history writer Patrick Barkham. I had just read his book, *The Butterfly Isles*, so was particularly interested to meet him. Having fed numerous visitors over the summer, it was requested that Patrick cook for us in exchange for overnight accommodation. He was dropped off by boat on a rainy evening, sleeping bag in tow, along with ingredients for a vegetarian curry. Being a naturalist, Patrick asked us informed, detailed and probing questions. The theme of his article was to be 'Do we still need nature reserves?'

In his article, Patrick wasn't shy to mention the challenges of dog walkers and the need for pest control. He even mentioned our April helicopter visit from Jay Kay. Although Steve Downes had been told the story, it was requested that he did not publish it. Time having passed, it was mentioned quite offhandedly to Patrick. Inevitably, news reached Steve that the story was out and so he wrote an article about it in the *EDP*, despite it having happened five months before. The article probably attracted more interest than his whole 'Point Break' feature and was also picked up by the *Daily Mirror* and the *Daily Star*. We put our version of events on the blog, emphasising our key wildlife messages.

6

September
and Beyond

AT THE START OF September, I headed to Great Yarmouth for a day to help at the Maritime Festival. I took the beach display with me and some Blakeney leaflets. One visitor saw Blakeney Point on a leaflet and remarked how that was where Jay Kay had landed in his helicopter. I suspected they had read the story in the *Star* or *Mirror* rather than the *Guardian*.

I was the only one of the four of us not to be quoted in the *Guardian* article, so when Clare Gogerty from *Coast* magazine visited the Point to write an article, I was given the opportunity to show her around and have the chance to get my name in print. Although my experience had increased markedly over the season, I still had far less bird knowledge than the others, but there was obviously a lot more to the Point and I had paid attention to everything I had been taught, from botany to history. Clare noted down frantically as I covered the Point's habitats and associated species. She seemed more relaxed, careful and open-minded than some journalists and I felt that she really listened to what I said, which was largely about the need for conservation.

A week into the month, autumn wildlife was apparent. Among the forty species caught in our moth trap was a brown-spot pinion, a characteristic autumn species. But the season was truly heralded when the first skein of pink-footed geese flew over the Point. We rejoiced at their arrival. There is something so special about hearing the calls of 'pink feet!'.

With autumn declared and the school holidays over, summer was in many ways done. My five-month contract reached its end on the second Sunday of September. Eddie organised an end-of-season jolly for Paul, Joe, myself and little tern ranger Al. We headed to Blickling Hall to view a collection of stuffed birds that had originally been on display in the Lifeboat House. They were removed some years ago as stuffed animals aren't to everyone's taste, being much better admired alive than dead. After examining the taxidermy, we lunched at the Fur and Feather in Woodbastwick, part of Woodforde's Brewery, whose real ales we loved so much. I was designated driver for the day, but other members of the party made the most of the opportunity.

Mid-September produced the first snow bunting of the autumn, which I was thrilled to see from the site of the old sea hide. Joe had knocked in a couple of posts and nailed some wooden planks to them, forming a screen to sea-watch from behind. Birds seen from it included a puffin far out at sea. By now, pink-footed geese were a daily sighting and winter thrushes were starting to appear: the odd song thrush or fieldfare, a redwing or two and the occasional ring ouzel.

Northerly and easterly winds combined with rain on the penultimate weekend of the month and produced a fall of autumn migrants. The avian cast included a number of the scarce signature migrants that Blakeney Point birders hope for in September: red-breasted flycatcher, barred warbler and ortolan bunting from Europe along with yellow-browed warbler from Siberia. As well as birds coming in off the sea, a large bat was observed, an impressive sight in broad daylight. Less wonderful was the impact the blustery conditions had on seabirds, namely gannets. A note in the bird log records the following near the sea hide, 'one dead Gannet; one dying Gannet; one Gannet with only one foot'.

Winds switched from east-south-easterly to south-westerly on the Monday and rain persisted. This resulted in one of my most special moments of the season. It was not the rarity of the birds it brought that was so special, but the sheer abundance of them. At this time of year, large numbers of thrushes and chats migrate to Britain from Scandinavia, but species such as redwings tend to fly over high during the night. The relentless grey drizzle brought the arriving birds to ground on the Point throughout the course of the day.

As we walked along Far Point, song thrushes dropped out of the sky into the Suaeda bushes in front of us. We estimated a total of 340 of them, alongside more than 100 common redstarts, sixty robins and twenty wheatears. I hadn't imagined that a damp and grey autumn day would turn out to be one of the most magic of the whole season, but it truly was. It really gave a sense of the battle migration can be for small birds crossing the North Sea in challenging weather conditions.

The reduced visibility focuses your attention on the area immediately in front of you and changes your perception of your surroundings. You get a sense of the birds' strength and also their vulnerability.

But they were safe on the Point, an ideal place for them to make landfall and rest for a while before continuing inland to feast on berries. The Point itself wasn't without its blackberries, which we had been encouraged to resist picking so that they could provide necessary forage for exhausted migrants who needed them far more than we did.

That day, as well as the four of us, the true Blakeney Point birders were also out helping us record numbers: Richard, Andy and James. Nobody else was on the Point and we were all careful not to unnecessarily flush these birds but merely admire and record them.

'Thank goodness for Professor Oliver,' I thought to myself. Over the course of the centenary summer, I had learned a lot about the wardens of old and also the foresight of Oliver, who ensured the Point was saved for the nation and for nature. Had it been bought privately in 1912, maybe it would have been developed, damaged or destroyed. A thought that didn't bear thinking about but, at the same time, did need to be kept at the back of our minds.

It wasn't just birds on the move. Eddie and Bee headed up to northern Scotland for two weeks, Joe headed to Malta for a week and I went up to Northumberland for a job interview. Following the end of my seasonal contract, I needed to find my next job in conservation. A six-month contract with Natural England at Lindisfarne took my fancy – a similar habitat to Blakeney but with some major differences, such as an impressive castle and a bizarre tarmac road across the saltmarsh to the island, covered over by every tide.

Heading back down the A1 after the interview, a call came through saying that *Autumnwatch* would be filming on the Point the following day. That was my lift back to the Lifeboat House solved, I could take my supplies up in the Land Rover along with the BBC crew's filming equipment. At the barn, I met presenter and filmmaker Richard Taylor-Jones, renowned wildlife sound recordist Gary Moore and two young cameramen.

From Cley beach, we drove right out to the beach beyond the gap to film the seals at low tide. After doing a low-tide seal count on film and sharing the figures, we spent a while watching the diving gannets. There was obviously a good supply of fish in the channel because dozens of gannets, both adult and immature, were engaged in a feeding frenzy, dropping beneath the surface with speed and agility. If they hit the water at the wrong angle, they risked breaking their necks.

Richard Taylor-Jones was to return to the Point later in the year to film grey seals during the pupping season for *Winterwatch*. His September day's filming with us would feature in *Autumnwatch* as a teaser of what was to come. Part of the *Winterwatch* hook was whether we would reach 1,000 pup births this winter. The trajectory of the past decade suggested this would almost certainly be the case.

Just before Richard and his crew headed back to the mainland, my phone rang and I was offered the Lindisfarne job. I would be starting in two weeks' time. Everyone in the team was very pleased for me. Graham jokingly said I was heading to the 'dark side', technically becoming a civil servant.

It was a relief to have another job to go to and exciting to be able to embark on a new coastal adventure. Although I didn't know it at the time, that summer on the Point had been the end of a chapter. Times were changing.

Change had actually been impossible to ignore throughout the season. Subtle changes in the reserve's staffing structure coincided with wider changes. Across the nation, wardens were being renamed rangers, this having started in the Lake District. Some of the 'old-school' wardens were not too fond of their new title. This was not, however, change for change's sake. The name change signified a move from a focus on conservation to a focus on conservation *and* engagement; the latter being increasingly recognised as an absolutely key tool to facilitating the former.

In little over a decade, the Point's management had changed markedly. It started in the mid-1990s when Joe Reed's role progressed from Blakeney Point warden to property manager for Blakeney National Nature Reserve and Brancaster. He probably had a challenging time juggling this broad role with the demands of implementing the Point's predator control programme. With office work increasing, Marilyn was taken on to assist him in the late 1990s and then Dave was employed as the new Point warden in 2002. By then, Joe and his wife, Janet, no longer lived in the Lifeboat House in the summer and the tearoom, which Janet had managed, had closed. Since being opened by Bob and Alice Pinchen in 1923, the tearoom had closed during the Second World War and for four years in the early 1980s but this time it had closed for good.

Joe Reed was a warden at heart and didn't enjoy the more desk-based side of the role. Marilyn remembers some fun times in the office with him. An attempt to change the toner in a new photocopier resulted in a cloud of black covering Joe's face and shirt. His philosophy had always been to only invest in what he believed in. Then along came the world of emails. Joe told Marilyn that the day he had to send an email to her, in the same room, would be the day he handed in his notice.

That day was inevitable, and he was true to his word. The world was changing. He took early retirement in 2003. Meanwhile, warden Dave filled the predator control element of his job and local boy John took on the property manager role. Marilyn and Graham maintained that this was the most significant personnel change they witnessed at Blakeney during their twenty-plus years there. In fact, the only bigger change in the history of the Point's management was probably when Ted Eales retired in 1980, ending the continuity that Bob Pinchen had started back in 1901.

Thanks to Dave having worked alongside Joe, continuity was not to be lost this time. Protection of the breeding birds – and also seals – continued, although the number of guided walks gradually dropped off. In the 1990s, between May and July there were often several different schools visiting on a single tide, but a few years into the new millennium, whole weeks could pass without a single booking. Dave continued Joe's philosophy of keeping the promotion of the Point to a minimum to keep visitor numbers manageable. Eddie continued this when he slipped into the Point warden role, three years later.

The centenary year had seen a major national feature on *Countryfile* and now further national coverage was afoot with *Winterwatch*. This was an excellent opportunity to spread conservation messages. A harder message to communicate was pup mortality. One of the pups Richard Taylor-Jones followed was abandoned. It happens. It is nature. However, a studio-out comment about how the rangers do not intervene did result in viewer complaints coming to the office. This is something you have to manage when you get national exposure and more people questioning your management. Greater exposure can bring greater support and awareness, but also brings greater criticism. This does, however, present the healthy opportunity to justify and review practices; ensuring they are appropriate, relevant and effective.

In the Lifeboat House at the end of September, we were preparing for another big change; one so major it meant moving practically everything out of the building. From late October through to the following March the building was being renovated. This was a long-overdue project, funded by the Enterprise Neptune appeal, the patron of which was none other than the Duke of Edinburgh. The renovation process would involve completely recladding the building with a robust, synthetic material that would not require the repainting that the original corrugated iron did.

The building had last been painted five years previously. A cherry picker had been hired and transported along the spit by tractor and trailer. Back in the 1930s, it had been done with ladders by father and son, Billy and Ted Eales. In his memoirs, Ted recalls that it would take 15 gallons of paint and about a week to complete the job, providing the weather was good. Once, when both men were painting, Ted said something to annoy his father, who shouted back at him from above, his top teeth flying out as he did. They slid over the wet paint into the gutter and had to be washed off in petrol.

In the 1930s, the building was painted dark Admiralty grey on the roof and light Admiralty grey on the sides. Colour photographs from the 1960s and 1970s show it looking a very light shade of grey all over, except for a white trim. By the late 1980s, it had turned a deep blue, presumably because that colour was the easiest available at the time. It remained blue from then onwards, sometimes darker shades, sometimes lighter, but constantly referred to – and very much loved – as 'the blue building'.

Discussions took place about how it technically made sense to revert the building's colour back to its original Admiralty grey. The large double doors were to be reinstated at the front of the building, using photographs from 1905 and 1915 for reference. The original doors had been removed during the 1921–23 renovation of the building when the National Trust acquired the building and converted it into the tearoom, museum and warden's house.

There was much debate about the colour of the new cladding, the building having become so iconic in blue and depicted in countless paintings, cartoons and motifs. I was firmly in the blue camp at the time. Indeed, blue was chosen in the end. However, the traditional colours of lifeboat houses meant that light Admiralty grey and red had been a contender, like Tenby Lifeboat House, for example. Given the choice again now, I would actually choose light grey and red as they would make the building stand out even more, as well as matching other lifeboat stations.

As September reached its end, the cold wind gave the Point an undeniably autumnal air. The barred warbler had been in the garden for a whole week. Pink-footed goose numbers now exceeded 1,000. On one occasion, we spotted two barnacle geese among them. There were still quite a few Sandwich terns around, feeding out at sea and flying past on passage.

Rough seas can lead to shells, weed and crustaceans washing up. On this occasion, we found over fifty sea potatoes washed up on the beach – this is a type of sea urchin that is common around the British Isles. They bury themselves in sand and feed on organic waste, and their lifespan is thought to be over ten years. Their heart-shaped shells are so thin and fragile that finding them intact on the beach is quite rare. We therefore proclaimed, on the blog, to have what could be heading towards Europe's largest intact sea potato collection.

Throughout the summer, a whole manner of different things had washed up on the Point. From intact sea potatoes to dead birds to shoes – always singles, never pairs – to starfish, a dead muntjac and unopened, in-date packets of crisps, chocolate bars, cans of soft drink and even Guinness. Food and drink in sealed packaging that washed up was part of our 'Tideline Challenge' game, nominating each other to consume them. On 1 October, a grey squirrel washed up on Middle Point. We thought this was a first for the Point. However, Graham recalled a previous occurrence when, as a bait digger in the late 1970s, he had seen one sat on top of the buoy at the end of Morston Creek.

The following day, we removed the maps, identification charts and posters from the Lifeboat House walls in preparation for the upcoming renovation. This seemed to symbolise the beginning of the end of the season.

On 9 October, my final day on the Point, exactly six months after moving in, I had one last walk around the dunes and one last look at the Lifeboat House under a brilliant blue sky. The next time I would visit, whenever that would be, the corrugated iron cladding would be gone forever.

Joe, just back from Malta, took me down to Cley on the quad bike. I sat on a fish box in the trailer with my belongings wrapped in bin liners to keep the dust and grit off them. The tide was fairly high up the beach and at one point a big wave hit us. At the office, John said it had not been an easy year, with all of the changes, but complimented my ability to get on with everyone. Just twenty-four hours later, I was moving into my new home in Berwick-upon-Tweed.

Joe moved off the Point two days after me. Eddie and Paul both moved off on the last weekend of October, ahead of renovation work commencing the following Monday. The first grey seal pup of the winter was born on that Saturday.

Up on Lindisfarne, 22 and 23 October were foggy, with a north-easterly wind across the east coast. In the dunes, I witnessed a big fall of hundreds of redwings, blackbirds and robins and thousands of fieldfares. This was undoubtedly my most special moment on the island. On the Point, an estimated 25,000 redwings, 4,000 fieldfares, 3,000 blackbirds, 3,000 song thrushes, 280 robins, eighty goldcrests and thirty ring ouzels were recorded. It was truly spectacular to witness such large numbers of birds in Northumberland and know that my friends over 200 miles away were experiencing the same spectacle.

In between chasing after escaped sheep and cattle on Lindisfarne, I spray-painted white-fronted goose decoys, transforming them into pale-belled brent geese for a satellite tagging research project. I also set up the very first Natural England blog, my Blakeney blogging experience having been a been a factor in securing the Lindisfarne post.

During the first week of December, the thousandth pup of the season was born on Blakeney Point, which Richard Taylor-Jones named 'Millennium'. He and the *Winterwatch* team were staying in the Old Lifeboat House as the Lifeboat House was being renovated. With scaffolding erected, the old iron cladding was peeled off in the middle of the month. It was evident that the harsh environment had taken its toll on the lookout tower and its timber was severely rotten. Fortunately, extra funding was secured to completely rebuild it, it being such a useful vantage point.

Big migration of thrushes, October 2012. (Richard Porter)

Being back in East Anglia with my family for Christmas, I couldn't resist visiting Blakeney at the very end of December. It was a welcome chance to catch up with friends and former colleagues as well as seeing seal pups and the progress made on the Lifeboat House renovation.

There was more to catch up on than I realised. Eddie and Bee had some big news. The pair had accepted a shared job on Skomer Island in Pembrokeshire. Eddie thought I should seriously consider applying for the Point ranger job. It sounds ridiculous now, but, until that moment, I had never really considered that I might have the opportunity to apply for this role.

I was interviewed for the post in February. My preparation had revealed that, during my time as a volunteer and seasonal assistant, I had learned all of the key elements of the role. I also realised, privately, just how much I wanted this job. I had some new ideas and an overwhelming realisation that this was my dream job. Of course it was.

It all became so clear in my mind that this was what I wanted. I simply couldn't imagine myself doing anything else.

I waited and waited for a phone call from Blakeney. I held on for a whole week. But the waiting was instantly forgotten when I was offered the job.

Five weeks later, I moved from Northumberland back to Norfolk. The Lifeboat House renovation had not yet been finished, having been delayed by the weather, so I was put up in the volunteer accommodation, where I had begun my Blakeney journey four years earlier. It was great to be back.

Part 3

Seabird and
Seal Seasons –
A Dream Come True

1

Preparation

BY THE TIME THE first Sandwich tern calls are heard over Blakeney Point, preparation for the forthcoming nesting season should be well under way. Getting ready really starts in the winter. By Valentine's Day, the beach is eerily quiet, the last grey seal pups having long since left. Before the first ringed plovers take up their territories along the main shingle ridge, vehicles track slowly up and down it to complete various maintenance tasks.

There are many things that need servicing, cleaning, fixing and organising before the start of April to enable the ranger team to take up residence and begin round-the-clock bird protection. Some of these preparatory tasks are rather mundane, but they are essential if the season is to run smoothly.

Emptying the septic tank is a key task. If it were to overflow in the middle of the summer, we would be quite literally in the sh*t. Just getting the tanker successfully up and down the Point can be a drama. Although the shingle ridge may look consistent from Cley beach to the headland, this is not the case. There are looser patches where vehicles can all too easily sink in if they are carrying too much weight. On one occasion, a tractor and empty tanker failed to get more than a few hundred metres along the spit before becoming stuck, simply because it had the wrong tyres.

There is a patch of shingle near the Hood that is particularly loose. Former property manager, John, remembers being the only one in the office one day and receiving a call requesting him to bring the tractor to the Hood to tow a contractor's tractor and its tanker back to Cley. It was a slow and sweaty journey, with the tractor engine becoming progressively hotter until Cley beach was finally reached.

Having the chimney swept is a much less stressful job to complete. The renovation of the Lifeboat House had included the installation of a wood burner and therefore the reinstatement of the chimney, which meant annual sweeping was added to the job list. A family-run Norfolk business were recommended to us by our colleagues at Blickling. Father and son Geoff and Mark would come out each year and do a great job, passionate about traditional sweeping methods. They also enjoyed the ride up and down the Point, which included a stop halfway so that the Watch House Trust did not have to organise the same services separately.

The Watch House chimney is not always treated well due to a whole variety of driftwood in different states being burnt in the open fire by the many people who stay there. Back in the twentieth century, the Lifeboat House also had an open fire, and wood from the wreck of the old *Britannia* houseboat was burned on it – literally history going up in smoke. We tended to burn seasoned logs from Bullfer Grove, which were stored by the Friary Farm barn. At the start of each season, I would transport a load up to keep us going. We stored it in a large agricultural bin by the back door.

The annual gas inspection is another legal requirement, which Fakenham Gas have been doing for many years. This is usually done in March, giving them a lift in the Land Rover and stopping off at the Watch House, the Old Lifeboat House and sometimes even a hut or two on the way. Another father and son business, the son would sometimes come out by kayak if he had to visit during the breeding bird season.

One sad day, the old gas lights were disconnected. Even after we had solar power, I liked to use the gas lights occasionally. They gave a much nicer, warmer and more subtle light that matched the spirit of the building. But they became very outdated, and every light fitting had some degree of leakiness. After several seasons of patching them up, the decision had to be made to disconnect them. As nice as they are, they don't justify setting the building on fire. In fact, getting hold of the correct-size mantles had become a challenge. I challenged Blythe and

Wright of Sheringham and they managed to find a single box, which appeared to be the last ones available in the country. They were very fragile and broke so easily.

Hand in hand with the gas inspection, we would order our supply of gas cylinders for the year. I would ring the UCL, the Watch House Trust and the hut owners to take their orders and then Marilyn would send them an invoice. We would get the occasional request from a hut in the middle of the summer and sometimes even give them one of ours. It became clear – after a few were never paid for – that organising it all at the start of the season and recording it in a logbook was the way forward. Then, like a milkman, I would travel up the Point and drop off cylinders to whoever had ordered them.

Following the addition of solar panels, there were a few other routine services to get sorted at the start of each season. These included fire alarm inspections and the servicing of both the storage batteries and the back-up generator. The Norwich-based company that installed the system unfortunately became bankrupt after just a couple of years. We eventually found an Essex-based company who took over the maintenance of our system.

When serious flood warnings were issued in December 2013, the whole electricity system was switched off in case of saltwater inundation. Fortunately, the water didn't come quite that high. However, the whole system was switched off long enough for the batteries to become completely drained of charge, which is not good for their health. After being drained of power, they no longer held their charge as well as they had before. In the later months of the subsequent two seasons, with reduced sunlight hours, the batteries would frequently let us down, causing the generator to kick in. The generator itself wasn't in great condition either.

Impressively, almost three years after the tidal surge, we were still able to claim the batteries on insurance because the fault could be directly linked to the surge event. Once the necessary paperwork had been completed, we set about the task of moving heavy batteries. They were 3ft high, 1ft in diameter and weighed over 50kg each. There were twenty-four old ones to remove and replace, which meant a lot of lugging.

First, we carefully and slowly negotiated their transportation along the top of the shingle ridge. This took several journeys due to their weight. A tracked telehandler had been hired for the job, but it overheated before even reaching the Watch House. Such are the challenges of moving heavy things along Blakeney Point.

Then there came the fun of negotiating the steep dune on which the battery shed is located. We made a ramp out of wooden railway sleepers and used a sack barrow to wheel the batteries up and down, forty-eight times in total. Fortunately, no backs were injured in the process.

According to my diary, the operation took place between 5 and 7 April, so we were really cutting things fine. Needless to say, it was a huge relief when the batteries were all connected and successfully switched on, just in time for the start of the season. The seasonal assistants started the following Monday; they had not experienced the suspense, strain and pain of making sure there was power.

Vehicle servicing is another winter job in preparation for the season. We would scrape barnacles off the bottoms of both boats and apply anti-foul. Servicing would usually be done by Neil Thompson Boats, whose boatyard was nearby in Glandford at that time. The boats would then be launched in late March or early April.

I experienced a number of challenges and dramas with the Bonwitco boat. There were several occasions where it nearly cut out, and two when it actually did. The first time was during an evening tern survey with assistant ranger, Sarah, who conveniently happened to be rather good at rowing. The boat was rolling about in the waves, making us both feel dizzy, but we got into a good rowing rhythm. As soon as we re-entered the harbour, the water was beautifully still, like a millpond. A serene rowing trip back to Pinchen's Creek ensued.

The second time – after it had been allegedly fixed, I might add – the engine cut out in a similar place, this time during the middle of the day. Fortunately, wildlife crime officer and predator control volunteer Jason was nearby and kindly towed us back. We felt embarrassed but relieved and very grateful.

As well as the boats, there was the Honda quad bike and later the Polaris Ranger sit-in all-terrain vehicle. Servicing for both vehicles could often be expensive due to inevitable salt corrosion. Even wax oiling and regular hosing down wasn't enough to protect it, due to the harshness of the environment. The trailer suffered too, and numerous pairs of footwear have perished through salt corrosion. But it was all part of the challenge of living and working on Blakeney Point.

There would always be a few items to purchase each season. We would constantly need new metal road pins for breeding bird cordons as well as a few rolls of agricultural baler twine. An extra lump hammer would never go amiss as the odd one would get put down on the shingle, never to be found again.

At the start of my first season as Point lead, we had a lot of items to buy for the Lifeboat House following its renovation. I was advised there was budget for the purchase of new cutlery and crockery. However, I was very attached to the old Maidstone crockery and so salvaged as much as possible because most of it was in perfectly good condition and had more character than plain white plates and bowls.

Maidstone plate from the Lifeboat House crockery set. (Ajay Tegala)

We bought a lot of things from Blythe and Wright in Sheringham: from a wok and saucepans to a new kitchen bin, brooms, coat hooks and generally anything we spotted in the store that could be useful, such as a 'private' sticker to go on the front door. This would hopefully reduce the frequency of visitors walking into our kitchen – I remember one day finding a man in our kitchen, whose wife or girlfriend was cheekily using our bathroom despite the toilet block being open and just a few footsteps away. They hadn't even knocked on the door.

The old sofa bed and matching chair had been thrown out because they did not meet the increased fire safety standards. I managed to find a nice armchair from the Benjamin Foundation in Holt and was advised to contact Debbie from the holiday cottage team, who lived near Felbrigg Hall. She had a second-hand sofa bed that we could have for free. I drove the HiLux over to her barn to collect it along with assistant ranger Matt.

I will never forget carrying the sofa from her barn to the HiLux, with a donkey in attendance. While passing the donkey with the sofa, the dear thing decided to bite me. News spread, and when speaking to Marilyn on the phone, her opening line was, 'I hear you were nibbled by a donkey.'

After wrapping up and taking the sofa bed along the Point by tractor and trailer, we found it was an inch too big to fit through the door. It stayed in the visitor centre for a few days before being taken back to the mainland. We also struggled to get a new bed into the smallest bedroom, the one by the stairs, because the turning circle was too tight. Graham found a small bed and mattress that was being thrown out of one of the Friary Farm caravans – this fitted nicely.

I was against getting rid of too much of the old furniture because it was in good condition and matched the character of the building. There is a wonderful driftwood shelf in the living room that simply has to stay there. The dresser had to be moved out of the kitchen to make space for new cupboards, so it was relocated in the living room next to the seldom-used television, which sat on an old workbench that had washed up on the beach some years ago.

Employing seasonal staff is a rather important pre-season job. From my point of view, I needed people who were reliable, punctual, flexible, committed and easy to live with. Working and living in close proximity in a remote location is not the same as a nine-to-five office job. Luckily, the many applicants each year were – for the most part, although not exclusively – dedicated nature lovers.

It was always hard having to turn down dozens of great candidates. I liked the combination of having someone who knew the Point and the job well alongside somebody new with fresh eyes and enthusiasm, in need of their first leg-up into a career in conservation, like I had been. This proved to be an ideal arrangement for a number of years.

For new team members, prior experience monitoring wildlife and communicating with visitors is essential. Although, if experience is limited, that is not necessarily a huge problem so long as they are motivated. Someone with a good attitude and a willingness to learn can make a great team member alongside other experienced staff. In fact, probably the best seasonal assistant I worked with was Sarah because her attitude was terrific; she was a real pleasure to work and share accommodation with.

One of the last jobs to do at the very start of the season is to turn the water back on. Water comes off the mains at Morston and passes underneath the harbour through a pipe that was laid in 1974. On the Point side, the water is turned off and drained ahead of winter, so that no water sits inside the pipes, freezes, expands and leads to the pipe splitting.

Laying it in the first place had been quite a task. A digger sank on Morston Marsh and a second sank trying to retrieve the first.

Forty years after it was laid, the pipe had begun to degrade in the under-harbour section. There had been a couple of historical cases of boats dragging their moorings, which had exposed the metal casing that protects the pipe. There had also been a leak at the Morston end, which was easy enough to access. The leak that occurred during my time was not so easy to locate and repair.

R. & S. Whiting, a Norwich engineering company, were tasked with the job. Lee from the company spent many hours helping me. First, the pipe was isolated by the coast path on the head of Morston Marsh and also on the landing ridge, dividing it into three separate sections. An old bait-diggers' causeway facilitated access to the head of Morston Marsh for a lightweight digger.

Getting the digger out to the Point was to be more challenging. The trailer it sat on didn't really have suitable tyres, but in my desperation to fix the water leak before the start of the season, we chanced it. I would soon learn that playing it safe is usually best when driving on loose shingle.

We made it beyond the Watch House but got very stuck in the looser shingle near the Hood. With the aid of the tractor, we managed to get the trailer back to Cley. Unfortunately, the wheel bearings had been damaged by the shingle and the cost of repair work had to be added to the bill.

The worst case of getting stuck I experienced was one evening in early autumn. The relatively new all-terrain vehicle, a Polaris Ranger, cut out on the beach beyond the Watch House in the dark as the tide was rising. There was sufficient fuel, so that wasn't the issue, but it simply wouldn't start. The immediate response whenever we got into any form of trouble was always to ring Graham. He was in North Walsham so suggested I try Willie Weston, Jim Temple or Bernard Bishop, all of whom had tractors they could bring up to tow the vehicle out with. Willie didn't answer his phone, but Jim did, 'I'd help you if I could ... but I'm in Scotland!'

Thankfully, Bernard was able to come, having to tear himself away from a Rugby World Cup match. It was a horrible situation to be in. It didn't bear thinking about how the vehicle could become submerged in the sea: a horrific scenario from an environmental perspective, as well as an inconvenience, expense and damage to reputation.

Thankfully, Bernard was happy to help a neighbour out of a muddle, as we all were on the coast. He towed the Polaris up the beach onto the top of the ridge. I bought him a large bottle of Bell's whisky to say thank you and, from that day on, never took any vehicle below the high-water mark unless it was dead low tide and daytime. That way, if we did get stuck or break down, there would be time to walk to Friary Farm and return with the tractor.

The problem with the Polaris turned out to be a loose connection underneath the seat. It was to bring us other challenges over the coming year or so. The following summer, it overheated quite spectacularly, with coolant spurting out like a fountain. Like the previous autumn, it had to be left between the Watch House and Hood overnight and collected the following morning.

The water pipe challenge continued when we discovered the leaking section was under the harbour, which is the hardest part to access. With the breeding bird season now under way, we considered just paying an increased water bill in order to get water out to the Point. However, there was concern that saltwater could enter the pipe and flow back to Morston village, contaminating the village's drinking water supply.

An agricultural 1,000-litre water container was brought up the Point by tractor on a farm trailer and left tucked behind the Old Lifeboat House. We used this water, along with rainwater, to flush the toilets. Water for drinking and washing up was brought out in 5-litre bottles, which we regularly returned to the mainland for refilling. Inevitably, as we were not putting quite as much water down the pipes as usual, a faint odour did start to creep into the building after a few weeks. There was also the inevitable septic tank blockage later in the season, which thankfully was solved using drain rods, which were kept on the Point for such occasions. Not a pleasant job but certainly satisfying when it works.

It was June before we had running water. I endured nearly three months of only being able to shower every few days, resurrecting an old shower in the mainland office. Amazingly, I entered a serious personal relationship during that period – I suppose it was a good test, as we've now been happily married for some years. It was also handy being able to get my washing done each week until we were able to use the machine in the Lifeboat House again. Over the years, I'm sure thousands of visitors have spotted ranger laundry drying on the line strung between the Lifeboat House and public toilet block. It was eventually replaced with a rotary one, tucked a little less conspicuously in the garden.

Seabird reserves like the Farne Islands do not have mains water and manage okay. We adapted quite well and got used to a new routine. The public toilets had to be closed. We enjoyed not having to clean them, but their closure obviously didn't go down too well with locals, especially the seal ferry operators, whose customers used them. I was always surprised at the number of people landing off the ferries who would make a beeline for the toilet block.

Original warden Bob Pinchen wrote in his book, 'For a good many years, fresh water was carried down to us in small tubs, jars or bottles.' He described how increasing student field trips from UCL led to a shortage of water. The solution was to dig a well in Glaux Low near the UCL laboratory, which had been built in 1913. After digging down 4–5ft, fresh water welled up.

Initially, water was conveyed to the Lifeboat House by a handcart and whatever form of vessel was available. It was decided that a well should be dug near the Lifeboat House, too. In fact, four more wells were subsequently opened close by. The surface of the water would rise and fall with the tide, but the taste was unaffected. Even in the driest summers, there was water for all requirements. The only problem was encountered during the First World War: the soldiers stationed on the Point 'did not trouble to keep the sand clear, with the result that the wells filled up'.

After the water pipe had been laid in the mid-1970s, the wells all fell into disrepair. One can still be seen in the Lifeboat House garden, full of sand and covered with a concrete lid. I have not been able to find any trace of the one by the lab. The idea of digging a new well to supply our own fresh water appealed to me. However, the pipe really did need to be fixed.

In a normal year, water is not a worry, but food is always an important consideration. Especially for new rangers. A weekly shopping routine must quickly be formed to ensure sufficient supplies. The obvious thing to do is to bring in a good stock of non-perishables at the start of the season. Paul once started a season with no fewer than seventy tins: several months' supplies of beans, sweetcorn, soup, chopped tomatoes and the like.

On 1 April, the Point's seasonal dog restrictions begin, which last until mid-August. Dogs have been excluded from the tern nesting areas since at least the Ted Eales days. Birds perceive dogs as predators and are therefore disturbed by their presence, compromising their breeding and chick-rearing success. The Point is carefully zoned so that the most vulnerable areas for nesting shorebirds are dog-free but leaving some of the least vulnerable areas accessible to responsible dog walkers, keeping their canine companions on a lead.

There are no fewer than fifteen dog signs to go up on 31 March. Unless Easter is early, the seasonal staff generally don't start until April is under way. I would always try to get the Far Point fence lines up before the end of March in advance of the Sandwich terns starting to settle. In later years, my partner would help. We would move to the room above the woodburner because this was the warmest, thanks to a radiator containing water heated by the burner.

One year, the assistants didn't start until the second week of April. Being single at the time, it took quite a while to get the fences and signs up, but I enjoyed the solitude, working at my own pace, and the feeling of being the sole person in charge of such a wonderful and important place.

During his time as Point lead, Dave had a period of a few weeks on his own. I imagined what this would be like. It did appeal in some ways, during the quiet moments. But, of course, you would need to be in two or three places at once at the height of the season. A team of three is only just enough to safeguard such an important bird-breeding site when it is also a popular leisure destination.

2

Nesting

THE BEST WAY TO get to know a nature site is to spend multiple seasons there. That way, you can tune in to the rhythm of nature through the changing seasons. Although no two years are the same, there are certain things you can almost set your calendar by.

Key events can be delayed or brought forward by weather conditions. Blakeney Point is defined by the changing seasons, dynamic weather, shifting shorelines, and wildlife that behaves in response to all three. For birders, the thrill is seeing which migrant birds will turn up, and looking at weather charts to see when conditions are best to look for them.

Finding the first nest of spring is one of my favourite things. The first few weeks of the year can often be bleak with strong northerly winds blowing straight from the Arctic. All through the winter, coveys of grey partridges are encountered, sometimes totalling well over twenty birds. When they start separating off into pairs and begin taking up their territories, this is an early sign of spring.

Every year I spent on the Point, the first nest to be found would invariably be that of a mallard on Far Point. After the stormy tides of February had passed, I would plan where precisely to locate the fence line around the tern colony area. Each year, the area would reduce in size, as the seaward edge of shingle was rolled further inland, burying more and more Suaeda bushes and even uprooting a few.

It would usually be during these March fencing recces that a mallard would be flushed from her nest beneath a Suaeda bush. What may have seemed like a quiet spot when the mallard nested, would become a dangerous predator-laden neighbourhood by the time the eggs hatched.

It was quite a surprise, one July, when a trail camera on a tern nest captured eight ducklings on the very tip of the Point. That year, a female domestic mallard also nested in the ternery, laying eleven infertile eggs. It returned for several consecutive years.

As the years rolled by, there seemed to be more and more cock pheasants appearing along the Point. In the course of a tractor or Land Rover journey from Cley beach to the Lifeboat House in late February, multiple territories could be observed and, occasionally, birds fighting over territories, with their spurs out.

At the same time as seeing an increase in this non-native, not-completely-wild species, I sadly also saw the loss of another nesting species. Prior to the refurbishment of the Lifeboat House, a pair of stock doves had nested in the roof for many years, gaining access through a gap in the corrugated iron cladding. Calling could often be heard from the upstairs bedrooms. A little loud first thing in the morning, but nice to know they were there, technically, sharing our house.

After the refurbishment, there was no longer a place for the pair to nest. Or, rather, no longer access into the roof. We saw a pair prospecting on the Point for three consecutive springs, but they did not go on to nest. I looked into erecting a nest box on the Lifeboat House. Permission was required from the Trust's curator, who approved, providing the nest box was painted blue to match the building. So a tawny owl box was acquired, painted and installed.

As well as initial concern about the nest box standing out to visitors, there was also concern that it could attract the wrong sort of occupant. In 1974, a kestrel had nested in the roof. Literally hundreds of dead victims were stored under the roof to feed their chicks, resulting in an unpleasant odour filling the bedroom below. Warden Ted Eales cut a trapdoor through the roof to remove the rotting carcasses and discovered five large chicks.

In three weeks, the parent kestrels brought in an estimated 150 little tern chicks to feed their young. Noticing a dead young rabbit near their nest being torn up to feed the chicks, Ted ensured a regular supply of rabbit carcasses in order to divert them away from the tern colony. Eventually, four chicks fledged and 'happily left the Point with their parents and preyed on the black-headed gull colony on Morston Marshes'. The fifth chick had fallen into a water tub and never recovered.

These were the first known raptor chicks ever to have hatched on the Point and none have been recorded since. In spring 2019, a pair of marsh harriers began nest-building on the saltmarsh off Far Point, only to be washed out by a big tide. They then made a second attempt, suffering the same fate, and consequently abandoned the Point area altogether. This did make an interesting addition to the list of attempted breeders. This list also includes an unpaired laughing gull, which took up residence among the black-headed gull colony on Near Point in 1999. It attempted to breed with black-headed gulls and occasionally a young Mediterranean gull. It even constructed a nest beneath a Suaeda bush.

After four years of playing swift calls to try to attract them to nest in boxes on the lookout tower, we admitted defeat. Perhaps the Point was too isolated a spot for them. We were becoming tired of the constant recordings on loop each day. A visiting artist who was commissioned to paint a mural capturing the Norfolk coast's 'spirit of place' even depicted a swift above the Lifeboat House because she associated their calls with the building.

Interestingly, the year we ceased playing swift calls, a pair of starlings took up residence inside one of the swift nest boxes. This was the first breeding starling record in almost thirty years. It gave me the idea to modify the swift boxes slightly in the hope of attracting other birds. We had already had some success with swallows nesting on shelves and a pair of pied wagtails using a nest box on the shed each year. I widened the opening to allow larger birds in. Two years later, I was delighted to hear the news that a stock dove had taken up residence after a six-year absence.

These little experiments and anomalies were interesting, but nothing could compare to the fascination of our characteristic shore-breeding terns and waders. I once spotted the exact location of a redshank nest from the quad bike as the adult took off from among the grass on the edge of a dune. A quick inspection revealed four speckled eggs, elongated at one end, the pointed end of each egg facing the centre of the nest. The beauty of redshank eggs in a nest is rivalled only by the cuteness of the newly hatched chicks.

Redshank and ringed plover pairs often return to similar spots on the Point to nest each year and some oystercatchers choose almost the exact same spot. Due to the variety of behaviour shown by oystercatchers, individual birds can be recognised.

There was a particularly aggressive bird who nested in Great Sandy Low for numerous years. When you came too close to her nest site, she would fly quickly towards you and hover above your head intimidatingly. We noticed she had a metal ring but, despite her coming quite close, we never managed to read the full code, just the first two letters: 'FA'. So, I nicknamed her Fatima.

Between 2012 and 2016, we found a few dead oystercatchers with metal rings on their legs. All of them had been ringed in the late 1980s in the Wash, making them over 20 years old. Knowing that some of these dead birds had been part of the Point's breeding population, a possible theory was raised that we had an ageing population. For the first decade of the century, around 130 to 150 oystercatcher pairs nested each year. But, in the second decade, this started to drop, falling below 120 pairs, then fewer than 100 pairs to around 80. There is always a margin of error in our surveys, but there was no denying that the number of breeding pairs in, say, 2015 was significantly lower than it had been ten years previously.

There had also been a number of years with low productivity. One year saw 100 oystercatcher pairs fledge just twenty young. Another year, eighty-five pairs fledged only eight young – and not all of these fledged birds would survive to breeding age. With known birds return-ing to the same spots each year, I worried that eventually these birds would die out and not be replaced. However, because they were long-lived birds, productivity did not need to be high every year. I was seeing a snapshot in time, but it did look like a downward trend was emerging.

Ringed plovers were also showing a definite and worrying decline, over a longer period of time. From the end of the Second World War through to the end of the 1980s, there were regularly over 100 pairs nesting across the Point. This number rapidly halved during the first half of the 1990s and has been under twenty pairs since 2000.

More detailed research over a longer period of time was neces-sary. This was one of the many possible research areas I would love to explore. I could easily have spent all of my time researching breeding behaviour and population dynamics. However, as some of the older staff rightfully pointed out, you could 'count down to extinction' – we had to protect first and monitor second.

There is, however, a very good argument that monitoring is, of course, needed to prove the need and validity of the protection methods adopted. I was always keen to collect as much useful data as we could to aid conservation. After all, this is why I was doing the job: to protect our breeding birds as well as possible.

I was in no doubt that human disturbance needed to be minimised to give our breeding birds the best possible chance. History had proved this. The birds already had weather, food supply and predation to battle with.

In fact, it was the gull predation of oystercatcher chicks that I was worried was having a significant impact on the population. Especially when common gulls would fly up and down the beach, often in pairs, hunting out oystercatcher and ringed plover chicks. They had become specialists. We would shout at them and wave our arms to try to scare them off, it was instinctive.

The avocets on the Cley end of the Point were admirable in their response to predators. I often saw them having a good go at any black-headed gulls that came too near. Like ringed plovers, they also adopt a clever broken wing display. Locating themselves a safe distance from their eggs or young, they feign a broken wing, to lure the predator, only to make a miraculous recovery at the last minute. This behaviour can successfully draw a predator further and further away from where the wader doesn't want them to be, thus saving their eggs and young.

While checking on the avocet colony during the second week of May 2016, a little ringed plover was spotted. This was actually a Point first for me. They had returned to breed on nearby Blakeney Freshes two years previously, after a twenty-year absence. The Point bird was seen regularly throughout May and in fact turned out to be a pair. Within a month, a nest was located containing four eggs.

During Eddie's first year as an assistant, ten years previously, he had discovered the very first little ringed plover nest on Blakeney Point. He found it on the patch of shingle between Far Point and Middle Point. Reporting back to his colleagues, they assumed he was referring to a ringed plover that was little, not a little ringed plover. They did not believe him until they saw the bird for themselves. This nest, however, was predated at the egg stage by common or herring gulls.

Protected from gulls by the avocet colony, if the 2016 eggs could hatch, these would be the first-known little ringed plover chicks to hatch on Blakeney Point.

Our hopes were answered on the day of the Summer Solstice. Three of the four eggs hatched. The youngest chick died in the scrape, but the other two were seen regularly. By the middle of July, only one chick was present. There is a chance that the pair split the brood or perhaps one chick had died. However, it was a true delight to be able to say a little ringed plover had fledged on the Point for the very first time.

Because of our exceptional interest in the little ringed plover nest, coupled with its location, some of our volunteers and regular birders were able to monitor it carefully. On the headland, however, we had such a number of various other birds' nests that we couldn't monitor many as closely as this one. This is one of the reasons we invested in some trail cameras, so that we could effectively have twenty-four-hour surveillance on a number of nests.

There seemed to be no end of fascinating behaviour going on all around. Trail cameras are a brilliant research tool and gave us a deeper insight into the lives and habits of the nesting terns and waders. In fact,

Oystercatcher nest containing six eggs laid by two females, May 2016. (Ajay Tegala)

they helped us to prove a theory we had about an oystercatcher nest of particular interest.

In May 2012, we observed an oystercatcher scrape near the Lifeboat House, which contained five eggs. While many Blakeney Point birds tended to lay four eggs, five was exceptional. We wondered whether a female had actually managed to produce a fifth egg or if these were the eggs of two females. The following May, we found another five-egg scrape in almost exactly the same location. A day later, the scrape contained six eggs and the day after that it contained seven! While a female laying five eggs in five days was just about believable, seven eggs in seven days was impossible. This surely had to be a case of egg dumping by a second female. Much to our surprise, a few days later, we found a six-egg oystercatcher scrape not far away on the end of Near Point.

The seven-egg nest was predated before any of the eggs had reached the hatching stage. In early June, five more eggs were laid in the same scrape. Noticing that there often seemed to be three birds in the vicinity, a trail camera was positioned by the nest to find out more. We were careful to locate it far enough from the nest that the birds were not put off by its presence. Bird welfare *must* come first.

The footage showed one bird literally pushing another off the eggs to incubate them. It appeared the trio of birds were made up of one male and two females apparently fighting over incubation duties. We were able to capture incubation changeovers between a male and female at a 'normal' nest for comparison. Here the birds were far less reluctant to change over. We hoped that having two mothers would mean the chicks would be well protected, if this second clutch could only make it to hatching. One egg was predated, although we did not manage to capture the culprit on camera.

On 8 July, the remaining four eggs began hatching. By the following day, two chicks were seen walking around on the shingle – a 50 per cent reduction in brood size in less than twenty-four hours. We had hoped for better, having captured some examples of good parenting on the trail camera.

On three occasions, conflict between oystercatchers and grey partridges was captured. When the partridges walked too close to the oystercatcher nest, they were aggressively seen off. We witnessed grey partridges behaving aggressively too, on 16 July. We stumbled upon a pair with sixteen very young chicks in the dunes. Determined to protect their newly hatched young, the adults behaved quite intimidatingly towards us. They fluffed themselves up to look bigger, made loud, fierce calls and kept jumping up towards us. We soon got out of their way.

In 2014, the oystercatcher threesome was still going strong. The beach profile had changed a little, but they still nested together in the same vicinity, again producing a clutch of five eggs from which two chicks fledged. Another six-egg nest was observed on Near Point too, this one failing, either due to flooding or predation. A camera was not located on that nest because of the fear of it being damaged by the tide. However, trail cameras on other nests did reveal predation incidents.

A pair of ringed plovers chose to nest directly underneath an information board in front of the Lifeboat House ramp in 2013. We worked hard to keep visitors from accidentally flushing the incubating adults off their nest. I saw the situation as an opportunity for engagement and education. During each high tide, we would take it in turns to position a telescope at a safe distance, focused on the incubating bird. We were able to have positive conversations with dozens and dozens of visitors, many of them genuinely excited to see the ringed plover up close and impressed at how camouflaged they are when sat tight.

We monitored this nest for the BTO Nest Recording Scheme. Knowing when the eggs were laid, we were able to predict the day they would hatch. On the day they were due to hatch, we had a glance at the nest on our morning rounds. To our great disappointment, we found an empty scrape.

The trail camera was able to shed light on what had happened. It showed a common gull gobbling up the eggs, one by one, shortly after dawn that July morning. We had witnessed numerous common gull incidents that season with the victims ranging from mallard to meadow pipit. At least we had captured the evidence.

Due to their decline across the coast, ringed plovers were also a focus of the Norfolk Little Tern Working Group. We were able to share the footage with our neighbours, many of them having witnessed the same thing. That year, we entered a five-year Little Tern Life Project funded by the European Union. The project had the ambitious aim of increasing the population by the end of the project. As partners, we used some of our funding to purchase more trail cameras, which we positioned on little tern nests.

The first little tern egg predator we caught on camera was, in fact, an oystercatcher. As well as being victims of nest predation, they were also clearly guilty of it. One individual was seen literally zigzagging between nests, hammering into the eggs and feeding on their contents. Such is the complexity of the relationships between the Point's breeding birds.

A survey of the very tip of the Point, on 1 June 2014, would reveal a curious interrelationship between little terns and another tern species. While carefully counting the little, common and Arctic tern nests, we

discovered a scrape containing two little tern eggs alongside a common
tern egg. A trail camera was positioned overlooking the scrape and we
waited eagerly to learn more.

The eggs were being incubated by a pair of little terns. However,
common terns were present at the scrape on a regular basis. The
common terns made several attempts to incubate their egg. Each time
they tried, one of the little terns would attack, driving them away.

Within three weeks of discovering the nest, both little tern chicks
hatched and were subsequently predated. Frustratingly, whatever took
them was not captured by the trail camera. This was a recurring frustration we seemed to be experiencing. With the little tern parents now
having abandoned the scrape, the common terns were able to resume
incubation of their egg. It began hatching but the chick died inside the
egg. Curiously, the camera captured an adult little tern by the common
tern egg on two occasions after the chick inside had died.

We wrote an article about the shared scrape for the *British Birds*
journal. My research turned up examples of two female common terns
sharing a scrape, common and roseate terns dumping eggs in each
other's scrapes and even little terns sharing a scrape with ringed plovers. As far as we were aware, however, this was the first known case of
common and little terns laying in the same scrape.

In mid-June the following year, we were again surveying the tip of Far
Point when we made another surprise discovery. This time it was a scrape
containing one little tern egg alongside an Arctic tern egg. Needless to say,
we positioned a trail camera overlooking the scrape. This revealed that
the eggs were being incubated solely by an Arctic tern pair.

On 9 July at 4.45 a.m., the camera captured images of a little tern
chick. It was fed and brooded by the Arctic terns. The little tern chick
was fed sixteen times in ten hours before the Arctic tern chick also
hatched, at around 3.00 p.m. Both chicks were recorded at 7.20 p.m.
but had disappeared by the time the camera was next triggered, two
minutes later.

An adult Arctic tern was then captured repeatedly searching the area, which indicated the chicks had been predated, most likely by a gull, although unfortunately not captured by the trail camera. As far as we were aware, this was the first-known case of an Arctic tern attempting to raise a little tern chick, albeit for just one day.

During the period that both chicks were present in the scrape, each was fed twice. Little terns showed signs of poor feeding on the Point that June. This led us to speculate that the little tern egg had been abandoned. The mean incubation period for both species is three weeks, therefore, the eggs must have been laid within approximately a day of each other to hatch within twelve hours. This suggests that the little tern egg was abandoned very soon after laying. While the Arctic tern could have forced the little tern to abandon its eggs, this is not typical behaviour and no instances of aggressive behaviour between the two species had been witnessed on the Point.

Arctic tern pair with little tern chick, July 2015. (National Trust)

The very tip of Far Point is one of my favourite places during the summer, simply because four species of tern all nest in close proximity. It is this close proximity that has led to these interesting inter-species relationships. Indeed, in the mid-1970s, Ted Eales discovered a hybrid pair consisting of a female Arctic tern and a male common tern. He actually managed to film the pair sharing incubation of their chicks. The footage appeared in the Anglia Television programme *Point of Departure*, as well as footage of the kestrels that nested in the Lifeboat House roof.

My first two seasons on the Point – one as assistant and then as lead – were both reasonably successful for nesting, on the whole, and were certainly free from catastrophe. Indeed, the second had effectively been a trial, which culminated in me successfully securing the permanent Point ranger post after a successful interview that September. The following three years were to throw a broad range of challenges at me and the team.

My first major television appearance was filmed with Tony Robinson on the eve of my 24th birthday. As we filmed a walking shot along the landing ridge towards the Lifeboat House, Tony said that people must be 'green with envy' that this was where I lived. Indeed, I always felt extremely fortunate to call the iconic building my home. But it was far from a holiday home, as the next season would demonstrate.

This was the first breeding season during the Little Tern Life Project. By the second week of June, chick provisioning research conducted by Al had shown poor attendance at the Watch House colony, suggesting poor feeding. On top of this, there were big tides and strong onshore winds forecast for the next four days. This was a great concern for the beach colony, which, as usual, supported by far the largest proportion of little tern nests on the Point.

Over the winter, the beach profile had changed. As a consequence, the little terns had nested further east in a slightly lower area of newly deposited fine shingle. As part of our licensed monitoring, we carefully entered the colony in late May and marked twenty-four nests. After tidal flooding at the end of May, three nests had been washed away, six scrapes contained broken shells or yoke and all other scrapes contained cold eggs. The incoming flood water had put the little terns up off their nests and given common gulls the chance to dive in and dine.

Immediately prior to the spring tides in mid-June, there were sixty-seven active little tern nests on the beach and we knew that all were certain to be flooded. The thought of complete breeding failure made us feel sick. What could be done? We knew that the Long Nanny colony up in Northumberland faced flooding each year, due to its location beside a small river that was gradually changing its course. I had visited the site when I worked at nearby Lindisfarne and had learned all about its management from ranger Jane.

There, they raised nests up and even brought eggs in during big tides, returning them after the floodwater had receded. Because part of the Life Project involved experimentation and sharing ideas, we decided to attempt the Long Nanny approach on the Point. Our motivation was knowing that these nests were sure to be lost anyway, so effectively we had nothing to lose but potentially a lot to gain. After all, with a vulnerable and declining species, every nest counts.

We amassed empty egg boxes and filled them with cotton wool. Blank sticky labels were put on each box, so that we could record the corresponding nest number of every egg and chick collected.

A total of eight tides flooded the colony. We developed a routine: taking the quad bike and trailer to the edge of the colony, collecting the vulnerable eggs and young, wrapping the egg boxes in a duvet and keeping them warm for an hour or so by the log burner in the Lifeboat House before returning them to their scrapes after the water had receded.

Five nests were abandoned after the first tide. By the time the last flood was over, we were left with just seven active nests. Although we had kept eggs and chicks safe, many were still abandoned or predated by common gulls after we had returned them. There was obviously still a window between us returning the eggs and the adult little terns returning to incubate them – an opportunity seized by the clever common gulls, who raided at least twenty-five nests.

It was a fascinating and valuable learning process, but we concluded that attempting to move so many nests over so many tides was a bit too ambitious and neither sustainable nor productive. However, there was a little consolation knowing that the seven nests that were saved would certainly have been flooded otherwise. Some of these nests contained small chicks in the second week of July when onshore winds blew sand through the beach colony. It buried all of the remaining eggs and killed all the chicks. By the middle of the month, the colony had been abandoned.

Elsewhere on the Point, at least five incidences of a hobby taking an adult little tern were recorded. Two UCL students, Jodie and Devanshi, spent a few weeks based in the Old Lifeboat House and we helped them position trail cameras on eight nests near the Watch House for their Master's degree research projects.

With a recent weasel sighting in the area, we were curious to see if any mammalian predators would be captured. None were recorded. However, a photographer in full-body camouflage was captured walking through the colony at six o'clock one morning. The image was circulated widely but the man was never identified. Our fear, of course, was that this was a potential egg thief, which was the very last thing we needed.

But it certainly wasn't all bad news for little terns that year. Building on Al's enthusiasm, a team of dedicated little tern volunteers were recruited specifically to help warden the colonies on the shingle ridge near the Watch House. Recruits included Nick, who I had met on a guided walk two years before, alongside Bill, who came over from Thetford Forest twice a week throughout the breeding season.

Thanks to our newly formed team of little tern volunteers, there was an increased presence across a wider part of the reserve. As a result, so many potential disturbance incidents were prevented by raising awareness about the camouflaged, fragile birds nesting on what many visitors saw solely as a pleasure beach.

Despite the remoteness and isolation, our small team developed a real love for that part of the Point. Nick told his friends about it. Each year, more and more people would get in touch asking to get involved.

Interestingly, many of them were not necessarily birders but all developed a great affection for the little tern.

In preparation for the following season, we discussed what we could do to boost productivity. What methods of conservation could be adopted without having to physically move nests? Through the Little Tern Working Group and Life Project, as well as my own experience in Northumberland, we were aware of a number of sites where decoys were being used to attract little terns to nest. This was often done on artificially created areas of habitat, such as floating shingle platforms. But could we use decoys to attract little terns to less flood-prone parts of the Point?

This was also an opportunity to get the Blakeney Primary School students involved in little tern conservation. I gave them a talk about terns: their migration, their nesting habits and the challenges they face. The helpful potters at Made In Cley kindly donated some clay for the children to make their decoys from. They also offered to fire the decoys for us in their kiln. It was brilliant to have a local business supporting our conservation work.

A place to locate them sprang to mind easily. After the flooding of the beach colony, two pairs had re-laid just east of the gap. We were able to protect and monitor them nicely from our watch point. In fact, we observed two young reach the fledging stage. This area was far less likely to flood than the beach colony. In the 1980s, the little tern colony had been more or less in this location. It seemed the perfect place to trial decoys.

Sure enough, thanks to the decoys, or perhaps by pure coincidence, ten pairs went on to nest in our new gap colony and managed to fledge twelve young. This exceeded the Life Project target of 0.75 productivity per pair. The following year, however, there was significant erosion to this area of shingle. Such is the dynamic nature of the shoreline.

Suddenly, the gap colony was less suitable for little terns. Instead, we located decoys – along with a solar-powered tape lure on loan from the RSPB – on the main shingle ridge between the Hood and Long Hills. We chose an area of habitat apparently similar to the areas the birds normally occupied but located a little further west. This turned out to have zero success. It could have been that the location was not close enough to a decent foraging area, as little terns tend only to fly a maximum of 6 miles to forage.

I was conscious that we shouldn't go too far in the way of intervention and become 'tern gardeners'. Blakeney Point is already a suitable site for little and Sandwich terns in its pure and natural state. Altering tern behaviour so much that they become reliant on us to prevent their nests from flooding is not beneficial in the long term. The problem is that man has greatly reduced the available habitat so much, through development and disturbance, meaning that suitable breeding sites are fewer and farther between than they once were.

3

Necessary Evil

WORKING AS A RANGER on Blakeney Point, you can't help but become interested in its history. There are lessons to be learned.

A recurring theme that becomes clear is that all introductions were a mistake. The most notable example being Spartina grass. Despite being instrumental in conserving Blakeney Point, Professor Oliver saw the purpose of ecology as not to feel closer to nature but to assist the exploitation of resources. In a paper from 1913, he classified areas not currently put to productive use as 'waste lands', including the Point, calling for such areas to urgently be devoted to economic use.

Thankfully, Professor Oliver did not plant conifers extensively on the Point's sand dunes, which could have happened and indeed did at nearby Holkham. This may have benefited migratory birds but would have completely destroyed the natural integrity of the Point's rare habitats. He proposed that marram grass should be harvested for making paper and that bulbs and vegetables should be grown commercially in the dunes.

Oliver also proposed that mudflats and saltmarsh should be reclaimed for agriculture. This is how the Blakeney freshwater grazing marshes had been created. Oliver suggested planting an invasive hybrid grass on the saltmarsh – Spartina, also known as cordgrass and rice grass – for cattle feed and the manufacture of paper. He had a great interest in experimenting with non-native plant introductions to understand which plants would be best suited to the Point. The legacy of these experiments is the Plantation, yucca, tamarisk and the extensive Spartina marsh.

By the post-war years, the saltmarsh was changing remarkably due to the invasion of the very vigorous Spartina grass, which was spreading at a remarkable speed. This resulted in the accumulation of mud and silt, raising the level of the marsh. With no fungal parasites to keep it in check, Spartina growth completely bypasses the growth of native glasswort and aster.

The monotonous, uniform Spartina meadow is devoid of native saltmarsh plants, such as zostera, or eel grass, that ducks such as wigeon feed on. By the time I became a ranger, the only remaining zostera was one very small patch in Stanley's Cockle Bight.

The best way to manage the Point is to let natural processes shape it. That is the charm and the value of the place – it is ever changing, shaped by nature. It can be argued that unmanaged coast is the closest to true wilderness we have left in the British Isles, all areas inland having been impacted on by man. While it is only natural for people to wonder what influence they can have on a place, the excitement of being involved with places like Blakeney Point is the surprise that nature alone creates. Managing the Point appropriately means reducing man's impact and observing nature behaving, well, naturally.

As well as plants, non-native animals can also have a negative impact on nature reserves. Indeed, history shows how rabbits on the Point inhibited important vegetation and insects associated with that unique vegetation. The 1913 Blakeney Point management committee report states, 'The sand-hills on the Hood and headland have for years been infested with rabbits, which browsed on and destroyed much of the vegetation.' Small areas were enclosed to exclude rabbits and 'showed that the rabbits exerted a profound influence on the plants, notably the Suaeda bushes'. That autumn, Pinchen 'appreciably reduced' the number of rabbits with great results.

In 1952, Doctor White wrote about how rabbits may jeopardise the stability of even established grey dunes, allowing the wind to blow away sand and form blow-outs, citing an example of a very large blow-out on the main dune ridge of the Point from which many tons of sand had been lost. Small areas of bare sand may be recolonised by dune-forming grasses, but large blow-outs tend to remain permanent features.

Blakeney Point was designated a Site of Special Scientific Interest in 1954 and a National Nature Reserve in 1994. The former made protecting the Point's flora, fauna and physical features a legal requirement and the latter resulted in a formal management plan. With over four decades of management experience, successes and mistakes were both clear. Indeed, the current management plan lists Spartina as an undesirable feature. Eradicating it would improve the reserve's conservation status. However, being flooded twice every day, it cannot be given chemical treatment, and physical uprooting, besides being a mammoth operation, would lead to significant salt-marsh erosion.

Essentially, management of the Point centres around preserving and allowing natural processes to take place and reducing all non-natural processes as much as possible. Contrasting with the intensive practical management of many inland nature reserves, a non-interventionist approach is adopted on the Point to let natural, coastal processes take place. The Point's habitats and native, adapted species are rare, vulnerable, unique and important. They are best preserved by man's impact on them being reduced as much as possible.

This is why footfall is channelled off the dunes and onto the boardwalk. This is why people, dogs, kites and planes are kept away from breeding birds. This is why very careful consideration is given to the impact of any new structures. Ideally, even banana skins or apple cores should not be dropped on a Site of Special Scientific Interest.

Nature faces so many pressures across the planet, principally caused by habitat loss and fragmentation. Therefore, our nature reserves are essential, as are all areas of green space that help connect them together.

Although the Point itself is well protected, the tidal waters that surround it face lots of pressures. Every tide washes up more litter, much of which is small pieces of plastic. Dead seabirds wash up regularly. Fulmars we collected were found to have stomachs containing an array of plastic. Toxic chemicals find their way into watercourses, impacting on the fish that the Point's birds rely on. As much as we can allow nature to thrive on the Point itself, it is still at the mercy of so many wider factors we cannot as easily influence.

As tempting as it may be to exclude people from places like the Point to keep them wild and natural, it is essential that people are able to access, experience, appreciate and value these important places. We all need nature. We cannot underestimate how much our actions to the detriment of wildlife are all eventually detrimental to us too. Like woodland, saltmarsh captures and stores carbon, removing carbon dioxide from the atmosphere and mitigating greenhouse gas emissions.

The battle to create a healthier, more sustainable future involves not just acting responsibly in the present and future but undoing the damage done in the past. This is why there is one exception to the non-interventionist management approach on Blakeney Point. A necessary evil. Predator control.

Killing any wild animal may seem contradictory to nature conservation, but everything must be seen in context. The problems faced by rare and declining bird species are a consequence of man's actions going back many, many years. This applies to the availability of habitat and food and also safety from predators. It is humankind who has drastically reduced the areas of suitable habitat for terns and waders. It is humankind that has reduced the populations of fish that the terns feed on. It is also humankind that has indirectly caused an unnatural increase in the numbers of predators affecting our truly wild birds.

This is why we have a responsibility to make our seabird colonies as safe from predators as we can, because we have caused the problem in the first place. Just as humankind has reduced the spaces available for little and Sandwich terns to nest, we have increased the number of foxes, crows and rats in the British countryside. A double whammy.

With greater habitat availability comes higher resilience against predators. Safety in numbers. With reduced habitat and food availability, predation poses a greater threat to productivity. This is the situation that faces Blakeney Point and many other reserves.

When Bob Pinchen became watcher of the Point in 1901, a key part of his role was to 'keep down the rats and other vermin which destroy a great number of eggs and young birds'. As a consequence of this, along with preventing egg theft and shooting, the number of nesting common terns rose from 140 in 1901 to 203 in 1913 and oystercatchers returned as a breeding species in 1906, following a fifteen-year absence.

While a high proportion of people are repulsed by rats and have no issue with them being controlled, some people may want to just let them be. The problem, however, is that humans have transformed the world in ways that favour certain pest species but do not favour several bird species. If no predator control had been done on the Point in the twentieth century, I believe there is an extremely high chance that breeding terns would have been lost altogether.

It could be argued that nature would have found a balance, but with humans having tipped the natural balance, it is really not worth the risk of not intervening and losing the terns altogether. We are indebted to them. While, in a sense, the killing of any animal can be called evil, in the case of the Point, appropriate predator control is a necessary evil.

More widely loved than the rat is the fox. Their coats are a lovely orange colour, their legs slim and dainty, their tails bushy and their general appearance similar to beloved pet dogs. Research, in 2013, even showed that their faces have some of the same features that humans find desirable: flat face, small nose, delicate jaw and large forehead. We find their cubs cute and appealing, like puppies. However, we also regard foxes as crafty, cunning and sly.

In contrast to the more overt tendencies of the more recent urban fox, rural foxes display 'sneaky' behaviour and are very discreet. Their homes are usually burrowed underground or in a hollow and they are primarily night-hunters. These behaviours have led to them being branded 'sly'. With their night vision, they became enemies of humans by running off with chickens, rabbits or other livestock. In defence of foxes, they are opportunists and, like us, have to feed themselves and their young.

Chicken farmers have to ensure their birds are kept in firmly fox-proof enclosures because foxes can be very determined when they find prey. They will not simply take one or two birds, but often go on mass killing sprees. This behaviour is, in fact, not so different from humans rearing and slaughtering chickens for the supermarket shelves, only for a proportion to go out of date before being sold and ending up being thrown away. As a fox never knows when its next meal will be, seizing the opportunity to secure a large number of birds is merely instinctive forward-planning.

Losing pets and livestock to foxes can be greatly upsetting and financially painful. So, imagine dedicating your life to protecting one of the nation's most significant colonies of vulnerable and declining terns and finding fox tracks.

This first happened relatively recently, in the early 1970s. Assistant warden Paul Cobb found footprints on the Point and signs that a fox had clearly been hunting rabbits. The first recorded actual sighting was made by Ted Eales in September 1974. Interestingly, Ted also made the Point's only recorded sighting of a coypu the same month.

A few years later, Joe Reed attended a seminar predicting that reducing numbers of gamekeepers controlling foxes on shooting estates would result in fox populations increasing and expanding their ranges, reaching nature reserves and impacting on ground-nesting birds. Joe subsequently began to prepare himself for a predator that was to dominate his time as protector of the Point. His preparation involved the purchase of an appropriate calibre rifle and silencer.

Joe's 1995 report makes interesting reading. He describes the season as 'almost certainly the busiest on record ... with an estimated 55-60,000 people visiting this summer'. Considering that media attention might be attracting greater visitor numbers, he writes that 'television companies offering an opportunity to promote the Trust's management role would be given priority'. One such programme, which he took part in himself, 'was specifically about foxes and the impact they are having on nature reserves'.

This was a very relevant topic as breeding foxes were discovered on the reserve for the first time that spring. A litter of cubs were found in the dunes on the Long Hills in April. Nightly vigils took place. During one, a fox was observed swimming across the channel onto Blakeney Freshes, probably where the pair originated from.

Joe noted that Cley had 'quite a high fox population' and:

Events at Scolt Head over the last few years have illustrated the impact foxes can have on the tern colonies, and while fox control might be quite an emotive subject, I feel that every effort should be made to prevent similar events from occurring on the Point.

This was easier said than done. The original pair having been removed, another two established a territory by February 1996. Regular night visits were made to the reserve to eradicate the foxes before the terns began to arrive.

But the topography of the Point makes it incredibly difficult to secure a reasonable rifle shot. By mid-May, there were around 1,000 pairs of Sandwich terns incubating eggs and the wardening staff were enduring many sleepless nights on patrol to keep the vixen away. Their efforts continued until the end of the breeding season, 'with at least two members of the wardening team working for ninety consecutive nights'.

Their dedication was rewarded with the knowledge that their efforts had enabled 3,500 Sandwich terns to fledge 3,000 young. The memory is preserved for perpetuity in the form of a painting on a piece of driftwood, kept in the Lifeboat House to this day, titled 'Year of the Fox': a cartoon depicting what life had been like during that most challenging of seasons.

The immense effort Joe and his two assistants, Mark and Nick, put in that summer could hardly be expected every year. Predator control being a controversial issue, one school of thought is to 'let nature take its course'. However, Joe felt 'we have already had such an impact on the environment and any natural balance which might exist, that there are occasions when positive management measures need to be introduced to redress this balance'.

Foxes had again re-established themselves by early 1997. It appeared they were now going to be an annual problem. Joe began an eradication campaign at the end of March, made much easier with the purchase of new night-sight equipment, meaning he could work alone, unlike the previous years when at least two people were required. Within two weeks, two vixens had been shot but it took another forty nights until the dog fox could be shot.

Of course, the idea of shooting foxes is met with disgust by a great number of people. I take no pleasure in the idea of animals being killed. But this method of control is absolutely humane. By the time the sound of the shot reaches the fox, it will already have been hit and as soon as it is hit, death occurs in a split second. This does, however, depend on a clear shot executed at the right time and aimed accurately at the right place. This is why fox control on the Point takes so much time, because the right opportunity has to present itself for the shot to be fired, otherwise the trigger cannot be pulled. So, fox control on the Point involves hours and hours of waiting, even when a fox is in sight. Just seeing the fox can be very difficult in such challenging terrain.

Sure enough, another pair of foxes were present on the reserve by November 1997.

The 1998 season was to be easier than the previous three, thanks to Joe having learned fast and grown in experience. Baiting was used to attract foxes to a particular location. Scraps of meat refreshed with boiling water create a strong scent to lure a fox. Locating the bait near the Lifeboat House meant the shooter could be positioned in the shelter of the building. This worked well and the resident pair were eradicated ahead of the breeding bird season.

When Joe retired, Dave took on the mantle. Indeed, I recall during my first year of volunteering that he shot a pregnant vixen from a bedroom window in March, enabling a successful tern breeding season to follow. Chatting to him a few years after he had moved on from Blakeney, he told me that the fox control work he had undertaken was probably the most effective tern conservation work he had done in all of his time as warden.

Being a confident and competent marksman, Dave maintained his fox control role even after progressing to mainland-based head warden of the wider Blakeney reserve and Norfolk coast property. This meant that, until his final year on the Point, Eddie did not have to worry too much about foxes. A year later, when I took over from Eddie, the Point's fox control now involved a few local policemen, who were keen deerstalkers. They were very generous to volunteer their assistance, although obviously they could not dedicate as much time as an employed warden. Fortunately, Bernard Bishop was controlling foxes at Cley, and Blakeney Freshes had a dedicated gamekeeper since the late 1990s: Barrie. This meant that foxes in these areas adjacent to the Point were removed before they could get there.

A lot of nature reserves with ground-nesting birds protect nesting areas from foxes, otters, badgers, mink and stoats by using electric fencing. Indeed, this has been considered for the Point many times as it takes away the need for lethal control. That is, if it can be effective. The challenge Blakeney faces is its topography and tidal nature with terns spread out across numerous colonies: sometimes as many as six distinct areas. The main ternery is invariably located amongst vegetation, undulating dunes and areas prone to tidal flooding, which simply makes electric fencing impractical. In 2018, we did begin using electric fencing at the little tern colony on top of the shingle ridge near the Watch House, which succeeded in keeping foxes out and indeed humans too. However, this protects just a fraction of the Point's little terns alone, not to mention the Sandwich terns.

The first two years after Dave had left were very quiet on the fox front. My first year as Point ranger was a good one for Sandwich terns with no fox issues while the terns were rearing their young. In fact, my first season was seen as a success, aided significantly by the continuity of having Paul as assistant and the invaluable support of Graham plus long-serving volunteers such as Richard Porter. But none of us had predicted just what a challenging winter lay ahead.

4

Storm Surge

IN OCTOBER 2013, I began what was to become a pattern for several years: moving into my 'winter residence'. As much as I would have loved to stay in the Lifeboat House for as far into the winter as possible, I had several mainland-based responsibilities.

Local artist Godfrey Sayers and his wife, Judy, had a holiday chalet in their garden, which I was able to rent each winter for a reduced rate. They were keen for it to be lived in through the winter. Located in Wiveton, just a short walk from the reserve office, it was ideal. Away from the road and surrounded by trees, 'Rosemeade' is in a peaceful spot. There would often be a soundtrack of tawny owls at night. During my first stint, there was also a firecrest overwintering in the garden hedge.

The Lifeboat House having been renovated and fitted with a wood burner, it was now more hospitable during the grey seal pupping months, so I would also try to spend at least one night out there each week. In fact, through my first November as Point ranger, I spent every weekend out on the Point, increasing my seal knowledge and experience of the grey seal rookery.

On the morning of Thursday, 5 December 2013, I was on Far Point conducting a pup count and planning to spend the night in the Lifeboat House. News came through that the Norfolk coast was under serious threat of coastal flooding that evening. Potentially the most serious tidal surge in thirty years was forecast. A low-pressure system had formed off the west coast of Iceland the day before and the threat was now moving south, towards the east coast of Scotland and England.

An Environment Agency flood warning map showed all of the Point and Freshes at risk of being completely flooded.

With this serious warning, we abandoned the pup count and began preparing for the worst. The Bonwitco powerboat had already been taken out of the water a couple of months earlier, but the tender was still on the landing ridge. We brought it to the Lifeboat House garden using the quad bike and trailer, anchoring it on the edge of the dunes. All of the gas cylinders were disconnected and secured in the storage cage. We didn't honestly expect the Lifeboat House to flood but, because it was a possibility, we moved all fragile and valuable items upstairs and our books were stacked on the highest shelves, just in case water trickled into the building.

By early afternoon, the Point had been evacuated. I brought the quad bike back to Friary Farm, making sure there were no walkers heading up the Point as I drove off. The quad trailer had been left on a small dune opposite the Old Lifeboat House as it was not road legal. I dropped by the fridge in my Wiveton winter accommodation to return the cottage pie I had pre-made and taken out to the Point for that night's dinner.

I bumped into Godfrey, who was in his flood warden role and warning that the imminent flooding could be as bad as 1953. The difference, thankfully, being that this one was forecast and so people in homes at risk of flooding could evacuate in time.

Godfrey urged me to move the Blakeney parish hut higher up Friary Hills. The hut, owned by the parish council, housed a car park attendant in the summer months and a pay machine is attached to the side for use during the winter. Moving the hut off Blakeney Carnser car park during big tides was something we helped with regularly.

Graham had moved the hut earlier in the afternoon, but Godfrey thought it needed to be stored on higher ground to be safe. I intended to do this but, in all the frenzy, had been requested to do a sweep of the car parks along the coast between Salthouse and Stiffkey, to make sure any cars vacated immediately.

Two hours before high water, I pulled up by the Spar shop on Westgate Street. It was dark by now, so at first I didn't realise why an *EDP* photographer was taking pictures of the King's Arms. When I

saw that the water had already reached the pub, I realised how serious things were becoming. A phone call then came in to say that the
Lifeboat House fire alarms had gone off. We rushed to Morston Quay to
try to see what was happening on the Point.

In the darkness, with adrenaline running high, I ran towards the
information centre, only to realise I was suddenly in ankle-deep water.
The water was almost as high as the flood bank. We couldn't really get a
clear look at the Lifeboat House in the dark. It was still there, but something didn't quite look right about the front of the building. I stood on
the bank for a moment, watching the water rush past from west to east.
A few chunks of white polystyrene floated past, looking a bit like seal
pups. Oh crikey, the seal pups. How were they faring?

We zoomed back along the coast road to Friary Farm to move the
parish hut. Graham and I took the Land Rover onto the top of Friary
Hills, noticing the water had already reached the bottom of them and
was waist deep at the Wiveton end. It was too late to move the half-
submerged parish hut, the car park machine on the side was already
partly under water.

We then saw that the Manor Hotel had been flooded. Standing on the
High Street overlooking the quay, we watched in horror and disbelief as
the water crept up towards the top of the sea wall. It just didn't feel real.
I felt like I was watching a film.

It was difficult to see the sea wall being breached because of
the darkness. But, as high water approached, the level appeared to
drop suddenly. This was the point where water began to flood into
Blakeney Freshes. Effectively, this saved the villages of Blakeney and
Morston from much worse flooding. The Freshes filled up like a flood-
relief reservoir. Around 9 p.m., we decided to call it a day and come
back first thing in the morning to start sorting out what to do. The
BBC ten o'clock news was dominated by Nelson Mandela, who had
sadly died the same day.

At first light on Friday morning, I stood on Wiveton Bank and
gazed across the saltwater reservoir that once was Blakeney Freshes.
Fortunately, all livestock had been moved off a month ago for the winter.
The water level was only a few feet below the top of the secondary bank

parallel to the coast road. This bank was now higher than it had been during the 1953 flood when a lady had sadly drowned in her Wiveton home. Thankfully, no lives were lost in December 2013.

There was no power at the Friary Farm barn, so we sat in semi-darkness, coordinating staff and volunteers to cover Stiffkey to Salthouse looking for displaced seals and documenting any damage. Among the team of people who had turned up to help were the two lads who Graham and I had helped retrieve their flooded Land Rover from Morston Marsh three years previously. They reported thirty to forty boats smashed up in a pile near Stiffkey Freshes Creek.

My task was to survey the bank around the former Freshes, which had been breached in thirty-seven places. Boats and jetties from Blakeney Quay had washed up on the western bank. We could only get as far around as the cart track before facing a deep hole blocking our way. One of the two Environment Agency sluice gates was jammed shut. Calculations were done as to roughly what volume of water may be trapped and how long it would take to pump it out.

Inspecting the breaches, it became apparent that water had flowed over the bank at various points and the back-swirl had scoured out the bank from the inside. The force of the water had not punched through the bank from the seaward side as one might have imagined. It became apparent that the bank was too steep to be strong enough to withstand breaching. A wider bank with a shallower slope would be stronger against the force of water washing over it. But, at this early stage, of course, nobody knew when or whether the breaches would be fixed. Godfrey had suggested leaving the Freshes to revert back to saltmarsh and tidal mudflats and withstand any future storm events that were likely to increase with climate change.

We spotted a weaned seal pup in a pool on the Freshes. It stayed there a few days and received quite a bit of attention. Being fully weaned, we decided not to take it to RSPCA East Winch, who were already overrun with orphaned pups from east Norfolk. Eventually, the seal found its own way into the harbour and out to sea.

The Horsey and Winterton rookery had suffered badly in the surge, but at Blakeney, very few displaced seals were found. One of the few ended up practically in Bernard Bishop's front garden, by the side of the coast road in Cley, which was under water, as, of course, was the Beach Road, making the Point inaccessible even by tractor.

Bernard and I caught the young pup using a seal stretcher and I drove it back to Friary Farm on the quad bike, with it sat in the fish box on the front. A volunteer took it on to East Winch. The lack of displaced seals meant the rookery must still be on the Point, thankfully.

Sat in the Wiveton Bell that evening, we discussed plans for the next day. This would become somewhat of a routine for the days ahead. A priority for Saturday was to launch the *Whittow* and finally survey the Point. Although I was nervous to see what damage had been caused, I was itching to get out there and finally know what the score was.

With so much extra water in the harbour, we did not have to follow the tides so closely or land in the usual places. Iain steered the boat to Pinchen's Creek, where Graham, Paul and I hopped out to investigate the state of the building. It became clear that the force of the water had

Lifeboat House following the December 2013 tidal surge. (Graham Lubbock)

Damage to boardwalk caused by the December 2013 tidal surge. (Graham Lubbock)

forced the foundations of the ramp up out of the ground, pushing it into the building. A pup was sat on the damaged ramp. The double doors had remained closed, but the smaller door within them had been forced open when the ramp had been smashed into it, flooding the building in about 2ft of water.

I hadn't really anticipated finding such a mess around the building. Detritus, thatch and timber lay strewn around. The UCL Old Lifeboat House doesn't sit on stilts, so is a good few feet lower. Therefore, having much deeper water inside, the long table had floated around and knocked into the shelves and cupboards, creating quite a mess all over the floor. Outside, whole sections of the boardwalk had been torn up and were completely missing, having floated off with the floodwater.

There were saltwater pools throughout the main dunes. A young pup and its mother sat in the Lifeboat House garden; thankfully, they hadn't been separated.

Graham documented the damage with his camera, noting the overwhelming amount of tidying up required. Shocked by the mess, I struggled to imagine the clean-up operation. But, without a chance to dwell on this too much, we embarked on a hurried pup count.

Out on the beach, we found the fuel safe from the Lifeboat House shed. We later found sections of the boardwalk had washed up on the beach near Far Point, having floated off and then washed back up on a subsequent tide. Some weren't spotted until the following February, almost completely buried in sand. A door from Wells Lifeboat Station had also washed up on Far Point; we asked if they wanted it back and they said no.

There was so much rubbish strewn in the dunes. Thankfully, there were also 1,235 seal pups, a dozen or so clearly having been born since the surge. The rookery was intact.

We breathed a sigh of relief for the seals but still felt stunned by the state of the buildings and boardwalk. The Point's wildlife had withstood the surge far better than our man-made structures – an important lesson.

The natural topography of the Point had made it resilient. Sure, there was erosion to some of the dunes and a significant shifting of shingle on Far Point, but this is what Blakeney Point does, that is how it was created: shaped by the sea. We can only imagine that the seals were able to head to the taller dunes and onto ground high enough to not be submerged. Maybe they even had a sense of what was coming?

Data was later retrieved from the people counter located at the gap. Its thermal sensor detected a mass of movement at the time of the surge. This resulted in a theory that all of the seals had rushed from the beach through the gap to reach the safety of the dunes. With the rookery spread across a whole mile of beach, I just couldn't imagine that *all* of the seals would head through the gap. Surely, they would take the most direct route to the nearest safe dunes. I imagine a number of seals naturally headed through the gap, but only a fraction of the total. Of course, we will never know for sure.

The morning before, I had hurriedly tried to put a trail camera in time-lapse mode on the lookout tower to document the water coming in. However, this sadly had not worked. It probably would have been a social media sensation had it documented the floodwater coming in. We imagined what it would have been like to have stayed in the lookout tower. In hindsight, it would have been safe up there. However, when the ramp was smashed into the building, it would undoubtedly have felt like the whole building was at risk of being damaged.

The impact was devastating for those whose homes and business were affected. I felt like I had been punched in the stomach when I first saw the Lifeboat House, which I regarded as my home. Graham was affected by it, but optimistically pointed out that all of the damage on the Point was fixable. It was clear to see that the only negatives on the Point related to our man-made structures – the seals were more resilient. Aside from the sympathy and sadness I felt, elements of the event had actually been almost exciting, to some extent: not knowing just how much a natural phenomenon would change our lives and how dramatically it would alter the coastal landscape that fascinated me so much.

The impact on the shingle at Salthouse was fascinating. For a number of years, the shingle bank had been bulldozed up to maintain it as a flood defence. However, this had altered its natural integrity and actually made it a less-effective barrier.

Whereas the unaltered stretch of Blakeney Point itself had absorbed the shock and acted as a natural barrier beach, Salthouse had breached. A large hole let saltwater onto Cley and Salthouse Marshes with every tide. The Cley sluice was evacuating saltwater much quicker than the sluice on Blakeney Freshes. By Christmas, the breach at Salthouse had repaired itself through natural beach recharge. The car park at Gramborough Hill had been completely buried by shingle in the surge, thus bringing it to the end of its life.

For two and a half weeks after the surge, we kept very busy achieving as much as possible. We were fortunate to receive lots of support. Staff and volunteers from nearby Felbrigg and Blickling did a fantastic job helping us rake up thatch, pick litter and drag boats out of gorse bushes. We also assembled a group of helpers to spend a day reinstalling the boardwalk on the Point.

Using the tractor and some rope, I had been able to drag some of the washed-up missing sections back from the beach to the edge of the dunes. From there, as a team, we dragged the sections into position and reattached them. Among the helpers were former wardens Dave and Eddie.

In the middle of the clean-up operation, Graham had a pre-scheduled evening talk at a hotel in Cromer for a visiting wildlife photography group. It would have been easy to cancel, but Graham was determined for it to go ahead. I went along to help with the technical side. However, it turned out our extension lead was faulty. It tripped the hotel power twice, which didn't impress the duty manager very much.

The wildlife group were grateful that we had gone to the effort to go ahead with the talk in the middle of a busy and difficult time. They kindly made an extra donation to show their appreciation and support for our ongoing major clean-up operation.

On Christmas Eve, we were able to walk out onto Blakeney Freshes for the first time in three weeks. It was surreal walking down Marsh Lane and seeing litter in the trees above our heads. We found a few washed-up boats and a number of dead water rails, which had presumably drowned while hunkered down for the night. There was a ring of tideline around the highest point of the Eye field, the only part of the Freshes not to be submerged, just a few square metres in size.

Hares had already made a comeback. The fences along the northern fields were in a bit of a tangle and the northern fields themselves now contained a large amount of shingle, so would not be fit for grazing the following spring. In fact, spring was to see an assortment of saltmarsh plants growing in those fields. Samphire grew quite prolifically, as it tends to do on disturbed ground. The shingle also attracted a few pairs of opportunistic avocets to nest plus the first nesting little ringed plover on the Freshes since the early 1990s.

Between January and March, I monitored salinity levels each Friday. With access across the Freshes now possible again, I was able to devise a circular route that took in the key sea wall breaches and areas of standing water within the marshes themselves. We had been loaned a handheld piece of kit by the Orford Ness team. Using a pipette, a droplet of water is dropped onto a glass prism. Looking through the eye piece, a salinity reading is possible.

Predictably, salinity dropped progressively, to the point that it was no longer considered detrimental to the environment. I did find that, in some of the deeper, isolated pools, salinity was actually rising because evaporation was increasing the concentration of the salt.

The holes were eventually filled in by the Environment Agency when the sea wall was repaired. At one stage, there was a possibility that the breaches would be left. However, the rarity and national importance of freshwater grazing marsh habitat for wetland birds, combined with the value of tourism and popularity of the Norfolk coast path, meant that repair was deemed necessary.

Having learned from the way the breaches had formed, modifications were made to the bank around the Freshes. It was built a couple of inches lower with shallower sloping sides. This should allow future floodwater to flow onto the Freshes, so they can again act as a flood-relief area. The two sluices could then evacuate the saltwater over the following days, especially now that both were working; one having been seized shut at the time of the tidal surge.

5

Year of the Fox

THE FOUR MONTHS FOLLOWING the tidal surge were pretty full on. A year after its major renovation, the Lifeboat House underwent more works. This included re-varnishing of the visitor centre floor, tearing up and replacing the lino flooring in the kitchen, bathroom and office and replacing the sodden carpet in the downstairs bedroom. The ramp had to be completely rebuilt with new wood. I later used the timber from the damaged ramp to build a storage shed, with some help from handyman and hut owner Andrew.

Repairs were done to the public toilet block and, of course, in the Old Lifeboat House. Some of the same contractors from the year before returned to carry out the works on the Point, much to the horror of some of them. Coming all the way from Great Yarmouth and then creeping along the shingle ridge, before spending a day in the cold, wasn't everyone's cup of tea. Some of the team were very helpful, however, using their telehandler to help us retrieve buried sections of boardwalk from the beach and return them to the dunes.

I became heavily involved with the practical work on Blakeney Freshes. This included unfurling the mesh and barbed wire of the damaged fences, putting in new posts and tensioning new wire. Sections of geotextile and boardwalk were laid around the large holes by the sea wall in order to reinstate the coast path. Likewise, at Morston, we laid a geotextile path across sensitive saltmarsh to a temporary bridge replacing one that had been literally swept away by the surge, breaking into pieces with the impact. The temporary bridge allowed the seal ferries to operate as normal and the National Trust funded a permanent replacement.

On Friday, 4 April, I moved into the Lifeboat House, which – like the year before – was only just ready, following renovation work. I was impressed with what had been fixed and replaced since the surge and it felt terrific to be back in residence. What a joy it was to hear the sound of returning Sandwich terns over the Point.

However, beneath my sheer delight to be back on the Point, there was a slight feeling of frustration. With the whirlwind of activity going on at Morston and on the Freshes over the past few weeks, I felt like the Point had almost been overlooked. I had ended up doing a lot of preparation in my spare time. It took me a few days to unbox everything, set up the Lifeboat House and finish tidying up around the building.

But my spirits were lifted on Monday, 7 April, when the seasonal assistant contracts started. A herald moth was spotted, heralding the start of our season together. We finished putting up the breeding bird fencing and triumphantly laid the last section of the boardwalk.

Our final post-surge tidy-up task was to retrieve a shed from Yankee Ridge. It had originally been situated beside Pope's Hut and had been washed away by the surge. I spotted it on Yankee Ridge a few days later, but it was low down on the job list. A regular guest in Pope's Hut was Simon Garnier, former National Trust regional director. He was pleased to see the shed back in its correct location. Some years before, Simon's daughter, Mollie, had collected all the shoes she found washed up on the beach over the course of a summer, arranging them into a pile in the dunes. The shoe pile survived the surge, continuing to surprise, amuse and sometimes confuse those who came across them. It has since been removed but was the Point's secret art installation for over a decade.

April went well, with the breeding season starting off like any other year. There were concerns, however, about whether the reduced veg- etative cover on the shingle ridge would deter little terns from nesting.

We were worried that changes in beach profile towards the tip might also have a negative impact on them. Fortunately, sea sandwort recolonised the shingle at a surprising rate.

Sandwich terns settled on Far Point in good numbers, increasing throughout the month, which brought us a great sense of relief. The many impacts of the tidal surge had meant that fox control had somehow fallen down the list of priorities. A trail camera near Beach Way picked up a fox several times in March, usually during the early hours of the morning. Fortunately, Barrie had some fox control success on Blakeney Freshes, and this seemed to coincide with the apparent disappearance of the Point fox, leading us to believe it had been crossing over from the Freshes but was now no longer a problem.

I was still quite new to the job and still learning about the shear amount of work that had been put into predator control during recent years. As a property collectively, I think there was a feeling that we were on top of the situation, or perhaps just too focused on the many other things that needed doing as a consequence of the tidal surge. This blissful ignorance was to be abruptly interrupted at the start of May.

Black-headed gulls were on eggs and Sandwich terns had started laying. It had been almost four weeks since any fox signs had dried up – although we hadn't been searching every corner of the Point. On the morning of Saturday, 3 May, my heart sank when we discovered forty-one dead black-headed gulls, all having been killed by a fox. Our lives changed in that moment. The rest of the season was now going to be an ongoing battle that we faced on a back foot.

Nightly cover was implemented immediately. Our responsibility to protect the ternery meant no night could afford to go unwatched. Barrie's focus was moved from the Freshes to the Point. Our helpful volunteer marksmen were also approached, and a rota was put together. I tried to work it so that our shooters arrived and left by boat at high tide or by quad and trailer at low tide.

We were quite creative in attempting various ways of deterring foxes from the colony. But no bait could be greater than a noisy, smelly tern colony at the peak of the breeding season. We made a scarecrow with loose clothing that flapped in the wind. We played a radio loudly on the edge of the colony. We put motion-sensing cat scarers out. We researched scents to detract foxes. The problem is, once a fox latches on to the colony, it can lose its natural wariness of unfamiliar objects.

So, on nights when shooters were unavailable, rangers Sarah, Paul and I took it in turns to patrol the edge of the colony between dusk and dawn, just like Joe and his team had done before us in the 1990s. We had a small, camouflaged tent in view of the colony. It was fascinating to be inside it and witness the colony gradually quieten down for the night. As the hours ticked by, you grew accustomed to the soundscape.

One night, I must have half nodded off, because I was jarred by a sudden increase in sound coming from the terns and gulls. The birds were up and in a state of panic, which instantly spread to me. I just knew that a fox was there. Looking through handheld night-vision equipment borrowed from Orford Ness, I scanned the mass of Suaeda bushes but could not see the fox. After a minute or so, it emerged from out of the colony, a tern in its mouth.

Fox predating common tern eggs, June 2014. (UCL)

In that moment, although I knew the fox was only behaving naturally, I felt a strong feeling of anger at the situation. This was the enemy. This was what was terrorising the ternery. This was what was causing my sleepless nights, my worry and the dreadful feeling that the Point's precious terns were not safe. There it was, right before me, that b*****d fox. I let out a loud, primal shout, which came from deep within, vocalising my distress and frustration. The fox froze for a split second and then ran away from the colony. It had now gone for the night, but my presence had not deterred it from entering the colony. It would be back again the following night.

A UCL student group were in residence at the time and the accompanying staff set up a series of trail cameras around the colony, under my direction and supervision. Images from the same night I saw the fox revealed it at a number of locations immediately prior to the time I had seen it emerge. It became clear that the fox had arrived at the very tip of Far Point, sneaking up on the colony from behind and evidently giving me a wide berth. It was captured eating a common tern egg before walking through the main Sandwich tern colony.

'You really need to get rid of that fox,' lecturer Ben Collen agreed, as he shared what the cameras had captured. Various images revealed the same individual fox, which could be identified by its unusually shaped tail.

Somehow, we got through the 2014 season. The only time I left Norfolk that whole summer was to attend my paternal grandmother's funeral. There were certainly moments when I found myself quite literally pulling my hair out. About three-quarters of the Norfolk Sandwich tern population were nesting at Blakeney that year, with the other quarter on Scolt Head Island. Fortunately, Scolt experienced higher productivity.

The Point population managed to fledge just over 500 young, which can only be described as poor. However, it was not a complete failure and we considered every fledged bird a success; a small reward for what we went through.

Even after the terns had fledged, there was still fox activity on the Point. We had to seriously up our game over the winter and I was embarking on a very big learning curve.

As summer became autumn, there was a wedding to celebrate. In the middle of the difficulties and struggles of the season, seasonal assistants Sarah and Paul had fallen in love and enjoyed a Blakeney Point romance. With all that was going on, I hadn't really clocked the signs. In the second half of June, I had spent a couple of nights away from the Point, during which Paul had told Sarah how he felt, thanks to Dutch courage supplied by visiting hut owners Brent and Brigid.

I was food shopping in Holt only a few weeks later when I received a call asking me to bring a bottle of champagne out to the Point to celebrate their engagement. This may have been the first wedding proposal to occur inside the Lifeboat House itself.

I had already witnessed one on the beach, the year before. Doing some visitor engagement on the beach, I had approached a couple of walkers and offered them a look at the seals through my telescope. They weren't really interested in my telescope but asked me to take a photograph of them to preserve the memory. The gentleman had literally just popped the question to his girlfriend, who had said yes. I thought to myself, they would have had an incredibly long and awkward walk back to Cley if she had said no.

Our assistant rangers' love story was welcome good news to counter what was otherwise a rather grim time. Sarah and Paul, both in their mid-thirties, had first met on the Point in April, fallen in love by June, become engaged in August and were married in September.

September also saw me head to West Sussex for a firearms awareness course near Billingshurst. This was the start of a few months of both formal and informal training, which I underwent with the long-term aim of becoming the first competent marksman to live on the Point since 2006. It is a vast understatement to say that logistics of Blakeney Point fox control are simpler if the responsible person lives in the Lifeboat House.

My training involved target practice in an old, private quarry, a few miles inland. I also went shooting with Ed from Blickling and Norfolk's wildlife crime officer, Jason, who signed me off as competent. This enabled me to obtain a firearms licence from the Norfolk Constabulary, following a visit from the firearms officer.

I have never actually shot a fox. Some people are natural marksmen, usually because shooting is part of their upbringing. I am not one of those naturals, never having handled a rifle before I came to Blakeney, but I was prepared to do whatever it took to safeguard the reserve I cared about so much.

As luck would have it, gamekeeper Barrie was keen to take on the role of Blakeney Point fox control with me assisting and supporting. Barrie had decades of experience under his belt, which made him ideal. Over the coming winters, he and I spent countless hours on Blakeney Point in the dark and the cold. He was great company and had lots of entertaining stories to share, having loaded for royalty and celebrities. Barrie also socialised with Joe Reed regularly, so was able to pick his brains and benefit from his experience – and nobody had more relevant experience than Joe.

At the Blakeney Twelve Christmas event in the village hall, I chatted to Joe at the bar. He told me that lots of patience was required, but if I put the time in, then eventually I would get there. I felt encouraged and motivated by our conversation and proceeded to follow his advice. Joe's old baiting spots were resurrected, located in wide open areas with good visibility and clear sight.

After a day's work on the reserve, I would pop home, wolf down a quick and easy meal – usually pasta and pesto – then layer up with thermals, a thick jumper, hat, scarf, gloves, windproof overtrousers and a coat or two before dashing back to the barn to meet Barrie, load the Land Rover and drive carefully and inconspicuously up the Point.

There were varying opinions as to the most effective modus operandi. Some thought searching and lamping gave a greater chance of finding your fox, which works well on farmland after harvest. Joe and Barrie's experience in tougher terrain was to choose a good spot and wait.

Oh, the waiting and searching we did, scanning with our night-vision equipment. Barrie used the rifle sight, and I used a hand-held spotting scope, on loan from Joe. With the older equipment, you would look for eyes shining back at you. Mostly, we picked up the eyes of hares and sometimes even muntjacs. We also borrowed a thermal-imaging device, later purchasing one. Body heat showed up, and the shape and size revealed the species. It was fascinating to survey mammals at night.

Over a period of four years, I saw every hour of the night: through dawn patrols in summer and night work in winter. I never resented having to spend so much time waiting in the dark; that was an important part of my job. Every hour made you feel stronger, but time almost always seemed to pass very slowly.

One night, Barrie said he could feel the Land Rover shaking. I had forgotten my overtrousers and was shivering. Another night, as the temperature dropped below freezing, the grass began to sparkle as frost formed.

If conditions were right, we would go up the Point several nights in a week. When the moon was too bright, we would be too visible, although camouflage netting could be used to stop the windscreen reflecting the moonlight. If it was too windy, this could influence the shot trajectory, which was a risk we simply couldn't take because fox welfare was absolutely essential. The trigger could only be pulled with complete confidence that a lethal shot could be delivered. We had to take a hiatus between mid-November and the beginning of January due to the grey seal rookery taking over the Point.

January became February and February became March. I kept hearing Joe's words: 'Put the time in' … 'It won't be easy' … 'You'll get there in the end'. But I began to lose faith.

So, we changed our approach slightly, heading out later in the night and staying well beyond midnight. If there had been lots of activity on the Freshes, we would locate ourselves on Friary Hills where I would know when another hour had passed by the church bells.

As well as the desire to achieve our goal, I was kept going by the thought of what I would eat and drink when we finished for the night. Usually, a whisky mac and some crisps. In fact, I piled on the pounds over the winter because of my midnight snacking and frequent trips to the nearby Wiveton Bell when not on the Point. Suddenly, I gained a good 2 stone without really realising. I am pleased to say that I did manage to lose the 'winter insulation' in time for my wedding, a couple of years later, and I have not weighed over 9 stone since.

Finally, just after midnight, one night in late March, Barrie did himself proud. The feeling of euphoria and relief eclipsed the sight of a helpless carcass. The fox would not have known what had hit it. The terns faced a fox-free season. The phrase 'fox-free' was floated around in various meetings with other nature reserves, but I came to detest the phrase, realising it was a myth. This was a never-ending job. Every autumn, foxes would return to the Point. It became expected, part of the pattern of the year. We soldiered on.

I was pleased when Barrie agreed to start using the lookout tower on the top of the Lifeboat House. This was a great vantage point and made us more inconspicuous as well as being slightly warmer than the open back of the Land Rover.

It was well into March again the following year when our winter efforts finally paid off. I had spotted our target on the far end of the landing ridge. It took almost an hour for it to emerge fully from the Suaeda. This was certainly an exercise in patience and holding your nerve. Fortunately, Barrie was a master at this.

I enjoyed listening to his stories. There was the one about how he found a long-eared owl nesting in an old pigeon's nest at Stiffkey, when he worked for Lord Buxton. There was also the one about the time Billy Bishop was asked to look after the Prince of Wales on a shoot and had greeted him as 'Charlie Boy'. Another great story told of how Joe Reed had once declined a dinner invitation because he had a fox to catch on the Point. That night he got lucky and was able to join the dinner party in time for dessert. We were never *that* lucky.

But I was lucky to have the assistance and expertise of Barrie, the support of my colleagues and also the support of the local community. To many born-and-bred Blakeney, Cley and Morston residents, the poor breeding success of the terns was considered the trust's fault for not protecting them well enough. I never took this criticism personally,

I actually appreciated it because it provided even greater motivation to protect the terns as well as possible.

I understand that, to some people, the active control of foxes does not sit comfortably. I myself take no pleasure at all in fox control. They are a British wild animal and I adore all wild creatures. But humane fox control is an important part of conservation. It should absolutely *never* be confused with fox hunting – using dogs to hunt wild mammals has been illegal since 2004. This so-called sport causes animals a huge deal of stress before often slow and painful deaths.

Fox control for nature conservation does not cause them any unnecessary pain or suffering. Animal welfare is at the heart of conservation, with more and more humane ways of predator control developing as our knowledge and technology improves.

One of our staff members at Morston Information Centre wanted to translocate the foxes instead of shooting them. This would be ideal, if it was only realistically achievable. To humanely catch foxes on the Point would be a mammoth challenge. These are a world away from bold-as-brass urban foxes, and are as wily as they come.

Unlike the black cat that turned up on the end of the Point one October. To catch the cat, we did indeed use a live trap, baited with some cat food. Graham took pride in setting the trap, which had successfully caught the moggy by the following morning. It was taken to a veterinary practice in Holt and was found to live in Baconsthorpe, 10 miles from Far Point. The poor pet was clearly a lost, hungry stranger on the Point ... unlike a wild fox in its natural surroundings.

Another idea is to let natural resilience prevail. In some places, nature can still find a balance and the genes of the best-suited individuals get passed on. This was one of the reasons why we never took moving little tern eggs any further, because of long-term fears that it would reduce natural resilience.

The problem was, if we took a completely non-interventionist approach on a seabird colony such as Blakeney Point, there was a high chance we could end up losing our tern colony for good. Was that a risk we really wanted to take?

Our 'Year of the fox' had not been good for public relations; not just with the passionate locals, but in the wider world of conservation. We had a duty of care. While the nature of dense seabird colonies does pose some benefits against predators – safety in numbers – dense ground-nesting makes them vulnerable to mammalian predators. Unlike remote islands, the Point is too close to the mainland to be safe from mammalian predation.

With regard to foxes specifically, evidence came to light a few years later that showed how, once again, humans are to blame. I had not really considered just how much of an impact releasing pheasants into the countryside has on our native wildlife. There is no regulation of the numbers that are released, and therefore no limit. Research has proved that the increasing numbers of pheasants released since the 1980s have had a huge impact on our countryside. Of course, how can millions of introduced birds possibly *not* have any impact on the countryside?

Pheasant rearing has led to an increase in foxes and corvids. Other European countries with significantly less gamebird shooting have a much lower density of foxes and crows than Britain. While foxes are controlled as part of pheasant management, the sheer volume of pheasants in the countryside has led to an increase in fox numbers. These foxes do not just feed on pheasants, of course, they also predate a variety of ground-nesting birds too.

Just as taking away a top predator impacts on a whole food web in an ecosystem, so does increasing the population of a prey species, such as pheasants. A study showed that more than five times the number of pheasants were killed on roads in the 2010s than in the 1960s, which is indicative of the increase in pheasants in the countryside. Indeed, pheasants have found their way on to many nature reserves, where naturalised breeding populations have developed.

While the British population of foxes – estimated to be around 400,000 – could be solely supported by pheasants, the pattern of pheasant rearing and shooting affects their availability to foxes throughout the year. During the shooting season, predators may be elevated due to abundant prey over winter. But the end of the shooting season coincides with the nesting season for most wild bird species. This means that the over-abundant predators may have detrimental effects on nesting birds.

But introducing pheasants into the countryside each year is just one of a whole range of impacts we have on nature, with far greater ones being the development of built areas, the destruction of wild areas and the generation of pollution.

Conservation can be described as our efforts to mitigate for what we have effectively messed up. The importance of this mitigation is being realised and appreciated more and more, just as the impacts of our actions are having greater consequences on the environment and therefore on ourselves. Huge-scale loss of rainforest, woodland, mangrove and other habitats globally pushes wildlife into smaller and smaller areas, forcing species unnaturally closer together. We are, of course, to blame for this habitat destruction, as well as keeping various wild animals in cages in closer proximity to each other than would occur naturally. With the wild animal trade bringing people and livestock into closer contact with wildlife, the transfer of diseases between species and on to humans becomes inevitable.

Although the 2020 pandemic brought death, debt and devastation to the human race, the coincidental decrease in pollution, through lower vehicular emissions, had an undeniably positive impact on the natural environment. A lengthy period of restricted movement gave many people an increased appreciation of their local wildlife. Indeed, the benefits that nature can have on our mental health have become increasingly appreciated in recent times. But, for wildlife, their daily struggle is not about well-being, but survival.

6

Year of the Rat

WHEN I FIRST VOLUNTEERED at Blakeney, I would go along on winter trips up the Point to help look for rat prints, find their holes and put out poison boxes in appropriate locations near any activity. Throughout the 1980s and '90s, poison had been put out around the Point's buildings, an obvious place for them to head in winter. From 2000, rats began overwintering on the ridges, requiring more work and vigilance to control. This was possibly due to a combination of milder winters and the ridges having grown big enough to withstand tidal inundation throughout the year. By the time I had become a permanent member of staff, the grey seal rookery had grown considerably, which meant that looking for rat signs just wasn't possible on a large part of the Point during November and December. The increased number of pup carcasses were a valuable source of winter food for rats as well as gulls. I even saw a sanderling apparently feeding on seal afterbirth, or at least amongst it.

Just as trail cameras had captured foxes raiding tern nests the previous year, we were now capturing rats raiding oystercatcher nests on the landing ridge. At the start of that season, just like the previous few, we naively hoped that absence of evidence was evidence of absence. But we now had evidence of rats doing the very thing we dreaded.

An early *British Birds* paper tells how, in 1898, the terns 'were so molested by rooks and rats' that it caused them to leave the Point and instead nest at Stiffkey. A few years later, the very first Blakeney Point management committee report states how Bob Pinchen had 'done good work in keeping down the rats and other vermin, which used to destroy a great number of eggs and young birds'. Rat control has been a key part of protecting the Point from the very beginning.

Rats are adaptable animals and are present on all of the planet's continents except Antarctica. They have a wide diet, scavenging on a whole range of foods, many of them associated with humans. They are also prolific breeders, with a gestation period of less than four weeks, and are able to reproduce from the age of just 3 months.

Although the Point's geography gives it some island-like qualities, it is not isolated. Rats can easily make it across the harbour to recolonise, enticed by the strong scent of a dense Sandwich tern colony or grey seal rookery. With hundreds of pups now being born each winter, it was becoming clear that we could no longer rely on our previous spot treatment of rats.

Trouble manifested itself in late April 2016. By the 23rd, black-headed gulls had just started nesting on Far Point, providing their usual buffer on the eastern edge of the Sandwich tern colony. The following day,

Rat predating an oystercatcher egg, June 2016. (UCL)

I discovered a rat hole and cache on the edge of the colony. Having recently completed a training course on the control of pests with aluminium phosphate, I was licensed to poison these unwelcome rats.

Historically, along with the use of rat poison, this was the adopted method of rat control on the Point. It involves humanely poisoning rats with gas while they are in their burrows, a swift and effective method, providing the rats are, of course, in their burrows at the time. All other exit holes must be sealed off before the phostoxin tablets are applied. They are dropped into the burrow, using an applicator. When the tablets react with moisture, they release their toxic gas. Phostoxin is very poisonous to humans, too, and can result in death, so safety is vital. It must obviously not be used in wet weather and wind direction should also be taken into consideration. The treated area must then be left for a day before it is safe to return.

Fortunately, a day later, there were no further signs of rat activity in the gull colony. We couldn't afford to be entering the colony too often because of the risk of too much disturbance resulting in colony abandonment. However, rat presence posed an even greater risk of abandonment.

The colony was eerily quiet on the last day of April, as noted in my private diary:

> On arrival at the colony, it was immediately clear that all of the black-headed gulls had gone. A real shock and worry. Without the black-headed gulls, there is a strong chance the Sandwich terns will not nest, which would be a disaster after two consecutive very poor breeding seasons. A search next morning revealed rat activity. What a b*gger that we'd somehow missed one. Or maybe they had spread from the end of Near Point? It's frustrating, nay, infuriating, to realise that my most important job of all, protecting the terns, may be failing.

More poisoning followed, but we were fighting a losing battle by this stage. Time was not on our side. The disappearance of black-headed gulls from Far Point hadn't gone unnoticed, and word had spread in the community.

But the gulls hadn't completely disappeared. Small numbers were slowly returning, with twenty nests counted on 11 May. Alas, four days later, there was:

> ... a depressing return of the rats: I thought we were on top of them, but more have moved in. Surely the black-headed gulls won't establish themselves a third time? I think, as I suspected, we can write off all hope of Sandwich terns breeding this year.

Indeed, the black-headed gulls dispersed, some heading over to Blakeney Freshes to re-nest, some going to Arnold's Marsh at Cley and fifty-five nesting on the shingle ridge east of the Watch House. Thankfully, the gulls nesting near the Watch House did not make bad neighbours to the little terns. However, a kestrel family on the nearby mainland did take a considerable toll on them.

True to my suspicions, without a black-headed gull buffer, the Sandwich terns did not settle in their usual location on Far Point. This brought me down considerably. I remember an evening sat on a sand dune feeling particularly glum. However, it was some consolation to hear that Scolt Head Island were, like last year, having a much better year than us. I kept in touch with warden Neil; we would speak on the phone, sharing any notable Sandwich tern news to help give each other a coastwide picture of the breeding population. Thanks to Scolt Head, that year, the Norfolk coast Sandwich tern population, as a whole, actually had its highest breeding productivity in a decade.

Things even picked up a bit on Far Point later on in the season. Since the tidal surge, the very end of the Point had become larger, with shingle building up on the western side of the tip. By the end of May, black-headed gulls had begun nesting on the far end of the Point with a colony of around 600 pairs forming.

On 6 June, Sandwich terns began settling too. These late arrivals were terns from not just Scolt Head but the other side of the North Sea on the coast of mainland Europe: birds whose first attempt at breeding had failed and so they had come to a different colony to try their luck, much like the first arrivals at Blakeney that had gone on to Scolt.

During 'Year of the Rat', our late arrivals were a sweet icing on top of the otherwise hard-to-swallow cake that was the 2016 season.

There was no guarantee that these late nesters would manage to fledge any young, being possibly too small a population to withstand gull predation. However, adults were seen flying in with small fish from mid-July.

On the third day of August, I took volunteer photographer, Ian, out in the boat to photograph Far Point. It was a gorgeous morning, there were common seals hauled out beside a group of around 200 juvenile Sandwich terns. In the end, we had actually fledged more Sandwich terns than the previous year. This realisation cheered me up on my birthday. Having followed the progress of our Far Point terns throughout July, we were confident that these flying juveniles were birds hatched on the Point rather than birds hatched on Scolt Head, especially as they were only just learning to fly.

Of course, a mere 200 fledged Sandwich terns was clearly not the product of a good season. We knew we seriously had to up our game to prevent rats from continuing to wreak havoc in future years. Richard Porter suggested that we should get in touch with a contact of his, Tony Martin, who had rolled out a successful rat eradication programme on South Georgia. He was clearly the man we needed to be speaking to and was based not too far away in the Cambridgeshire Fens. We were elated when he agreed to visit the Point and offer his advice.

Tony proposed a systematic network of permanent baiting stations. With regular checks to replenish bait, any rat arriving on the Point would encounter bait and hopefully be poisoned before being able to cause any problems. This would achieve such a low number of rats that any damage they could cause would be negligible.

It would take a bit of work to implement Tony's proposals, but, once up and running, we would have an easy to manage, effective solution. After passing an online rodenticide course, I was able to purchase bromadiolone poison, which we stored in our secure chemical safe. A proactive media statement was then prepared and signed off. That autumn, a delivery of 280 bait boxes was made to the barn.

I made a 50m^2 grid map of the Point to plot locations for bait boxes. This way, as Tony suggested, rats above the high-water mark on the headland would never be more than 25m from a bait box. This meant putting thirty-five boxes along Yankee Ridge, for example.

I also devised a coding system for our records. So, the Yankee Ridge boxes were labelled Y1 to Y35. An 'L' prefix was used for the landing ridge, 'N' for Near Point, 'F' for Far Point, 'D' for the main dunes, 'H' for the Hood and so on. A custom-designed warning label was also stuck on the top of each box instructing people not to touch. We then left the boxes outside so that the weather and elements could take away the smell of new plastic and ink.

Things had come a long way since the Ted Eales days when gin traps were still legal. I had actually found a few of his old traps under the Lifeboat House and was amazed at how vicious they looked. Predator control methods and legislation have moved on considerably with developing technology, coinciding with an increased focus on reducing bi-catch.

When I first started out, Fenn traps were widely used in the British countryside to catch small mammalian predators. Now, traps are so sophisticated that the chances of catching the wrong species are confidently eliminated. We trialled self-resetting traps that send a text message when they are triggered, which seemed revolutionary at the time. We were sent some by someone who had read about our rat problems in the national press.

This was why a media statement was required before we could start our rat control programme. We called it a 'ground-nesting bird protection project'. With rats present across Blakeney Point, there is no avoiding the fact that death is inevitable: either a small number of invasive, non-native rats or an incredibly larger number of vulnerable, native birds of international importance. We were responsible for safeguarding the precious wildlife of the Point, therefore decided that the birds must be protected, which meant that the rats simply had to go.

With the bait stations in place, we began filling them with bromadiolone on Tuesday, 25 October. This was on the cusp of the grey seal pupping season. Our system had taken seals into account. There were two phases, the second being the rookery area, which would not have its bait stations installed until the last seals dispersed in the new year. Each October, these boxes would then be brought in to prevent them being damaged by seals.

The ranger team at this time consisted of myself, Graham and Mary. We were assisted by Barrie, his contract having been extended to help with the rat project. To begin with, we would check the boxes each week. This was actually a highlight of the week for all of us. We would pair off, Mary and I recording percentage uptake alongside Barrie and Graham respectively, helping us by replenishing the bait blocks as necessary. We established a routine and became rather efficient. Lunchtimes in the Lifeboat House were cheerily spent listening to Graham and Barrie's stories of days gone by.

Mary and I built up a set of data and produced a series of graphs showing how bait uptake accelerated at the start and then decreased as the bait did its work. As expected, there was a spike in uptake when we rolled out phase two in late January. While putting out the phase two bait stations, we spotted rat prints in the sand, undoubtedly lured to Far Point by the smell of the rookery, which had produced 2,400 pups that winter.

As the next spring approached and the baiting project did its job, we were confident rats would not be an issue. But we did have other things to worry about, namely whether the black-headed gulls would return to Far Point to nest after what had happened to them the previous spring. I was always keen to learn what we could from the past, spending many hours leafing through old wardens' reports reports as well as asking them for advice.

At the start of the century, decoys had been used to attract black-headed gulls onto Far Point after Near Point had been abandoned, and then become overgrown with dense Suaeda. Pigeon decoys had been painted to look like black-headed gulls. As luck would have it, we found some old pigeon decoys stashed away upstairs in the barn. So Mary and I merrily went about the task of transforming pigeons into gulls. We even made one into a Mediterranean gull. Most were painted during our spare time, knowing that attracting the black-headed gulls back could well be crucial for re-establishing the ternery and, therefore, of significant conservation importance.

7

Year of the Large Gulls

SCARCELY TWO WEEKS INTO January 2017, flood warnings were issued. While we discussed our course of action, snow fell outside the office window. It was Friday 13th, no less.

Darkness had fallen as I watched the tide come up at Blakeney Quay, uncomfortably reminiscent of December 2013. It came over the road, lapped at the wall of the ice cream shop and came very close to the top of the sea wall. Thankfully, it did not flood the Freshes:

Although Blakeney and Morston were pretty much fine, the Salthouse and Cley Marshes were flooded, with Beach Road about seven feet underwater. This meant that, to check Blakeney Point, Sabrina and I had to walk along the coast path from near Cley Windmill. The shingle ridge had altered with the impact of the weather. There had been erosion to the seaward-facing dunes. A mixture of shingle and sand had been washed into the low near Beach Way, much like in December 2013. The Old Lifeboat House had about two feet of water inside. Pope's Hut narrowly missed being flooded and a very small amount seeped into the corner of Clarke's Hut.

Two months later, we were graced with a visit from National Trust Director General Dame Helen Ghosh and the board of trustees. We took them on an evening seal ferry trip. On Morston Quay, she mentioned how the trust 'worked me hard', with reference to my many appearances in publications, on posters and in the media. My role that evening was to give a running commentary over the microphone.

I followed the very reasonable request not to use emotive terms – namely the word 'devastating' – to describe natural occurrences. The word 'devastating', however, did describe how it felt to see 500 large gulls roosting on Far Point. The ternery site was occupied by a mixture of herring and lesser black-backed gulls, with not a black-headed in sight. So, this was the be 'Year of the large gulls': infamous predators of tern eggs and chicks. We had our work cut out.

The best place to start was by chatting to other wardens around the British Isles who had been confronted with similar situations. During the previous month, we had hosted a two-day predator workshop at Brancaster, attended by reserve staff and ecologists from all partner organisations of the Little Tern Recovery Life Project. I had given a short presentation:

It was to an audience of experts. But, confident in my own specific knowledge and experience, I was able to come alive and deliver my talk with energy, enthusiasm, openness and honesty. The whole workshop was a good opportunity to share ideas and experience. I had some good conversations with some interesting people from across Britain. I believe there will be renewed confidence and focus on predator control, which is what we need.

Large gulls on tern colonies were covered at the workshop, with the RSPB's Coquet Island warden presenting his up-to-date experience. As with foxes and rats, the same challenges had been faced on the Point a couple of decades before. But times and laws had changed since then, with herring gulls now listed as a species of concern due to a national decline in coastal breeding. However, the national data, on which the herring gull protection was based, did not take into account the increase in urban-nesting birds. We heard stories of a large warehouse in Milton Keynes with a sizable herring gull breeding colony on its roof.

Just like foxes, and certainly rats, gulls are an adaptive species that have evolved to exploit urban environments and their numbers have been influenced by humans. Historically – although there is a lack of data – large gull numbers were probably inflated by the herring fishing industry, with birds following boats and benefiting from easy access to fish. The decline in the industry occurred when herring stocks were massively depleted by overfishing. Gulls adapted by moving inland and utilising open landfill sites as foraging grounds. We speculated that the recent closure of nearby Edgefield landfill site had prompted herring and lesser black-backed gulls to now exploit Blakeney Point.

On Coquet Island, up on the Northumberland coast, laser hazing had been trialled as a method of deterring large gulls. This was adapted from a method used at airports to prevent birds coming into contact with planes. Shooting a powerful laser beam towards a sitting gull prompts it to fly away. This was combined with another cunning technique, which involved playing recordings of herring gull alarm calls in the colony. They had rigged a system whereby they could ring a phone to set off the alarm call recording at any time.

Encouraged by the laser-hazing approach, we set about borrowing a laser from the RSPB, putting together a media statement and risk assessment – a powerful laser shone from Far Point could be a hazard to walkers on the coast path, therefore, direction of aim had to be controlled to prevent this.

As with rats, herring gulls were largely seen as a pest by the wider public. This was fuelled by their growing habit of stealing chips from alfresco diners in seaside towns. Our message was not that we don't want herring gulls to nest ... we just don't want them to nest on Blakeney Point. Our issue was not with them being a pest to humans, but rather to terns and waders.

By now, I was a representative on the Joint Nature Conservancy Council's seabird monitoring group. At their annual autumn meeting in Aberdeen it had been encouraging to learn that plans were being put together to survey gulls nesting in towns and cities. There was talk of photography from unmanned aerial vehicles, known more commonly as drones, 'but let's use their correct name,' insisted one of the senior participants.

In the meantime, at Blakeney, we applied to Natural England to have our herring gull licence amended. Previously, we had been permitted to take a maximum of ten nests per year, to deter them from breeding. It looked likely that there would be a lot more than ten nesting this year ... depending on how successful the laser would be.

The laser arrived with us in April, the same month that we said good-bye to Graham after more than two decades working on the reserve. His retirement party was held at the Blakeney Harbour Room, which was filled with numerous people from the community as well as reserve staff, past and present. Mary was now ex-Blakeney, having left a few weeks previously to take up an ecologist position.

Former Cley Marshes assistant warden Carl was recruited as assistant ranger. We got on really well as colleagues, just as I had done with the many other attendees at Graham's bash. I reflected how it was extremely unlikely that so many members of the community would ever turn out again for a member of reserve staff. Graham was so well thought of in the community, having grown up there and contributed so much to it. We no longer had any north Norfolk born-and-bred rangers employed at the property, which did make a difference to the community.

Seeing Graham leave felt like a big door closing. He had been a mentor, a bringer of good humour ... and some appalling jokes. I benefited greatly from his knowledge, experience and enthusiasm. He and Marilyn had become my good friends. Marilyn was to retire two years later.

Just a few minutes after Graham's leaving do had finished, I received a call from my agent, David – who had just taken me on – with an opportunity to appear on BBC primetime television alongside Chris Packham and Kate Humble. It was quite a day.

Back on the Point, herring and lesser black-backed gulls were now being lasered. An evening session worked a treat at clearing the colony. The laser worked best in low-light conditions. You could move the large gulls off nicely at dusk – but by the morning, they would be back.

Although the laser was effective at causing birds to take flight, it became apparent that it wasn't disturbing them enough to make them leave the Point completely. Efforts continued in the hope that persistent, repetitive lasering might eventually cause the gulls to vacate the area for good.

May Bank Holiday arrived and spirits were low. There was a complete absence of black-headed gulls and Sandwich terns on Far Point. Instead, there were herring and lesser black-backed gulls on eggs. Their tie to Far Point to breed was strong enough to overcome the inconvenience of being laser-hazed daily, which was an interesting learning point for us.

The large gull colony extended from the westernmost dune along the shingly tip of Far Point, clearly visible from the seal ferry trips. Over the years, photographs of herring gulls perched on 'No landing' signs had ceased to raise a smile. In fact, one year I rolled out a programme of sticking upturned bottles onto any possible predator perches near the tern colonies. The idea came from the RSPB Winterton little tern colony.

The highlight of the May Bank Holiday weekend on the Point for me that year was watching a cuckoo perched in the garden brambles, feeding on caterpillars. Meanwhile, the former Far Point ternery lay rat-free but sadly also tern-free, overlooked by nesting large gulls. The only black-headed gulls on Far Point were the plastic decoys that Mary and I had painted.

I suspected that the persistent large gull laser-hazing had indirectly also disturbed any prospecting black-headed gulls and Sandwich terns. Another possible factor was the change in topography of this part of the Point. Each winter, more and more of the ternery disappeared as shingle was pushed higher up the beach and stormy seas uprooted more and more of the Suaeda bushes that the black-headed gulls had previously nested on.

With large gulls on eggs, the next step of deterrence work commenced. We had been unable to keep them away, but we had a licence to prevent them from rearing any young. It wasn't game over yet. Just shy of fifty lesser black-backed pairs nested and well over 100 herring gulls. However, not a single chick fledged. That was thanks to an amendment to our licence from Natural England.

For a decade, our licence to prevent up to ten breeding herring gull pairs from rearing young had been sufficient as this exceeded the number nesting. Our argument that we needed to increase this quota – and include lesser black-backed gulls – was taken on board as it was for the necessary conservation of little and Sandwich terns.

For my first four seasons on the Point, the number of herring gull breeding pairs ranged between three and six. A single pair of lesser black-backed nested on the edge of the ternery each year but never seemed to rear any chicks – they could have been infertile. I continued Eddie's practice of removing the herring gull eggs from the nest as early as possible. He would smash them below the high water mark for the tide to wash them away, preventing the possibility of attracting predators.

It seemed a shame to waste eggs when they were perfectly edible. Herring gull eggs are larger and more conical than a chicken's. They are greenish blue with speckling. The yokes are a deep orange. The taste is very similar to a chicken's egg. We had them fried, scrambled and even in an omelette. Black-headed gull eggs were once a delicacy.

Graham Bean told me how he used to collect the first clutches of black-headed gull eggs from Morston Marsh and sell them to London restaurants. They were said to make excellent cakes. We didn't attempt any cakes with herring gull eggs. Most people thought we were strange enough for having them fried.

But, for us, this was part of our Tideline Challenge. One day, we found a large, raw German sausage in orange wrapping washed up on the tideline. It must have fallen off a boat. There was no 'best before' date visible, but the sea had kept it nicely chilled and it appeared to be relatively fresh. We cut a few slices off and fried them. Delicious. We even mentioned it on our blog, which my grandma found amusing.

In the first half of the twentieth century, a whole manner of things had washed up on the Point. Billy and Ted Eales had once found a load of oranges, which they consumed, so some of our traditions went way back ... just like a number of our conservation challenges.

Herring gulls had first bred on the Point in 1972 and lesser black-backed in 1978. Throughout the 1980s, more and more pairs began nesting. By the end of the decade, the damage they were doing to the terns had become increasingly apparent and so the birds were deterred from nesting. The 1998 warden's report records 150 pairs of herring gulls, stating, 'control methods used, but it is difficult'. The control methods referred to involved removing eggs and raking out nests to deter breeding. This was done under general licence.

Like with fox and rat control, a thorough decision-making process was gone through to assess the best management approach. And just like with foxes and rats, herring and lesser black-backed gulls were confidently identified as a very serious threat to the much more vulnerable, internationally important tern populations. Various committees were involved on a national level and government licensing tests were conducted, granting permission for large gull control in favour of the terns. This was a problem being faced across the British coastline. It was perhaps ironic, however, that great expense was gone to at Orford Ness in Suffolk to protect a large gull colony whilst the Blakeney team, 80 miles away, were working hard to detract them.

In 2000, a whopping 170 herring and 180 lesser black-backed pairs nested on the Point. Consequently, only 75 Sandwich terns had nested, fledging no young, and 115 little terns fledged just six. But 2001 saw a staggering 240 herring and 171 lesser black-backed pairs nesting. Again, every egg was removed.

Persistence paid off, as no gulls nested on Far Point the following year. That's not to say they had abandoned the Point altogether. Much to warden Dave's horror, during his first year in charge of the Point, dozens of large gulls began nesting in the dunes east of the boardwalk.

Due to some recruitment challenges that year, he was out there on his own for a few weeks. His solitary morning routine consisted of raking out every nest. This time, persistence really did pay off and the gulls finally seemed to get the message. In the following ten years, not a single black-backed nested and herring gulls also stopped nesting after a few years of just single numbers.

Facing a similar situation, we found ourselves treading similar ground, thanks to the Natural England's consent. With so many birds involved, we quickly found that removing eggs simply led to birds laying second and even third clutches. I tried replacing eggs with round stones, but it wasn't that easy to fool the gulls. So, we adopted the widely used egg-pricking approach. There does come a point where the incubating bird realises their egg is not going to hatch, but it buys significantly more time.

That year was a write-off for Sandwich terns, with just three late arrivals nesting on the tip and failing to fledge any young. This felt as sickening as the stench of pricked gull eggs festering. The trouble with pricking scores of eggs is that any leaked yoke starts to stink in the hot weather. Assistant rangers Luke and Ryan did a grand job in stomach-churning conditions. Working on Blakeney Point certainly isn't all roses and is not for the faint-hearted. But there is always room for improvement. The following year, eggs were oiled instead of pricked.

Oiling eggs is commonly used to prevent Canada goose eggs from hatching. The most notable major implementation of Canada goose egg oiling occurred in America in 2009, when an investigation into a plane crash determined it was caused by striking a Canada goose. Coating eggs in oil was found to be 95 per cent effective. Oil blocks the pores in the eggshell, thus asphyxiating the embryo inside, preventing the transfer of oxygen and carbon dioxide between the embryo inside the egg and the outside air. Some sites used paraffin, but cooking oil was used on the Point as a relatively inexpensive solution.

Only three lesser black-backed gulls nested the following year. Herring gull numbers were also reduced, although forty pairs continued to nest for the following three years. Sandwich terns made a comeback, first with 165 pairs, rising to 788 the following year, 2,425 the next and then 3,134 in 2021; exceeding 3,000 for the first time in eight years. Interestingly, they were now occupying a new colony site, which may well have been in response to habitat change. A healthy population of black-headed gulls had established themselves in this new location and the Sandwich terns followed.

This colony was located near the former little tern beach colony. The low-lying beach had become increasingly prone to tidal flooding. However, higher up the beach, embryo dunes had developed considerably, no doubt aided by a few seal pup carcasses helping sand to gather. Historically, the tern colony had moved progressively westwards as the

Point grew. Until 1918, the common terns nested in Great Sandy Low, moving to Near Point in 1919. At the beginning of the twenty-first century, they moved onto the westernmost dune on the present Far Point and crept onto the very tip. Now, they had moved a few hundred metres east, thanks to suitable, naturally formed habitat.

After a series of tough tern years for different reasons, I looked back at what other predators had caused problems historically, wondering whether maybe stoats or short-eared owls would be the next cause of grief after the large gulls. A stoat had been seen near the Watch House, so we kept a careful eye on the little terns nesting there.

In fact, there were lots of careful eyes on the little terns by now. Our volunteer team had continued to build, with many new recruits having heard about the role and wanting to get involved. Unfortunately, none of our many enthusiastic new volunteers were to see a flying little tern chick in 2018. A pair of kestrels nesting on the mainland had latched on to the colony, just as they had done in the 1990s.

For the kestrels, the little tern nestlings were an ideal food source that was available at just the right time. The adult kestrels could commute from their nest to the colony, their mere presence flushing the brooding little terns off their chicks. These unprotected, small and helpless chicks could then be plucked from the ground and carried back to the kestrel's young. It was an ideal-sized prey for them. Back and forth they went, until every chick had been taken.

At a time when the volunteers could have been watching tern chicks taking their first flights, they were instead confronted with an empty colony. Some had tried to scare off the kestrel, but this was pretty much impossible. Kestrel problems are common at numerous little tern colonies, so we were able to learn from other sites.

Diversionary feeding was a favoured technique in east Norfolk and Suffolk. Carl and I put up a feeding table on Blakeney Freshes. We knew the birds were flying over the Freshes on their way to the Point. Day-old chickens were put out for them, and we positioned a trail camera to capture any activity. Unfortunately, we didn't have any luck diverting the kestrels, probably because we had started too late in the season when they had already latched on to the ternery. The following year, diversionary feeding would start earlier.

Proactive wardening is the key, as Graham always said. Reactionary wardening means you are always on the back foot. By now, we were proactively controlling foxes, restricting dogs, engaging with visitors, baiting rats, lasering gulls, feeding kestrels, decoying little terns and putting out chick shelters.

Next came the global pandemic, which meant that human disturbance to ground-nesting birds was reduced dramatically for the first time since the Second World War.

Some of the little tern volunteers felt somewhat disheartened that, without any volunteer protection, little terns had their most productive season since the 1990s. However, with hardly any human visitors during the 2020 breeding season, their usually important work of preventing human disturbance wasn't needed or even legally permitted.

Of course, it wasn't solely the lack of visitors that had resulted in a good little tern season: an absence of predators was pretty key and a good food supply nearby was arguably crucial to their high productivity, with 154 pairs fledging 201 young. In years when food supply is good near the Point, a greater number of little terns will colonise.

Following the pandemic, the role of the little tern volunteers is as important as ever, due to more people visiting nature reserves for the first time – people who are unfamiliar with ground-nesting birds. Those volunteers who perhaps felt that they couldn't do much to help little terns are now in a position to really make a difference by educating a new audience of visitors and preventing them from accidentally disturbing terns and waders.

Talking to visitors on the ground has the potential to be extremely powerful. In just a few minutes, mindsets can be altered, and lives changed. Anyone who gives their time to help educate and raise awareness is arguably a conservation hero.

8

Blubber on
the Beach

DESPITE THE MANY CHALLENGES presented while trying to protect breeding birds, it was still my favourite part of the job. Few things could rival the joy of finding nests and the satisfaction of watching juveniles fledging. Although one thing came close: grey seal pupping.

The first live pup is invariably born in the last week of October, no later than 1 November. There would sometimes be outlying early births, presumably to first-time mothers. In my experience, these have always been found dead, with one usually found each October. The earliest I recorded was on the 10th.

During my first winter at Blakeney, when I was a volunteer, the 603 pups born seemed like such a big number. The following winter, numbers rose to 789, of which a memorable 747 were weaned. The year after that, 973 pups were born. With this trajectory and the state of Britain's seals in favourable condition, the anticipation of reaching 1,000 pups the next year was no surprise. Indeed, this is what had attracted *Winterwatch*, who were indeed able to film the thousandth pup of that season.

The growing rookery expanse was to be the subject of recurring news articles for years to follow. In addition to the numbers of pups being born and their cute appearance, the behaviour of the bull seals was another big attraction not just to film crews, but to radio, too.

In the aftermath of the tidal surge, it was decided we could still accommodate a prearranged visit from Trai Anfield to record an episode of BBC Radio Four's *Living World*. Trai, her sound recordist and I were able to tuck ourselves in the dunes and record the impressive sounds of bulls fighting. The cries of pups were also recorded, which sometimes sound strangely like human babies. But it was the fighting bulls that were considered prime animal drama.

The reason the bulls fight is entirely over females, their sole aim is to mate. The pupping season is a unique window in the grey seal calendar in which animals spend three to five weeks almost entirely out of the water. So, it makes sense that mating should take place at this time.

The cows come into season just days after pupping. Like zebra, for example, dominant males hold harems of multiple females, maximising the chances of passing on their genes. They do not, however, have any paternal instincts and no research has proven that they have any sense whether a pup is genetically theirs or not. Grey seal parenting is a very brief affair, with pups weaned after just three weeks. Pups weigh about 14kg when they are newborn and triple in size by the time they are weaned, feeding solely on their mother's extremely fat-rich milk.

Mothers can be very protective, snarling at and attacking other cows with their clawed front flippers if they come too close. They can also be quite hostile to other pups if they stray into the wrong territory. In contrast, occasionally a cow will allow another pup to suckle. This makes sense if they have lost their own pup. On more than one occasion, I have observed two pups suckling from the same cow together. It was tempting to speculate the possibility of twins.

Historic research shows that twins are extremely rare, but occasionally two foetuses have been present in females that were killed while pregnant. Grey seal pups are adapted to put on weight very quickly. Conversely, the cows progressively lose weight and appear quite gaunt after weaning their pup, in stark contrast to balloon-like pregnant cows who are about to pup. The chances of a cow being able to produce enough milk to successfully wean twins seems low.

In 2015, a cow was observed feeding two same-sized pups around the coast at Horsey. Far more accessible than the Blakeney Point rookery, with a car park just metres from the beach, Horsey attracts literally hundreds of times more visitors. Needless to say, the alleged twins received lots of attention. The abundance of visitor attention may well have led to the cow abandoning the pups after ten days, although the sheer drain of double feeding could also have been a factor, exhausting her milk supply in half the time.

I remember thinking it was unlikely that they were twins, because live twins had never been recorded before. However, their abandonment presented the opportunity to take DNA samples while they were being hand-reared at RSPCA East Winch. Hair and blood samples were taken and sent to Norway's Institute of Marine Research. Amazingly, this proved that they were indeed twins: the first proven occurrence of live grey seal twins in the wild.

This discovery caused quite a sensation and made Horsey even more well-known. Fortunately, the Friends of Horsey Seals were well established by this time with over 100 volunteer wardens helping to make sure the seals are not disturbed by the hordes of visitors.

Of course, occasional incidents are inevitable, but volunteer wardens are able to jump in and make sure that parents do not let their children throw stones at seals or try to put their child on a seal's back for a photograph. That sort of behaviour is truly shocking, not just the level of disrespect for a wild animal, but the sheer irresponsibility.

Seals are dangerous animals. In 2003, a marine biologist was tragically killed by a leopard seal in the Antarctic while snorkelling. I was once told a story about a very drunk solider in the Falklands who jumped on the back of an elephant seal. The seal literally tore his face off, resulting in his death, which was recorded as 'death in service', omitting the gory and somewhat embarrassing details.

At Blakeney, I managed a growing team of volunteers, many of whom helped protect little terns in summer and switched to seals in the winter. Fortunately, we never had any incidents of people attempting to put a child on a seal's back. Our mobile little tern hide doubled up as a seal hide in winter; not so much to see seals from, but as a landmark, housing for information boards and shelter from the elements.

The idea for a mobile hide came about after changing habitat and nesting habits rendered the tern hide on Near Point relatively useless and the sea hide almost fell into the sea. The nature of the Point means a hide's location may only be suitable for a limited number of years. So, a hide on wheels would be more cost-effective and could also be used to aid predator control. North Norfolk Engineering in Holt took on the task, making our idea into a reality.

Volunteers also had the Land Rover to shelter in. We didn't expect them to walk up and back, although Bill sometimes did.

The pleasure and privilege of minding this impressive rookery for a day meant that the rota always filled up quickly. Whereas doing the little tern volunteering rota involved trying to make sure every day was covered, the seal rota was more a case of sharing shifts out fairly between all of the volunteers.

On Christmas Day, the countryside staff take it in turns to be on call, which requires being within thirty minutes of Blakeney. When my year came, I intended to spend a solitary six hours on the Point, my family being an hour and three-quarters away in Lincolnshire. But friends in Brancaster Staithe very kindly insisted I spent Christmas with them.

The sight of a beach full of seals is such a spectacle. In my early days, we were able to take guided parties out to the gap to view the beach. However, as the dunes became engulfed by the rookery, it was clear that this was no longer sensible. We decided we would not make any exceptions in order to keep the message clear that access to the rookery is unsafe. A protective mother can be surprisingly speedy and the chances of being caught up in the middle of fighting bulls is too great a risk.

Some fights are borne out of bulls attempting to mate with cows that are not ready. This can lead to an almost comedic flipper-slap in the face or a more aggressive roar of disapproval, followed by a hasty retreat. It is during these heated retreats that I have seen pups get accidentally knocked by cows, sometimes even by their own mothers. Human disturbance can have the same impact, while many cows will rear up at you and hiss, some of the less-experienced mothers bolt instinctively towards the sea with fear.

Persistent bulls may chase an uninterested cow, in the hope she will submit. Research suggests that bulls are stimulated by the presence of oestrous cows in the rookery in general, rather than being attracted to a particular individual. Therefore, a strong sexual drive is needed for a bull to overcome the aggressive responses frequently displayed by cows.

An uninterested cow may well submit when a bull bites her neck and pins her down. Such fast, fierce and frantic sessions are balanced by mutually consenting copulation when both animals may be still for a moment while intertwined. On numerous occasions, I have noticed visitors taking sneaky photographs of a bull with his impressively sized genitalia on display!

A month into the breeding season, the drama reaches a climax. The birth rate peaks around the third week of November and drops considerably by the middle of December. This window is the optimum mating time and also the peak bull fighting time. Dominant or master bulls will establish territories early on, holding harems typically ranging from three to seven cows. Unlike land mammals that hold harems, such as wild equines, the bulls do not round up their cows. The cows do not tend to move too much, conserving their energy.

Master bulls must defend their territories from challenger bulls, which may be lurking on the periphery and will enter a master bull's territory when they spot an opportunity. Mostly, the master bull will assert his dominance and see off the intruder, but a secondary bull might just overthrow him. In the process, blood is frequently shed, with bulls biting each other's necks with their sharp teeth as well as scratching with the claws on their fore-flippers. This is the behaviour that Mike Dilger came specifically to film for the *One Show*.

Some secondary or bachelor bulls may carefully pick their moment to creep into a master bull's territory. While the master bull is engaged in copulation, or sleeping, the intruding bull can sometimes sneak in and successfully mate with a cow. This is a clever method of passing on his genes with minimal effort. Holding a harem presents a much higher chance of successful mating but requires much more energy and strength.

As the years went by and the rookery grew in size, extending eastwards towards the Hood, bachelor bulls could easily be spotted. Later in the season, they would gather on the beach at the eastern edge of the rookery, spending some of their time at sea. Young cows could also very occasionally be spotted. These younger seals tend to be very skittish and will usually bolt towards the sea as soon as they set eyes on a human in their vicinity.

To count the pups, we would walk through the dunes. Initially, this was done by two rangers. Walking side by side, one would count pups on the beach and the other would count pups in the dunes. As the rookery expanded, I divided the headland into eight different zones. Walking along the dune ridge presents sufficient views of the whole beach, but deviations into the dunes were required as more cows headed further into them to find a spot to pup. Volunteers Bill and Al became trusty seal count assistants and developed a keen eye over multiple seasons.

Being amongst the seals is a fascinating experience, making eye contact with them and seeing how they react. To us, walking through, it was the cows that posed the greatest threat, displaying the motherly instinct to defend their pups. Many would rear up, hiss and even charge towards us. For this reason, we adopted an approach of continuous movement, trying not to loiter in one spot and carefully picking the best routes through. The latter became increasingly challenging, especially at some of the pinch points where animals were densely gathered, such as the shingly low between Far Point and Middle Point.

Bulls do not generally show the same aggression towards humans as the cows. They tend to ignore us or nervously shuffle away, intimidated by our height. The exception, however, is if two – or more – bulls are engaged in a fight. In the heat of the moment, they simply may not register a person in their path. This was one of the many reasons we had to prevent access into the rookery.

As with all breeding wildlife, human disturbance presents a very real threat. Protective seal mothers, with their sharp teeth and surprising speed on land, present a danger to people and dogs alike. In a fight situation, my money would be on a seal faring better than a dog.

When I first experienced the Point's pups, eight years after the rookery had established itself, a fence had been erected at the gap, deterring walkers from the westernmost half a mile of beach and dunes. At that time, this was the extent of the rookery. Four years on, when I became Point ranger, the rookery had spread significantly further east and also south into the dunes and some of the lows.

I recall, during my first winter, encountering some walkers heading along the beach towards the rookery. They were very much of the attitude that they had walked along the beach every winter for years, so why should they stop now? Well, a few years ago, walking along the beach at this time of year was no concern at all. But the beach was fast becoming a completely different place in the winter.

Grey seal rookery east of the gap, November 2017. (Ajay Tegala)

Seals experiencing such success is so exciting to witness. As a conservationist, seeing wild species recovering and thriving is what we strive for.

The foundations of this wildlife success hark back to the legal protection of seals in 1914. In fact, the grey seal was the first mammal to be protected by modern legislation, with the introduction of a forty-six-day closed season. This was extended to four months in 1932.

There was a time when payment could be earned per nose of seal killed to protect fishing stocks. Presenting a seal's nose proved it had been killed and was rewarded financially. They were – and often still are – seen as the enemy of fishermen. However, modern research has proved that they forage over wide distances. Tagging studies on the Norfolk coast revealed that common seals were foraging around the bases of the Sheringham Shoal wind turbines. These rock piles had become fish spawning reefs because the area could no longer be trawled. A number of the seal ferrymen are former fishermen, who now earn a much more prosperous and reliable living through seal tourism.

At the beginning of the twentieth century, the Farne Islands' grey seal population consisted of around 100 adults. Six decades later, this had risen to around 3,500 adult and sub-adult individuals. Located just over 150 miles up the coast, as the seal swims, this was Blakeney's nearest grey seal colony until the early 1970s when a rookery began to establish at Donna Nook in Lincolnshire, about five times closer than the Farnes.

The first grey seals started to spend time at Blakeney in 1985, with the arrival of five bulls. Three years later, the first grey seal pups were born on the Point. But it would be over a decade before a rookery established. When it did, it became clear how well suited the Point's topography is for breeding seals. The beach is easy to haul out on and the dunes provide shelter. Contrast this to the rocky shores and cliff edges of the Farne Islands or Pembrokeshire and it is no surprise that pup mortality is much lower in Norfolk: generally, less than 6 per cent.

Being top of the food chain, with humans no longer a threat, grey seal numbers have been increasing since the Conservation of Seals Act 1970.

Explaining this on the ITV *Anglia News*, I said that seals 'are very happy here'. This seemed like a natural comment at the time, but I was later teased by a friend who asked how a seal can be happy. Of course, I had slipped into anthropomorphism, bestowing human emotions on wild animals; something I have since tried to avoid.

Protection from disturbance is a contributing factor to the success of the Blakeney rookery. As with the terns, habitat and food availability also play a crucial role. There is no guarantee the habitat would be in such good condition had it not become a legally protected site. Although seeing a beach crammed full of hundreds of seals looks like an unstoppable feat of nature, the beach has to be available for them in the first place. This highlights how species conservation goes hand in hand with habitat conservation. A species cannot be conserved effectively without a suitable habitat.

Our role as site protectors had quickly progressed to seal protectors. Winter tourism was on the up in north Norfolk. Gone were the days of Blakeney being a winter ghost town. Festive coastal breaks were now popular and the hugely successful Thursford Christmas Spectacular was bringing more visitors to north Norfolk in November and December. Seal pups were an added attraction to tourists from near and far.

The buzz of anticipation when putting up breeding bird cordons is matched when putting up seal cordons, using the very same metal pins and baler twine, if it's not too tangled. You soon learn to take as much care as possible winding in baler twine to avoid lots of time lost untangling it.

It made sense to maintain the main access route between the Long Hills and Lifeboat House. So, I devised a line of fencing that ran from the north-eastern corner of the dunes, along the southern edge of Great Sandy Low to the boardwalk. At the end of the boardwalk, Carl and I erected a chestnut paling fence to create a viewing area for visitors, inspired by Donna Nook. Experience had shown that a string fence won't deter a photographer wanting to get closer, nor will it stop a seal:

they can all too easily bend a metal fence post by simply rolling over it.

Similar to fencing for little terns, best-guesswork was used when putting fences up prior to breeding, knowing that the colony could easily expand beyond the fenceline. The fact a fence was required, to keep breeding animals safe and wandering visitors at a safe distance, indicated that a ranger presence was also needed.

Despite it being a long walk on shingle and often with strong, biting winds, an increasing number of people were making the slog along the spit to see the spectacle of the seals. On a dry, bright weekend with a midday low tide, over 100 visitors might walk up between ten in the morning and three in the afternoon, especially between Boxing Day and New Year's Day.

Hut owners Andrew and Kay would often head out to their hut for a New Year's Day pheasant soup lunch on the Point and would invite me along. I was usually on duty on New Year's Day, with a pup count making an excellent start to a new year.

By the latter half of December, into January, just the newborn – and freshly dead – pups are counted and added to the previous total. This is because there comes a time when the earliest-born pups head out to sea. They do not do this the day their mother stops feeding them, though. Weaned pups will spend several days in the dunes, living off their fat reserves, before hunger drives them to forage at sea.

Late December can be the most entertaining time to be counting pups because there are so many weaned ones lazing about in the dunes. These round, 'fat weaners' lie about snoozing and even snoring. I have walked quietly past many without being noticed. Sometimes they will sense you, awaken and instinctively snarl, showing their teeth.

When it comes to ageing pups, there are various signs to look for. Pups that have literally just been born will still be wet and often a bit bloody. On several occasions, visitors have been concerned about bleeding pups, which were, in fact, healthy newborns. Pups have a distinct yellowish appearance for the first three days, during which the pink umbilical cord tends to be present, turning dark and shrivelled by about day four. For the next two to three weeks, they become progressively rounder and eventually shed their white fur, revealing a beautiful, mottled coat beneath. They typically start moulting around their eyes first, which can sometimes look a bit comical.

As early as 2009, I remember spotting a moulted pup with jet-black fur. This was my first sighting of a melanistic pup. As the population grew, so did the occurrence of melanistic pups, with approximately one in 400 pups displaying melanism: the increased development of the dark-coloured pigment melanin. Every black pup we encountered was successfully weaned. Very occasionally, we also spotted the odd melanistic adult on the Point.

It is generally believed that about 50 per cent of weaned grey seal pups survive their first year at sea. The seals that do survive their first year are usually long lived. Bulls reach sexual maturity at 6 years and cows at between 3 and 5.

A cow may be sexually mature for up to three decades, pupping nine years in ten. Studies on the Isle of May found that mortality of first-year males was slightly higher than females.

When it is being born, a pup's genitalia may be swollen, but sexing a young pup is incredibly difficult. By the time they are weaned, sometimes the more elongated noses of the males are noticeable. Quite often, during a December pup count, we would look at weaned pups and pick out some that looked like bulls and some that looked like cows, based on their face shape.

As the weaned pups head out to sea to fish for themselves for the first time, the adults also head out to sea to replenish their depleted reserves. For the cows, after a month of not eating while supplying fat-rich milk to their pups, feeding is very important and by no means restricted to the local area.

By the end of January, the beach is deserted and hauntingly quiet. Considering the mass of blubber that is present for ten weeks, little is left behind: just the odd pup carcass here and there and the occasional pile of seal scat. The marram and couch grass in the dunes remains flattened, and little hollows, some with exposed sand, are left behind. On the whole, their contribution to dune erosion is minimal and has not led to any notable blow-outs. The vegetation soon bounces back with spring growth. One thing that did strike me, however, was how much the old sea hide dune had slumped over a period of a few years.

Around the coast at Horsey, grey seals haul out to moult in spring, having replenished their fat reserves after two months of foraging out at sea. Now back in good physical condition, three months after impregnation, true pregnancy begins. The fertilised egg, hitherto free-moving, now implants in the wall of the womb. It then takes around 250 days to develop into a fur-covered pup. The phenomenon of delayed implantation occurs in many mammal species. Indeed, common seals follow a very similar cycle, albeit six months ahead of grey seals. Pupping in June, they moult in July and mate in August. Their true pregnancy begins around November.

With low-tide counts of hauled-out seals having been conducted during the spring and summer months continuously since 2005, a great set of data has been built up. Twelve years later, as a product of networking with both Donna Nook and Horsey, I set about the task of conducting adult counts during the pupping season, to reveal exactly how many seals were on the beach at the peak.

Between Al, Bill and I, we recorded 2,555 pups in the third week of November 2017, alongside 1,849 cows. This indicated that a minimum of 706 pups were weaned by this stage as the cow count certainly included some individuals who had not yet pupped but had come ashore ready to. Interestingly, 706 was the exact number of bulls we recorded that day, revealing there were just over one and a half times more cows than bulls in the rookery. There was not a common seal to be seen, as they wisely vacate the area at this time of year.

I found this data fascinating, although it was a real challenge to collect. Assessing and recording 4,080 seals involved three people spending over three hours in the rookery, which could be argued to be unnecessary disturbance. An ideal way to count them more safely would be with an airborne camera flying at a safe height above the colony. Indeed, the Sea Mammal Research Unit do take aerial photographs of the rookery each year, in which pups and adults can be counted. The topography and density of the rookery was reaching the point where ranger safety and seal disturbance were certainly factors to be given increasing thought.

The following year, the total pup count trickled over the 3,000 mark, four years after first surpassing 2,000 and six years after it had first exceeded 1,000. A year later, Carl and I did a count on 7 December, a day the pup count once again exceeded the previous year's total.

The year after, the decision was taken to cease whole colony counting and just monitor a sample area. I had been caught up in the excitement of number-crunching along with the rest of the team. We would take bets on what the final count would be. All along, as hard as I tried to correctly age pups, not double count or miss any, I always accepted that our figure simply couldn't be completely accurate; there was a margin of error.

I loved making graphs and tables, but I realised that knowing whether, say, 2,900 or 3,100 pups had been born was almost irrelevant to their conservation. What matters is that they are given space, peace and protection.

It is slightly different on remote islands with much smaller rookeries, such as Skomer in Pembrokeshire. There, the total pup count averages around 150–200, which is a manageable number to monitor closely enough to gain accurate data on survival and weaning: indeed, important research has been conducted there for many years.

Eddie and Bee took up the post of Skomer wardens at the beginning of 2013. This provided me not only with the opportunity to succeed Eddie at Blakeney, but to visit Skomer and assist with their pup monitoring. I spent a windy week on the island one October when the sea was only just safe enough to make the boat journey out from Martin's Haven. There, I clambered down rocky cliff faces to reach the caves, coves and beaches below where individual pups are marked with coloured aerosol sheep-fleece marker sprays.

Pups are marked when they are four days old, with daily surveys enabling the birth date of each pup to be recorded. They are not marked until then in order to avoid disruption to the important bonding between cows and their newborn pups. Different colours and markings enable individual seals to then be monitored through to the moulting stage. Once they have been marked, pups can be monitored through binoculars from clifftops, avoiding disturbance. Quality of care by mothers is also assessed.

Bee's meticulous report, from the autumn I visited, documented a record 215 pups. Back at Blakeney, we would have more than eleven times this number. The data, recorded by Eddie, Bee and their fellow ex-Blakeney Point assistant, Jason, indicated that three-quarters of pups survived through to weaning. Causes of death included abandonment by the mother, separation from the mother – for example, during a storm – stillbirth, drowning and occasional disease. In years with worse storms, the survival rate can be much lower, the island's rocky topography making it a harsh environment for a pup during stormy seas.

Scoring pup size and shape, to classify development relative to age, helped me get my eye in and hone my pup-ageing skills. I also found following the moult pattern of individuals very interesting. That year, mean moult onset was two weeks and mean moult duration was six days. It was also clear that pre-weaned pups are still able to swim, dispelling the myth that their white 'puppy fur' coats are not waterproof.

Even marking a sample of pups at Blakeney would be difficult, due to the density of the rookery. But we could contribute photographs to the national identification database. Primarily, adult females are photographed from each side and head on to record their unique individual markings. With assistance from volunteers Helena, Bill, Paul and Sarah, a few dozen cows were photographed at Blakeney, in the hope that individuals breeding on the Point might be sighted in other places or back at Blakeney in future years.

At Donna Nook, a particular cow, identifiable by rope tangled around her neck, was observed for several consecutive years. 'Rope-neck' would arrive at almost the same date each breeding season. Over the years, I witnessed a number of cows with rope or netting tangled around their necks, although never one consistently returning to the same spot.

One year, we spotted a cow who appeared to be blind in one eye but was still a more than capable mother, successfully weaning her pup. When hunting, seals use their whiskers to detect vibrations more than they use their eyes, their eyesight not being particularly sharp.

During two winters, BBC crews also spent a few nights on the Point, filming *Winterwatch*. Their second visit came two years after the first. This time, they brought with them a high-spec. night-vision camera. I went out with them to the gap after dark and helped look for cows that might be about to give birth.

Their aim was to film a birth, although simply observing behaviour at night was interesting enough, as it had never been filmed before. (Essentially, their behaviour isn't much different at night to during the day, except for a very different atmosphere, from our point of view, watching them in darkness. Being out after dark, under a full moon, was incredibly magical.)

Seals don't specifically give birth at night, it can happen any time, but there are more hours of darkness than daylight during the winter, therefore there is a higher chance of birth being between 4 p.m. and 8 a.m. than between 8 a.m. and 4 p.m. So, cameraman Lindsay McCrae and I spent much time watching pregnant cows. Do you pick one and focus on her, or watch several, but risk missing a birth?

We found one cow that looked so ballooned she had to be close. She also looked restless, which made us suspicious that birthing was imminent. She kept us waiting. In the end, we did not manage to witness a birth, but some cracking night footage was captured, and I found it an immense pleasure to spend time in the rookery at night, as did the crew.

As the East Anglian grey seal population has increased, an increasing number of people have been lucky enough to witness a seal birth. I myself have only observed a stillbirth. It was sad but still educational and statistically a much rarer sighting than a live birth.

Fortunately, sick and injured pups were also a relative rarity. The phone would ring mostly during the Christmas holidays when visitors encountered weaned pups turning up at Salthouse, Cley or even Sheringham beach.

Weaned pups are best left alone. If a seal is out of the water, it is usually there because it wants to be. In the case of a weaned pup, it is more than likely resting. So often, I would encounter people genuinely wanting to help seals but ushering them back into the water. This is not an appropriate thing to do: if a seal is not able to get itself into the water, there is a chance it may not be able to swim.

There would generally be between one and five pups each year that genuinely needed sending to RSPCA East Winch. For example, a very young pup that turned up on Morston Quay. It had no way of finding its mother and would have starved to death in the car park. At East Winch, pups are force-fed blended herring and eventually released when they reach a healthy weight.

As far back as the 1980s, before East Winch even opened, rehabilitated seals were released in the harbour. In fact, there is a theory that the grey seals that arrived at Blakeney in the mid-1980s were seals that had been released there. True or not, natural southward spreading along the coast from Lincolnshire was inevitable.

Being more established than us, we looked to Donna Nook for advice based on their experience. Chatting to Lincolnshire Wildlife Trust warden Rob was interesting and useful. He had a theory that cows would abandon their pups if they sensed something wrong with them. Instead of investing in an unhealthy pup that would die anyway, they would abandon it and try again the following year.

Donna Nook were more than happy to pass filming requests on to us, namely for *Winterwatch*. Visitors are much easier to manage at Blakeney, thanks to the seal ferries that enable close-up views without causing disturbance. Just as the rookery grew, so did the number of ferry trips run during the winter, where before, all boats were taken out of the water by Halloween.

The second *Winterwatch* to feature Blakeney was broadcast in the second week of January. The pre-filmed Blakeney footage was spread across two episodes. Fine weather the weekend after the broadcast brought dozens of walkers to the Point, only to find a practically empty beach.

My appearance in the two films, alongside Iolo Williams, resulted in me receiving lots of comments in the community and beyond. Iolo is a true gentleman and a pleasure to work with. But I nearly didn't appear on the programme at all.

The evening before Iolo's filming day, I was involved in a road accident on the A149 near Warham and my car was written off. Fortunately, despite witnesses exclaiming I was lucky to be alive, I had only very minor injuries and was determined not to let them stop me going to work.

The many Horsey seal wardens enjoyed seeing the *Winterwatch* footage. I did a talk to them at Martham Village Hall, a couple of weeks later. It was a great opportunity to forge stronger links between the two seal sites and get to know some of the team there. Little did I know that one of the Horsey wardens was a helper on my future in-laws' farm. She would go on to give them a favourable character reference prior to our first meeting.

The Friends of Horsey Seals made an outing to the Point later in the year. I joined them on a seal trip and led a guided walk during the hour-long landing. It didn't occur to me at the time, but the group saw me as the face of Blakeney Point. I was very much part of a team, although the Friends of Horsey Seals associated me with Blakeney Point. This was actually much more the case in the past when tourists could actually buy postcards with pictures of the warden on them.

I never made it onto a postcard, but my picture appeared in lots of local newspaper articles and there were a fair few local radio and television news interviews about the seals each year. I enjoyed sharing my enthusiasm about the excitement of helping to safeguard an impressive and charismatic animal that was doing well.

I remember squeezing in a short-notice visit from BBC *Look East* one afternoon. Hurriedly, I refreshed the fox bait near Beach Way as we passed in the Land Rover, taking the presenter back to Cley beach. In my rush, I spilled the stinky, bloody mess all over my hands and coat sleeves, making the journey back slightly smelly and awkward. Then, a couple of years later, I found myself sat with her at a dinner party. Little had I known, at the time of the fox-bait incident, that my future partner was good friends with a number of Norfolk presenters and journalists.

The Blakeney seals having become relatively famous, our Director General, Dame Helen Ghosh, visited the Point. I was pleased to learn she had travelled by train.

Dame Helen's visit came after all but the last few pups had vacated, so she didn't get to observe the spectacle of the rookery. It was still an interesting time for seals, although sadly for a more sinister reason. There had been another spate of the still-unsolved corkscrew seal deaths.

Two-and-a-half years after the summer when numerous common seal carcasses with spiral cuts had washed up on the Point, grey seals and also harbour porpoises started washing up along the Norfolk coast displaying the same corkscrew injuries. A total of twenty-nine carcasses were discovered between late January and early April 2013 – then it stopped. However, two corkscrew grey seals washed up on the Point just before Christmas, followed by another six between January and March. It then stopped once again and no more were found until December, when twenty-two corkscrew seals washed up on the Point, most of which were sent to the RSPCA at East Winch for post-mortem examinations.

A pattern was emerging, with Horsey also discovering carcasses in winter with the same distinctive injures. Just like at Blakeney, the Horsey carcasses were primarily yearling grey seals, plus the occasional pup. In collaboration with the RSPCA, Sea Mammal Research Unit and the government's Marine Management Organisation, we had to get to the bottom of this.

Research and Discovery

THE MYSTERY OF THE spiral-cut seals and porpoises caught the attention of the Zoological Society of London. We were invited to a porpoise post-mortem by the Cetacean Strandings Investigation Programme.

Early on an April morning, Graham, countryside manager Victoria and myself boarded a train from King's Lynn to King's Cross and walked through Regent's Park to London Zoo. We entered the theatre, where a python post-mortem was also taking place. What Rob Deaville had to show us was quite a surprise.

In addition to the obvious torn flesh of the porpoise, there were some small puncture wounds. These were in pairs, with a consistent space between the two round holes. He explained that he had seen this on previous carcasses and offered up the skull of a bull grey seal to reveal that the spacing of the holes matched the distance between the longest two teeth on its upper jaw. This was quite a breakthrough, a strong theory backed up with evidence, although it was quite hard for us to process at first.

Rob went on to discuss the torn flesh, pointing out the feathering, which showed that it had been ripped rather than cut. He demonstrated by pulling at the loose skin, revealing that the edge of the tear was consistent with being pulled. This also demonstrated the spiral of fibres, showing how simply pulling at a loose piece of skin caused it to rip in a spiral pattern around the body.

Although graphic and unpleasant, this was very interesting and important. It seemed to rule out the possibility of these injuries being caused by ducted propellers once and for all, instead pointing towards a cause that humans, for once, were not responsible for.

We left Regent's Park with our heads spinning. This changed our whole view of the situation but was a lot to take in and make sense of in our own minds.

Our attentions soon turned to the breeding bird season, with no further corkscrew carcasses washing up ... until the winter. In fact, that winter, similar carcasses also washed up on the Isle of May on Scotland's east coast.

Corkscrew seals had appeared on the Isle of May during the same time periods as all of the previous Blakeney occurrences. The RSPCA explained to us that seals were probably only washing up in the winter due to the carcasses being negatively buoyant during the summer.

It was on the Isle of May, that December, that a breakthrough was finally made. Footage was captured showing an adult bull seal grabbing a pup by the scruff of the neck, dragging it to a shallow pool and apparently attempting to drown it. It killed it and then appeared to feed on some of its exposed flesh.

Over a ten-day period, the bull was observed killing no fewer than five pups, with a further nine pup carcasses discovered in places where the seal had been observed. Amazingly, twelve of these carcasses had the characteristic corkscrew wounds, starting at the head and spiralling down the body.

Just days after the Isle of May incident, a carcass washed up on Cley beach near the east bank. It was a pup of around three weeks old with a live weight of approximately 40kg. It was sent for post-mortem and, sure enough, the laceration was jagged – not smooth – with apparent claw rake marks present and punctures consistent with grey seal bites. There was also much tissue around the thorax absent, potentially fitting with the new cannibalism theory.

Durham University suggested that the bull had developed a strategy of tapping into a food reserve. Instead of not feeding or risking losing his territory by going to sea, using pups as a food reserve could be a way of maximising reproductive success by potentially increasing copulation opportunities. It was calculated that a grey seal would need to consume just 28g of seal blubber to obtain the same amount of calories as 100g of herring.

Almost three years after the Isle of May footage had been captured, seal cannibalism was finally witnessed on Far Point from a seal ferry. It was mid-March, and Derek from Temple's Seal Trips saw a grey seal bull grabbing a young seal by the scruff of the neck, just like in the Isle of May footage. Two days later, a corkscrew carcass indeed washed up on the Point.

It was a strange feeling, now knowing what had happened to this poor seal. Yet, it was a natural phenomenon and not our fault in any way. After years of hoping to stop these carcasses from washing up, we now knew we did not actually need to do anything.

During my first year as Point ranger, the BTO approached us with a Sandwich tern colour-ringing proposal. I had two things very clearly in my mind. Firstly, that our primary purpose was to protect them and not do anything that might compromise their safety. Secondly, that there was still much more to learn about our Sandwich terns to help our understanding and inform our conservation efforts. It would be brilliant to learn more about their lives away from the breeding colony.

Satisfied that disturbance would be minimal if chicks were ringed when close to fledging, we agreed to host a trial ringing session in the colony. This took place in the third week of June, around four weeks after hatching had started, and about one week before the first chicks were capable of flight.

We entered the colony on a warm, still evening at low tide, just two days before the summer solstice. A midweek evening was chosen so that there was minimal chance of visitor presence. We spent just thirty minutes in the colony before retreating and leaving the birds in peace.

All of the adult birds went up as we approached the colony. The chicks were grouped together and quick on their feet, running into the Suaeda, tucking themselves down and keeping still – survival instinct kicking in. Fifty of the largest chicks were gathered up and put into boxes – this equated to about 2.5 per cent of the total fledged young.

The birds were quickly but carefully ringed, one by one. Each bird was fitted with a standard metal ring on one leg and a blue plastic colour ring on the other. Each plastic ring, known as a Darvic, had a unique three-letter code inscribed in white: KAA, KAB, KAC and so on.

It was these rings that made the project worthwhile. The standard metal rings can only be read if a bird is in the hand, but colour rings can be read with optics from afar, greatly increasing the chances of re-sightings. We hoped that we would be able to see some of our ringed terns returning in future years. We were also fascinated to discover where else they might turn up along their migration as well as where exactly in Africa their wintering grounds would be.

Before the summer was over, we started to receive news of colour-ringed Sandwich tern sightings. The first, KCC, was seen 150 miles east-south-east on the Dutch coast on 8 and 9 August. It was then sighted on Wanerooge Island, Germany, on 20 August and then on Vejers Beach, Denmark, on 13 September.

This was fascinating, as it showed that, rather than heading south towards Africa, the tern had actually headed north along the European coast, presumably visiting prime foraging spots to feed up prior to the long southward migration. Another advantage of taking this indirect migration route is that it gives birds the chance to locate areas of suitable breeding habitat for potential alternative breeding sites in future years.

A second bird, KAH, was observed on 11 September at Luc-sur-Mer on the northern coast of France, 250 miles south-south-west of Blakeney. Interestingly, KCC was also seen on the French coast, as a yearling, the following Halloween.

A year after the first ringing session, forty-seven more chicks were colour-ringed at the colony. This time, we decided to delay by three weeks until early July. This later point in the breeding season was considered better as chicks were larger and all of the later-nesting adults had finished incubation.

An early July session was to be adopted again the following year. However, various predator challenges in the following years meant that we were unable to continue the ringing project. But those ninety-seven birds ringed over two seasons were to provide us with a lot of interesting data.

One of the July-ringed birds was seen from a seal ferry, a week later, and then at Le Havre in France a month later. The birds provided numerous sightings. Just as they had done the previous year, birds headed north initially. Three birds were seen together 30 miles up the coast at Gibraltar Point, Lincolnshire, and another two were seen 230 miles away up at the Ythan Estuary in Aberdeenshire. One of the Ythan-sighted birds was then picked up at Port Seton, East Lothian, in mid-August, apparently starting to head back south. However, it then went further north to Findhorn, in Moray, where it was seen at the end of August.

Four others were observed at Findhorn throughout August plus a bird on the Dutch coast and one at Dawlish Warren, down in Devon, at the end of the month. Then, on 23 November, our first winter sighting was made. Some 2,900 miles south-south-west from Blakeney, KDK was spotted at Tanji in Gambia. This was a place I had visited nine months earlier during my Gambian winter tern adventure.

The following October, KD3 – which had been seen at Findhorn the previous August – was seen much further south. It was among a group of several other Sandwich terns on the coast of Storms River on the southern coast of South Africa. This was a major discovery, revealing that Norfolk-breeding Sandwich terns were capable of migrating much further south than West Africa, all the way to the southern tip of the continent.

While some people are rightfully cautious about the true value of ringing versus welfare, I saw great value in the information it revealed about our breeding birds. Over the years, I have found a number of rings on birds that had died and it has always been interesting and educational to learn about their life history. The 'Year of the fox' was a tough experience and finding terns dead in the colony was utterly depressing.

But one small consolation was that five of these predated Sandwich terns had been ringed, so we were able to find out valuable information, including where those ringed as nestlings had hatched and how old they were.

Three of the Sandwich terns we found had been ringed as nestlings in three different countries: the Netherlands, Oye-Plage in France and the Farne Islands in Northumberland, aged 14, 6 and 11 respectively. The other two had been ringed as adults, one in Belgium, eleven years before, and the other at the Scottish Ythan Estuary, three years before.

These ringing recoveries proved that the North Sea Sandwich terns were one population. It was reassuring to understand how the success of the Blakeney ternery was just part of a greater whole. This, of course, did not make the protection of our ternery any less important, it just put the international lives of these amazing birds into context.

As well as the Sandwich tern project, some small-scale little tern colour-ringing also took place on the Point during my second summer as ranger. This was part of the Life Project and was carried out by Sabine of the RSPB, who I knew of from her previous bittern research coordination.

In mid-June, four adults were caught at their nests in the Watch House colony and colour-ringed with yellow Darvic rings. Cage traps, which looked like top hats made of netting, were used to catch them.

Because of our dedicated efforts to protect little terns, with the support of a growing number of volunteers, we were incredibly cautious about this trial, while at the same time mindful that calculated risks can be necessary for a greater gain. Al put in a lot of hours of observation to compare nest attendance and chick provisioning by ringed and non-ringed birds at this colony. His data revealed low attendance by the ringed birds, with both adults often leaving chicks unattended to go and forage. This highlighted how poor feeding had a big impact on fledging success.

We monitored the nest of one of the ringed adult little terns, UP7, using a trail camera. One of its two eggs hatched, but the chick was not seen after its fourth day, on 3 July. The ringed adult was then photographed at Winterton, east Norfolk, on 15 July, showing that it had abandoned the Blakeney colony. This raised concerns and we declined any further at-nest trapping of little terns at the Watch House colony. With twenty-one nesting pairs, this colony was less resilient than larger colonies.

That year, an interesting discovery was made at the main little tern colony on the beach. A dead, egg-bound bird was found to be ringed. I submitted a ringing recovery and heard back that she had been ringed as a nestling twenty-one years previously, at Tetney in Lincolnshire. It was fascinating to see that she was still breeding at such a ripe old age. Indeed, the oldest ringing recovery was just a few months older than this bird – until a ringed bird, two months shy of twenty-two years old was found on the Farne Islands very soon afterwards.

One of the most enjoyable pieces of research I have ever done was little tern prey sampling. With enthusiasm, expertise and resources provided by ecologist and tern specialist Doctor Martin Perrow, we gained an insight into the fascinating world of what lay beneath the surface. While we had a pretty good handle on the influence of disturbance, predation and weather in a given season, prey availability was more difficult to ascertain. Al had been doing chick provisioning watches, seeing what size and species of prey were fed to little tern chicks by their parents and where the adult birds were foraging. This gave an insight into prey availability. Physically seeing what was in the water in the foraging areas would take our knowledge and understanding a big step further.

Ninety years before, pioneering research into tern prey had been conducted at Blakeney. This involved investigating the stomach contents of forty-one common terns, nine Sandwich terns and five little terns between May and September. Permission was granted by the Blakeney Point management committee because a notable decline in flat fish in Blakeney Harbour had coincided with the growth of the Blakeney Point breeding tern population, which had approximately doubled in the first two decades of the twentieth century.

Silhouette of tern with sand eel, July 2014. (Ian Ward)

The findings of the 1925 study concluded that the scarcity of flat fish at Blakeney Point was due to some other factor and for certain 'if the whole of the tern population of Blakeney Point were to migrate elsewhere, the result would not be marked by any increase in fisheries'. Indeed, no flat fish were found in the stomachs of any of the fifty-five terns that were killed. Nine of the terns that were killed had empty stomachs, so had sadly died in vain.

The primary prey item of both common and Sandwich terns was found to be sand eels, whereas little terns fed almost solely on crustaceans during the breeding season. Interestingly, about 2 per cent of the common tern diet was found to be cockchafers, which the report described as beneficial to humans due to them being 'injurious insects'.

Our prey sampling was to inform conservation, proving just how important prey availability is in relation to the selection of breeding locations and subsequent productivity. To see the whole picture throughout the season, surveys were conducted in May, June and July. Thanks to the shared passion of all involved, this was done for two consecutive years. Passion was certainly helpful as the survey work was quite full-on but, I have to say, an absolute highlight of my time on the Point.

The methodology involved seine netting. We used a 60m-long by 5m-deep beach seine, with 5mm mesh, unfurled in a semicircle using a rowboat. With floats on the surface and a lead-line on the bottom, a wall of net is created. Both ends of the net are then pulled ashore. Fish and crustaceans trapped within are gradually forced into a smaller area of water before being transferred into a large oxygenated tank. Species are identified and measured before being released back where they came from, unharmed. On some hauls, lots of time was taken unpicking dozens and dozens of small shore crabs and shrimps caught in the fine mesh.

During the first year, the harbour was sampled at various points along Pinchen's Creek, moving along it with the tide. Four different states of tide were sampled: high, falling, low and rising. So a day's seine netting was pretty intense.

The first day was beautiful, sunny and warm. Two of my friends on ranger internships, Pete and Bruna, were spending a week volunteering on the Point, so were able to assist with hauling nets and processing prey, along with Paul, Sarah, Al and I, led by Martin Perrow's team consisting of himself alongside Andrew, Richard and Joe; the latter two having both worked as seasonal assistants on the Point in previous seasons. Working as a team and getting into a good rhythm was almost as satisfying as seeing what the net had caught.

Shore crabs were the most abundant catch species in all three months. Both brown and Palaemon shrimps were scarce in May, but around 300 of each were caught in June and July. In fact, in July, Palaemon shrimps overtook shore crabs, with over 700 caught. We caught over 200 young sea bass in May, but far fewer in June and fewer still in July. This indicated that the harbour is an important nursery area for them before they head off to sea. Greater and lesser sand eels, the favoured food of common and Sandwich terns, were only caught in very small numbers during our surveys, showing why these terns tend to forage further out to sea. Sand smelt and sand goby were among the more abundant fish. Other species caught in small numbers in the harbour included a few young herring, flounder, plaice, very occasional pipefish, sticklebacks and a couple of long-spined sea scorpions.

In the second year, efforts were doubled to sample the sea as well as the harbour. This gave a full picture of the Blakeney little terns' foraging sites. Fortunately, we weren't short of volunteers. More trainee rangers from across the trust had heard about Pete and Bruna's week on the Point and were keen to help out. We also offered the opportunity to assistant ranger interviewees who weren't successful but might like the chance to gain a week's experience for their CV. I enjoyed the chance to work with a range of enthusiastic young rangers and they enjoyed the chance to spend a week on the Point.

Again, three sessions of surveying were conducted across the season: covering the courtship, incubation and chick-provisioning stages of the breeding cycle. We found the harbour to have greater prey abundance than the previous year, which correlated with an increased number of pairs nesting on the tip of Far Point: an impressive forty-eight nesting pairs that were actively foraging in the nearby harbour.

Coordinating the sea-based seine netting required a couple of additional considerations: sea state and tide height. The water needed to be calm enough to set the net effectively, so wind speed had to be minimal. It also needed to be a neap tide so that the tractor could be parked on the edge of the beach without fear of tidal submergence. The tractor and farm trailer were used to transport the rowing boat and equipment from Cley beach to near the Watch House colony.

We located our sampling site far enough away from the colony to avoid any disturbance to the nesting little terns, hence tide height playing a determining role as we would need to be parked above the high-water line when the tide came in.

Amazingly, we managed to complete all of the surveys that had been planned, recording a large number of fish species. There were key differences between the sea and the harbour and radical differences according to tidal state. These were overlain by seasonal changes reflecting the dynamic nature of the area. Martin and his team were great company, full of energy and knowledge. They were also brilliant at sharing their expertise, enabling us to develop our fish and crustacean identification skills.

The sea sampling produced some marine species that we hadn't encountered in the harbour. These included dozens of venomous lesser weever, reminding us that walking barefoot on the beach can be dangerous. Martin was surprised that we caught squid and little cuttlefish too. The latter, although little over 2in in length, changed colour with different backgrounds. We even caught a sea trout, which was released back into the sea, as indeed were all catches except for a couple of flounders that Martin allowed us to take back to the Lifeboat House and fry. The sea trout stood out as particularly large compared to every other fish caught. Another notable catch was a garfish, known as the 'green bone' in German because it does indeed have green bones

One of the most memorable hauls was one of the last in July. We were on the beach sampling a rising tide. The net seemed to be full of shining silver darlings. There were literally thousands of young herring and sprat: tern food. Shimmering in the evening light, they looked quite magical, and their presence was certainly good news. A beautiful sardine was recorded amongst the other fish, a species typically occurring much further south: its presence a clear sign of climate change. Over the two years, we did a total of sixty-nine seine net samples, which caught over 20,000 fish of twenty-six different species, of which 83 per cent were herring and sprat.

As well as facilitating and assisting with tern diet research, we were also involved with seal diet research. This was a very different affair and far from glamorous. It involved bagging up grey seal scat at the end of the breeding season. During my initial chat with the University of St Andrews, I learned how the ear bones of fish were separated out and analysed under a microscope. There was a request to avoid bagging up sand with the sample. Separating sand from scat was described as 'degrading' – I thought to myself that picking it off the beach in the first place was hardly joyous either. But we saw the value in finding out the breakdown of our seals' diets.

Interestingly, herring made up only a trace percentage of the samples collected. Research at Donna Nook in the mid-1980s had found sand eels to make up almost half of the seals' diet. However, this had reduced to less than a quarter, reflecting a distinct decline in this species. There was also a reduction in commercial species, such as cod and sole, which accounted for about 5 per cent each. In contrast, species such as drag-onet and short-spined sea scorpion had risen from 5 per cent in the 1980s to a quarter each. This was important evidence to demonstrate that seals are not a threat to fishermen.

We, of course, had also learned that, for the very occasional bull, pup blubber also made up a proportion of the winter diet, and Paul had once witnessed a seal take a duck from the surface of the sea. It swam up from beneath and dragged it under the water. This was another example of atypical behaviour that, nonetheless, showed how seals are opportun-ists and feed on a diverse range of prey.

In the late November of my first season monitoring the rookery, trainee ranger George and I discovered a breeding cow with a telemetry tag attached to the back of her neck. She was on Middle Point with her pup. I did a bit of research and contacted the Institute for Marine Resources and Ecosystem Studies in the Netherlands. They had tagged the seal in Texel that March and had been tracking her movements since. I was sent a couple of maps, one confirming her location on Middle Point and the other showing her complete movements over the previous eight months.

This amazing technology revealed that the cow had followed the coast of northern Europe from Texel to Dunkirk. She had then spent time for-aging off the coast at Dover before heading north and foraging near the Essex coast for a while. The seal then headed in a straight line across the North Sea back to the Dutch coast before crossing back again to come to Blakeney Point and give birth. The map perfectly illustrated just how widespread the foraging range of a seal can be within the course of a year, clearly not restricted to the waters of a single locality.

Grey seal cow with telemetry tag, Middle Point, December 2015. (Ajay Tegala)

Eight years previously, ten adult grey seals had been fitted with telemetry tags at Donna Nook. Interestingly, none of them came to Blakeney, despite its relative proximity. The Donna Nook seals tended to head north, with some recorded at the Farne Islands and off Scotland's east coast, as well as an apparently prime fishing spot around 100 miles north-east out to sea from Donna Nook.

I met a visiting conservationist from northern France during multiple winters. He was seeing a gradual increase in pupping grey seals on his native coastline and was convinced these were Norfolk-born seals dispersing further as the population grew.

In 2014, a small sample of adult grey seals were caught on the West Sands and fitted with telemetry tags by the Sea Mammal Research Unit in partnership with RSPCA East Winch. We were given access to the live data feed and were able to follow their movements around the North Sea. Indeed, they were very wide ranging. Some headed north-east, one directly east and another headed southwards towards France.

10

Tales of the Unexpected

WHEN WORKING WITH WILDLIFE, life is often full of surprises. The actions of humans and the subsequent consequences can also provide drama. I encountered a considerable number of unexpected dramas during my first nine months as Point ranger alone. One of these numerous 'Tales of the unexpected' could, in fact, almost have been expected as it had been a semi-regular occurrence for several decades.

During the Second World War, many Norfolk beaches were laid with explosive sea mines to prevent German invasion. These minefields started to be cleared as the end of the war approached. Around the coast at Trimingham cliffs, by 1953, no fewer than twenty-six men had lost their lives as a consequence of mine explosions. Half a century later, the discovery of mines on Blakeney Point was still a somewhat frequent occurrence, making the Point a relatively dangerous place. All new staff would be briefed on the appearance of mines and instructed not to touch them in case they should still be live.

Any mines discovered above the high-water mark are the responsibility of the police and any below the high-water mark are the responsibility of the coastguard. Mines would often turn up close to or literally on the high-water mark and so both the police and coastguard would attend, the relevant one leading a beach closure. Ultimately, the military take control, detonating mines with controlled explosions. We would be involved in the communication of information and facilitation of beach closures, ensuring visitors were kept safely away from danger zones.

My first encounter with unexploded ordnance was not a mine but an unspent military flare. Four of them, in fact. These were regularly used in training exercises conducted off the coast by the United States Air Force, usually on Tuesday evenings. If activated, the phosphorus within can cause life-threatening injuries.

According to my diary, one Saturday afternoon in October:

> ... a knock came on the Lifeboat House door saying there was some ordnance on the beach. We discovered two phosphorus flares, then another two. I tried to contact the Royal Air Force directly, but was unable, so I rang the coastguard who informed the police. A police officer then had to come to view the flare before the bomb squad could attend.

A photograph wasn't sufficient, it had to be confirmed by an officer, despite being 3½ miles along Blakeney Point:

> It was dark and rainy by the time they arrived. Graham had turned out with the tractor. As the story unfolded, I received countless calls. We put off dinner waiting to see if we needed to come down with the quad. In the end, the sergeant only viewed one of the flares, returning to Cley for over half an hour before deciding to return in the morning. Eventually, the next morning, she gathered the flares together and blew them up in a controlled explosion. All four were found to be live. We were not allowed to leave the Lifeboat House until afterwards. From the look-out tower, we watched a plume of smoke rise from behind the tallest dune after the earth-shaking boom.

That Sunday morning, Aylmerton Field Studies Centre happened to be out on one of their low-tide harbour rambles. Sometimes there would be a theme, with the leaders dressed up, usually as pirates. They would refer to me as 'Captain Ajay'. On this occasion, it was a Second World War theme, so the explosion really added to the atmosphere.

The afternoon following the flare explosion was much quieter. On a solitary ramble down Far Point, I finally saw my first long-eared owl. I had seen countless short-eared owls on the Point and barn, tawny and little owls on the mainland, but for years had ached to see my first long-eared. At last, there I was, alone with a bird I had dreamed of, the beautiful autumn sky behind. Long-eared owls are an almost annual October migrant to the Point from Scandinavia and I had finally managed to catch up with one. It was a bittersweet moment because two hours later, I was reluctantly moving off the Point for the winter.

What a winter that was to be, with the tidal surge and massive subsequent clean-up operation. A week into the new year, we were very busy tidying up Blakeney Freshes completely unaware that tragedy was about to strike just a few miles along the coast.

As usual on a Tuesday night, the United States Air Force were running a training mission off the Norfolk coast, flying their aircraft to the coast from RAF Lakenheath, about 45 miles inland. At around 7 p.m. on 7 January 2014, a Pave Hawk helicopter was flying very low over Cley Marshes when it crashed. It came down north-east of the east bank, killing all four airmen.

Controlled flare explosion, viewed from lookout tower, October 2013. (Ajay Tegala)

Pave Hawk helicopter parked beside crash site, January 2014. (Graham Lubbock)

Looking through telescopes from Friary Hills the following morning, we could see the crash site. A second helicopter was involved in the exercise and had landed beside the wreckage to assist. News soon filtered through that live bullets had been strewn across the crash scene, which was about the size of a football pitch. A 5-mile exclusion zone was put into place for all aircraft and an abundance of personnel from the United States Air Force descended on Cley. A large lorry only just made it around the tight bends of the coast road.

Manned checkpoints were instated in Cley and Salthouse and the Cley Visitor Centre was taken over by the air force. Cley warden Bernard Bishop had been helping escort rescue crews across the marsh.

The wreck itself was left untouched until all of the live ammunition had been retrieved. Very early on, there was speculation that a bird strike was the cause of the tragic incident, possibly a goose. We felt incredibly sad for the families of the four airmen who had lost their lives. It was difficult to understand why they should have flown so low over an area renowned for its winter wildfowl.

On the Thursday morning, members of staff from UCL came to Blakeney to examine and tidy their buildings following the recent flood damage. I rang up Cley Visitor Centre to request permission to travel along Beach Road and access the Point. There was an American accent on the end of the phone, requesting us to bring our passports as proof of identification. Graham found this particularly surreal. The furthest from Norfolk he had travelled was Berwick-upon-Tweed, now he needed his passport to go through the village he was born in to access the reserve he worked on. It showed just how serious the situation was.

As I arrived at Cley beach with the UCL staff, we saw four stretchers being taken out of a vehicle and carried east towards the crash site. We headed west along the Point in the Land Rover for the first time since the tidal surge had altered the ridge. The tractor had been up the previous week, to put a set of vehicle tracks into the newly spread shingle. Unlike the powerful tractor with its large rear wheels, the Land Rover was lower to the ground with six adults crammed inside. We barely got a third of the way along the ridge before it sank into a loose patch of shingle.

We now had to request permission for the tractor to come and tow us out. This was bad luck on a day when we were trying to keep vehicle movements to a minimum, but it could not be helped. Eventually, we made it to the Old Lifeboat House where the UCL staff catalogued the extensive flood damage. A few hours later, we headed back, the tractor leading the way to compact the shingle for the Land Rover following closely behind it.

Barely beyond the Long Hills, my phone rang. It was a message from the office saying we were to stop, wait where we were and not proceed any further until given permission to do so. The bodies had been retrieved from the helicopter wreck and we were not allowed to be anywhere near Cley beach until they had left the beach car park. It was a very grim feeling, knowing what had happened and what was going on just a few miles in front of us. Such a tragic, premature end to four lives.

We waited for a good half an hour near the Long Hills before being given the go-ahead to proceed forwards. Coincidentally, we were waiting literally a few metres from the site where there had been another aircraft crash. On 19 June 1940, four crew were on board a German Heinkel, which had been fighting a British Blenheim over Norfolk when an engine caught fire. The Heinkel's second engine then failed as it flew over Blakeney, forcing it to make an unscheduled landing in the shallow water just off the Point. Fortunately, all four on board survived. They were taken prisoner by the coastguard when they came ashore.

The rusting Heinkel wreck remained offshore for twenty-nine years until it was blown up by the order of Trinity House. Fragments of it were washed ashore and then buried by shingle deposited by the sea. Over the winter of 2012–13, there were unrivalled vehicular movements along the shingle ridge to carry out the Lifeboat House renovation works.

Tractors, four-by-fours and telehandlers went up and down the ridge multiple times a day for five months. This undoubtedly led to a section of shingle collapsing by the Long Hills. As a consequence, a large chunk of the Heinkel was exposed, thought to be part of the wing casing. It wasn't long before it was engulfed by shingle again, although it did reappear in November 2017. Mary and I brought it back to Friary Farm, where it went on to the trust's regional office to be stored alongside various historical and archaeological finds from across East Anglia.

Barely two months after the crew of the Pave Hawk helicopter had tragically lost their lives on the north Norfolk coast, another sad and unexpected tale took place. On the last Tuesday of February, I went on a birding holiday to Gambia during the quiet time between the seal pupping and bird nesting seasons. It was absolutely brilliant to see Sandwich and little terns on their wintering grounds.

The following day, things were far from quiet back at Blakeney. Bean's and Temple's were both running boat trips, with customers including schoolchildren on a trip with Aylmerton Field Studies Centre. While the boats circled around the tip of Far Point to look at the hauled-out seals, an unidentified object was spotted floating in the water. At first, it was dismissed as a dead seal, but its human-like appearance could not be ignored. One of the ferry operators insisted it was a rescue mannequin.

By the time police and coastguards attended the scene in a frenzy, it was clear that the floating object was sadly a human body.

In the heat of the moment, one of the ferrymen had grabbed an ankle to bring it ashore. Graham was swiftly at Cley beach with the Land Rover to transport the police to Far Point. The coastguards had already sped along the shingle in their vehicle, only to get stuck. Expecting Graham to help as he approached in the Land Rover, they were somewhat frustrated to see him zoom past without stopping. He was under police instruction to head straight to the body without delay. But by the time he reached Far Point, the inshore lifeboat crew had already recovered the body, taking it to Morston Quay, where it was handed over to the police.

The body was identified as a 70-year-old woman from Norwich with Alzheimer's disease, who had been missing for three days. She had last been seen walking by the coast near Blakeney. The lady was an avid walker and her death was concluded by the coroner to be accidental. It was, at least, a comfort to her family that she had died enjoying herself in a glorious place.

Due to the nature of the tides and currents, there have been multiple historical drownings off the Point. But many lives had been saved by the brave Blakeney lifeboatmen and other RNLI crews. The coastguard have also helped rescue injured walkers, and we have given a few people with sprained ankles lifts back to Cley beach over the years.

I was once on my own when news came through that a lady had slipped on the saltmarsh mud, falling and breaking her arm. Cley coastguard Cavin came to the rescue, taking her to safety. She was in agony. It just shows how careful you have to be if you're going to walk on the slippery mudflats.

A very strange occurrence took place during my first summer as Point ranger. It was the first weekend in June, when rangers, Paul, Matt and I were taking it in turns to do dawn patrols for potential egg thieves.

I remember cooking my grandad's chicken recipe for dinner, which we had on the ramp in front of the Lifeboat House. After dinner and a few drinks, we turned in for the night. It was Matt's turn to get up at dawn. He headed out at 4 a.m. to check the beach, returning to the kitchen about an hour later.

Not having seen anyone on his patrol, Matt was rather surprised to find a 50-year-old woman stood in the kitchen. She had bare feet, was wearing sunglasses and had a white scarf wrapped around her head.

The woman looked startled and began speaking in French, pointing to herself and saying 'Florentine'. Matt tried to explain that she was in a private building. Despite apparently being unable to speak English, he felt that she could still understand what he was saying to her.

Eventually, he managed to lead her out of the kitchen into the visitor centre. Now directly beneath my bed, I was woken up by her loudly saying, 'Matthei' repeatedly. In my semi-conscious state, I tried to make sense of this distressed-sounding French voice, so opened my window and looked out. Florentine emerged from the building and headed towards the toilet block. She must have crossed the harbour as it was low tide and we were satisfied she was not a potential egg thief.

Over breakfast, it dawned on us that Florentine could potentially be in trouble, especially if she was unfamiliar with the landscape and the tides. However, she had managed to cross the harbour to the Point and seemed to have a savviness and determination about her. We began noticing lots of odd little traces she had left behind. As well as helping herself to yogurt from the fridge and making herself a coffee, she had poured a discarded half-empty can of lager into a glass and thrown the can in the bin. It also seemed that she had removed the bin bags from the toilet block and put them underneath the building.

We checked all of the huts and also popped down to the Watch House to look for her. Near the Hood, two visitors told us they had seen a lady walking onto the marsh. From the lookout tower, we scanned carefully across the harbour, hoping she had made it safely back to the mainland. We contacted the police, just in case she had got into trouble in the mud.

Back at the Lifeboat House, we found she had left postcards dotted around the kitchen and visitor centre. On one, she had written '*Moi*' followed by an 01263 telephone number and an address for a house nearby.

Intrigued and curious, I rang the number and spoke to the owner, who I knew was an author. She was surprised and concerned, stating that she had no French friends who were unable to speak English. We agreed to contact each other if we found out any more information, but suspected we may never find out anything more about the mysterious Florentine.

Around 4 p.m., the coastguard rescue helicopter flew over Morston and Stiffkey. A call to the coastguard revealed that they were assisting the police in a search for a missing 52-year-old woman by the name of Florentine. The coastguard said he had heard about the lady who 'had a cup of tea' in the Lifeboat House. Surely this had to be the same person, coffee having changed to tea as the story spread between people.

I rang the author again. She was out but her son answered. He mentioned an unusual lady his mother knew who was 'mentally unstable' and had been admitted to Hellesdon Hospital. The interesting thing was, this lady – whose name I shall keep anonymous, changing it to Katrina – had rung her friend three times the day before, saying that she was in the Gunton Arms and had had her car keys confiscated by the landlord the night before.

Convinced that the missing lady was, in fact, Katrina, I rang the police to explain what I had learned and pieced together. They confirmed that they were indeed looking for Katrina – I was correct.

A little while later, the author called me back. She explained that the French part of the story had thrown her because she was unaware Katrina spoke French, but she had later thought it might be her due to the phone calls the previous day. Katrina was one of her creative writing students and had apparently wanted to visit her that day. However, she was having a birthday party for a friend and the last thing she wanted was Katrina there 'being mad'. She explained that they were sort of friends and that Katrina would write to her, sometimes in German, and often before her worst episodes. The most recent letter had been sent just two weeks ago.

I learned that Katrina used to have family nearby, which would explain her familiarity with the Point and harbour. The author also recounted an occasion when she had visited her at Hellesdon. Katrina ran out of the hospital dressed only in a nightie, followed the river out of Norwich, stole a horse from a farm and rode it bareback along the Dereham Road. 'Oh yes, she's resourceful,' said the author, explaining how Katrina was trying to ride the horse to her parents' home in south Norfolk.

A few months after Katrina had crossed Morston Marsh, a different kind of bird caused drama on the marsh. A sick spoonbill was reported to us. Graham, George and I crossed Morston Creek and searched the marsh. It was found tucked in one of the smaller tributary creeks: a juvenile, believed to be from the breeding colony 8 miles west at Holkham, as it was too early in the autumn for juveniles from mainland Europe to have reached Norfolk. At the time, Holkham was the country's sole spoonbill breeding site, with eighteen young fledging that year.

The underweight, injured young bird was carefully put into a large cardboard box and driven to RSPCA East Winch. It was found to have a fractured shoulder, probably the result of a collision. As they were unable to do anything for the bird, it had to be put down.

We, of course, felt sad but also had an idea that maybe some good could come from this. I asked if we could have the carcass back in order to clean up and keep the skull for our educational collection. We became the proud owners of a British-hatched spoonbill skull, which went on to make several appearances on guided walks and at educational events. It very nearly made an appearance on national television when the BBC were going to use it as a prop in a 2021 episode of *Springwatch* when I was working on the series.

Looking back on 2013, so much really did happen. The very first event of the season had been the annual beach clean, scheduled for the Saturday of the Easter weekend. My contract as Blakeney Point ranger started that day, three days after my temporary contract on Lindisfarne had ended. It was an early Easter, and the weather was distinctly wintry. On a blustery and snowy Cley beach, we made the decision to postpone the beach clean, largely due to the complete absence of any volunteers.

Over the course of the following two weeks – when the rescheduled litter-pick took place – stormy conditions and offshore winds had caused the death of a worryingly large number of auks all along the east coast. During the beach clean, as well as the usual food and drink packaging, helium balloons and small pieces of plastic, we counted over forty razorbills, ten guillemots and twelve puffins along a 3-mile stretch of the Point. The RSPB described the extensive puffin wreck as the worst in half a century, with birds perishing as a consequence of harsh weather impairing their visibility and stormy seas causing fish to go deeper, making it harder for seabirds to feed. On top of this, their energy was further reduced by the cold winds.

Seeing these dead seabirds didn't make for the most pleasant start to the season, regardless of the fact it was completely out of our control. However, that particular breeding season went on to be one of my favourites. I really enjoyed stepping up to fill the Point ranger role, taking forward the management and monitoring of the breeding birds. We gelled well as a team and were praised for carrying the baton and moving things forwards.

In a century of Sandwich tern breeding on the Point, that was the only year that breeding pairs exceeded 4,000, as proven by our nest count. Luck was on our side on the predator front too, with no serious issues. But my share of predator challenges were all ahead of me. I soon learned to expect the unexpected.

As much as I tried to plan and structure each working day, there always has to be an element of flexibility built in. You can't ignore wildlife in trouble. One Sunday morning in early July 2014, Sarah, Paul and I came across five abandoned shelduck chicks, huddled together and shivering in wet grass near the boardwalk. We imagined that the parents had been leading their brood from the nest into the harbour when they were disturbed, perhaps by a marsh harrier. As shelducks lay eight to ten eggs, we assumed the brood had split in two, the parents staying with half of their chicks but the other five being left on their own.

Knowing they would surely perish, we debated whether we should let nature take its course or intervene. How could we let these adorable little ducklings suffer? My affection for them increased further when they started following me in a line. I led them to the Lifeboat House, where we put them in a cardboard box lined with cotton wool and tea towels with a hot water bottle underneath to warm them. The idea of raising these cute, fluffy black-and-white chicks appealed to us, but research revealed we didn't quite have everything that was required to brood them. So, we sent them on a seal ferry to Morston, where they were collected by the RSPCA and taken to East Winch. There they were cared for, with two of the five surviving and going on to be released at King's Lynn, two months later.

If someone had told me, when I first started at Blakeney, that I would get engaged on the Point, I probably would have laughed. But I did. In the North Sea, to be precise, as the sun was setting. I also first met my future in-laws in Pinchen's Creek. The whole family came out on a seal ferry.

It was a pretty unique way of doing things, as was the way we introduced our parents to each other, which also involved seals. We took them up to see the pups in December. Travelling by Land Rover, we put the four of them in the back and left them to get to know each other along the slow westward trudge. They've been friends ever since.

11

Treasured Memories and Changing Faces

BLAKENEY HOLDS MANY MEMORIES for so many people. From tourists who come to escape to those who are fortunate to live and work in such a special place. The two things that stand out most for me are the nature and the people, arguably two of the most important things in life.

Blakeney and its neighbouring villages are special because they have a strong sense of community. It can sometimes feel like everybody knows everybody's business, but people genuinely keep an eye out for each other, especially those who have grown up working on the marshes and in the harbour.

As more and more homes have been acquired for holiday lets and second homes, the core community has managed to remain strong and united. Those who move to the area and get involved in the community have enriched it, as well as learning and benefiting from the knowledge of local characters. Visitors who make the effort to understand and experience the true spirit of the coast can find it most rewarding.

I once spent a summer's day leading an A-level group who were visiting from one of the home counties. A-level students can be a tough crowd; you can talk to them as adults but they don't necessarily have the sense of joy and excitement that primary school children do. When preparing for their visit, I decided I should take them across the harbour at low tide to immerse them in the landscape.

Undeniably helped by perfect weather, the trip was a success. The teachers were pleased, saying they would definitely be back. But the best thing was the feedback I received from one of the students. She told me it was the best day of her life. What a pleasure it was to be able to give someone such a meaningful experience and treasured memory.

Spending so much time in a prime wildlife spot has resulted in a wealth of treasured memories. These range from wildlife I have searched hard for, to moments where I have stumbled upon something special in the course of my work.

Both apply to one of my favourite rare birds: the bittern. Perhaps my best sighting came out of the blue while working on Blakeney Freshes, one February, with George. I noticed a bird in flight, almost dismissing it. But something about it subconsciously caught my attention, so I looked again, and saw a bittern disappearing into a wet, reedy area. A little while later, it flew just a few metres in front of us, its feathers shining as they caught the light. Magnificent.

Another impressive bird is the osprey, with its 1.5m wingspan. There are annual sightings of individuals on passage, usually over the harbour when they put up every wader in sight. We would often get calls from the Point's regular birders, alerting our attention to one heading in our direction.

On one September morning, I spotted a large bird perched on the telegraph pole by the lab. When it took flight, I saw it had a large fish in its talons. A few minutes later, I bumped into renowned bird artist Martin Woodcock, walking up the Point from Cley. In my excitement at what I had just witnessed, I recounted how I had seen an Osprey … with a fish. 'That's what they do, you know,' Martin replied, dryly. Of course, I knew that, but was so excited to have had such a wonderful view of a bird that I had previously only seen from a distance.

Martin was not the only local artist I had the pleasure of getting to know. Another was Godfrey Sayers, a former fisherman, who specialised in watercolour landscape paintings of the north Norfolk coast. He and his wife Judy sold his work from a large van on Blakeney Quay for many years. I got to know them both when I rented their garden chalet between October and March each year.

I loved staying there. In contrast to communal living on the Point, I enjoyed the peace and solitude of my Wiveton winters. Between May and October, Godfrey would swim in the sea almost every morning. Many was the occasion I would see him on Cley beach. He always seemed to be busy, hurrying from one thing to the next. But on the occasions we both had time to chat, I enjoyed listening to him share his knowledge of the coast and his great interest in its history.

In fact, he had written a wonderful book about not only the history of the north Norfolk coast, but its local characters. Delayed by the December 2013 tidal surge, which prompted an additional chapter, *Once Upon A Tide* was launched the following winter, accompanied by an exhibition of some of his paintings. I was given a private showing of a particularly special painting prior to the exhibition, in his garage. It was a painting from the early 1970s, inspired by the mission to Mars. Godfrey had discovered that shining an ultraviolet light on the painting in a dark place made the stars shine, bringing the picture to life.

Wiveton is a brilliant place to see the stars at night, there being no street lights. The North Norfolk Astronomy Society have an observatory in the village. But you can't beat seeing the night sky from Blakeney Point. Stood on the back steps of the Lifeboat House, I have seen multiple shooting stars.

I think the most beautiful night view I have seen there is the full moon reflected in the harbour. On moonlit nights in the spring, Sandwich terns forage into the early hours, their calls carrying in the air. It was always a great feeling to hear them from my room.

Before turning in for the night, I would look out of my window across the harbour towards the distant lights of the mainland. One year, I was in the Lifeboat House on bonfire night and had a perfect view of Blakeney's firework display, and for a week each August, Gray's Funfair would come to the village, cramming a few fairground rides and a food stall or two onto the quay. Seeing the hustle and bustle of mainland life from afar made the Point feel almost like an island.

Up in the lookout tower, watching a spring tide come in made the Point feel even more like an island. On a few occasions, I watched the

Spring tide, viewed from the lookout tower, October 2013. (Ajay Tegala)

tide trickle towards the Lifeboat House, bringing the occasional black-headed gull or turnstone right to the doorstep.

But the magic of a late-summer evening insect hatch in the dunes has to be the most special view I have had from the tower. When it starts, within just a few minutes the dunes are suddenly covered in hundreds of gulls. After filling themselves with the newly emerged insects, they rest on the grass, like picnickers at a beauty spot. Any resident hut or houseboat owners couldn't help but share our appreciation of the spectacle.

One Sunday morning, my partner was upstairs in the Lifeboat House and heard some visitors chatting in the visitor centre below. A voice remarked how much they would love to spend a night in the building. Such moments would always remind us how fortunate we were.

It had once been suggested to us that we could provide a unique bed-and-breakfast experience, raising funds to aid conservation. But this simply wasn't possible alongside our long list of important responsibilities and would have infringed on our precious downtime.

One request we were happy to permit was Folk on the Point. Blakeney Old Wild Rovers sea shanty group and a group of local folkies, some with guitars, landed from a seal ferry for a couple of hours to play and sing in the natural amphitheatre of a dune dip near the Landing Ridge in late summer. We went along to listen, enjoying the novelty of live music on our doorstep.

Thick snow is a rarity on the Point but truly magical when it settles, as it did at the end of February 2018. I spent the last Monday evening of the month on the Point, carrying out fox control with Barrie during a blizzard. Even in the shelter of the tower, it was pretty cold.

The following morning, Carl and I headed to Holt to collect pigeons for fox bait from Paul Reed, the butcher, who kindly supplied them for next to nothing, knowing they were helping protect the reserve his father used to manage. Coming uphill along a back road by Salthouse Heath, the road was so slippery that we only just made it up the hill. We were surprised to see a seemingly carefree old dear heading speedily downhill in a little car.

The next morning brought perfect whiteness: 5in of beautiful, crisp snow that crunched underfoot. There was a cold and hungry blackbird by the office door. He devoured my hot-cross bun crumbs.

I called on Mrs Rowley, in the cottage near the barn, to see if she needed anything from the shop. It would be a few days before she felt confident to head out herself.

The snow on Cley Beach Road was so thick that we weren't allowed to travel up the Point for a couple of days. New ranger Leighton had just started and was dying to head out to the Point for his first visit. We were finally permitted to take the tractor out there on 1 March.

Travelling along Beach Road, about 100m from the car park, we came across a car on the beach side of a deep snowdrift. It turned out the driver had thrown caution to the wind and decided to camp out, Bear Grylls style. In the early hours, he had changed his mind and decided to head home, only to get stuck.

Thick snow on the main dunes: a rarity on the Point, March 2018. (Ajay Tegala)

Approximately twelve hours later, we appeared: the first people he had seen since he arrived. We were able to clear the road with the front loader on the tractor and then help push his car through. He was so relieved and grateful that he hugged us. We were happy to help, although distinctly unimpressed that he had been so foolish in the first place. If the sea had over-topped the ridge overnight, he could have been in real trouble.

It was breathtaking to see the Point under thick snow, which had settled on top of the shingle ridge. It had started to thaw, but the dunes were still very white. Long icicles hung from the Lifeboat House gutter like stalactites. Inside, water had frozen solid inside the toilet cisterns.

We felt like Scot of the Antarctic. Time flew by and suddenly it was starting to get dark. A stormy sea was breaking on the ridge as we drove back.

In almost a decade, I had experienced all weathers and seen a whole manner of migrant birds on the Point. My favourite has to be the bluethroat.

May 2015 produced the most brilliant views of this beautiful bird. A well-marked male spent a whole Sunday in and around the tamarisk. Its bright pink flowers were in full bloom and contrasted perfectly with the blue markings on the bird. Throughout the day, we were able to get some cracking views of it.

My friends Pete and Bruna arrived that day to begin a week's volunteering. I took them straight to the tamarisk. To them, it could have felt that Blakeney Point was always like this in spring, but I assured them this was a very special sight. I was surprised more birders didn't walk up the Point to see the showy bird, we had it to ourselves for most of the day.

Earlier in the month, a much rarer bird had attracted a considerable crowd to gather around the Plantation. It was a Moltoni's subalpine warbler, which had only recently been separated as a species. This meant it was not only a first for Norfolk but for mainland Britain, too.

A little later that season, Blakeney Point's first known paddyfield warbler dropped into the Suaeda near the Long Hills, the fourth record for Norfolk. While both of these birds were major rarities, I have to admit that my excitement was eclipsed by the responsibility of crowd management at the height of the breeding season.

Twitchers around the Plantation tend to be naturally self-policing, but the paddyfield warbler's location put breeding reed buntings, oystercatchers, ringed plovers and little terns at risk of disturbance. We reduced disturbance as much as possible by maintaining a constant presence until the bird finally moved on. We breathed sighs of relief when it did.

I have a soft spot for the more colourful and flamboyant migrants, so it was a thrill to flush my first British hoopoe from the dunes one mid-September morning. With its striking black-and-white wings and exotic-looking crest, this unmistakable bird had only been recorded on the Point a dozen or so times. I was alone on the Point at the time. Andy Stoddart half-jokingly told me that, although they are pretty hard to misidentify, I wouldn't be believed until the Point's regular birders had confirmed it.

One of the most pleasurable things I did on the Point was simply enjoy quiet evenings. As well as relaxing times by myself and with my fiancé, I also enjoyed the company of visiting UCL folk and the various hut owners. Many of them have a shared appreciation and affection for the place.

There were many happy times with the Clarkes and the Popes. We often dined together, in the Lifeboat House kitchen and their charming huts. When the UCL came out with student groups, the rangers would always be invited for a dinner. Some of the lecturers would also visit with their families and we would pop around for drinks and games of Bananagrams. After all, during my five summers on the Point, I worked every weekend.

Our classic after hours Blakeney Point game was Kubb. Pronounced 'koob', the game is said to date back to the Viking Age and was brought to Blakeney by Bee in 2012. It involves two teams competing to knock five wooden blocks over by throwing wooden batons. Once the blocks have all been knocked down, the winning team is the first to knock over the king. Traditionally a lawn game, it works just as well on shingle – obviously when there are no nesting birds in the vicinity. Many a Kubb game was played when the Clarkes were in residence. Cards Against Humanity was another favourite game.

After Brent Pope had sold his Salthouse Marsh to the Norfolk Wildlife Trust, he and Brigid spent much more time visiting their hut and fishing for sea bass from the beach.

Andrew and Kay were the hut owners who visited most, during my time on the Point. Knowing the place so well, they were a great support during 'Year of the fox'. They even towed me behind their boat on an O'Brien tube for a bit of light relief on my birthday. (Despite going out well into the evening, I was still spotted having fun in the harbour. Nothing goes unnoticed, particularly in August.)

Attractive washed-up flotsam would soon disappear, especially driftwood. I once found a particularly beautiful, spherical green bottle, completely intact, of which Kay was very envious.

Visiting hut owners were extra eyes, helping us to keep on top of dogs off leads, people having barbecues or trying to set up tents. I set Andrew and Kay up as volunteers so they could conduct occasional formal patrols in branded clothing. They also helped me knock some sharp corners off the *Yankee* ruin using lump hammers. A Victorian steam lighter, which was later converted into a houseboat, it had rotted and rusted over the years. I enjoyed hearing their memories of equally happy times with Joe and Janet in the 1980s and 1990s.

I wanted to know as much as possible about the Point's human history as well as its natural history. So, I was thrilled when Professor Oliver's grandson visited the Point. Naturally, his family were given the grand tour. In return, they presented us with a copy of the Old Lifeboat House guestbook, containing signatures of visitors between 1910 and 1939, including some notable ecologists.

Later in the twentieth century, the UCL's Doctor White followed in Professor Oliver's footsteps, taking students out to the Point and continuing to study plant and bird life. I met his widow, Monica, who told me that Middle Point was man-made. Ted Eales had laid a line of hay bales to form dunes. Indeed, the dunes on Middle Point are suspiciously regular and some maps label them as 'Eales Bank'. Doctor White and Monica would spend many hours sat on a particular dune in the middle of Great Sandy Low, which was named White's Hill.

I also met brothers Peter and Steve Trudgill, whose parents had been close friends of Ted Eales since the 1940s. Their father, John Trudgill, took several photographs during their family outings to the Point with 'Teddy' and assistant Reggie Gaze. One captures the latter in character as 'Aunt Matilda'. Gaze was a renowned wildlife photographer and published several books containing photographs of Norfolk birds and nests, many of which were taken on the Point. He spent at least sixteen seasons assisting Ted on the Point, as well as helping out Ted's father and original watcher Bob Pinchen.

I was interested to learn about what happened to the wardens of old after they had spent several years working on the Point. I thought how strange it seemed that, after more than sixty years on the coast, Ted should move inland to Fulmodeston on retiring.

An *EDP* article from the early 1980s suggests he did not find it easy to accept that the management of the Point would change. He was quoted saying, 'My life's work has been wasted', criticising some of subsequent warden Ronald Pimm's decisions. But change is inevitable, especially with regard to the management of a high-profile nature reserve – and forty years is a very long time for one warden to spend on a remote shingle spit.

Ted chose to end his memoirs with his final breeding bird report, which boasted very good success for almost every species in self-proclaimed testament to his effective management work. Warden of Scolt Head Island Bob Chestney also wrote a book when he retired after many years managing the ternery there. His book, *Island of Terns*, ends with some bitter remarks and criticism of the site's management following his retirement.

Bob Pinchen's short-but-sweet memoir does not contain any negativity after his thirty years' work. Bizarrely, he and his wife moved from the tranquillity of Blakeney Point to a cottage right next to a railway when he became warden of Oulton Broad. Joe Reed, however, continued to manage the café on Morston Quay and worked on the seal ferries. He continued to assist with fox control for a number of years. Like Pinchen, having trained up and empowered his successor, Joe had a sense of handover, with continuity being so important.

Indeed, working with two previous Point wardens definitely helped me to smoothly transition into the Point ranger position, along with valuable support from Graham. However, it still took time to build up first-hand experience, which inevitably involved learning from mistakes. The truth is that some of the lessons I learned had already been learned by my predecessors, but not every bit of knowledge can be passed on. Times move on, attitudes change and society evolves. Change is inevitable. Being young and keen, I fully embraced new technology. I saw the value of spreading important conservation messages through social media and the helpful information that trail-cameras can provide. Of course, wildlife must come first. New technology must not have any negative impacts that contradict the value of the research; its purpose should be to be better protect and conserve. I know a lot of locals and former staff would like to see reduced vehicular movements on the Point and increased ranger boat use in the harbour, and I completely see where they're coming from. I also appreciate that locals may find it hard to understand why no native north Norfolk applicants have been employed on the Point for many years (the posts are so sought after, with strong applicants from across the nation). I was Blakeney Point's first 'non-white' warden, but nobody in the community ever made me feel uncomfortable because of my ethnicity. Wherever I go in the country, my name is so often mispronounced 'AJ'. Some of the ferrymen affectionately changed 'AJ' to 'OJ' ... there are locals with far worse nicknames!

I feel a great sense of sentimentality towards the Point, including the Lifeboat House. I adore that building, with its interior wooden cladding. I mourned the decommissioning of the romantic gaslights, although fully accepted that the pipes had perished and become a fire risk. After all, modern lighting has a much lesser impact on the environment and a place like the Point should be leading the way in sustainability and environmentally friendly practices.

One thing I found a little challenging was the progressively modern habits of assistants, volunteers and students. To me, hearing loud music played in the Lifeboat House just didn't feel right. I was fine with Radio Four and Classic FM, even North Norfolk Radio for its local relevance, but I felt Radio One clashed with the ambiance of the place. Ready meals also felt wrong out there. But compromise is key to harmonious shared living, especially in remote confines. Good leadership is also key to running a tight ship. Hygiene and cleanliness being important, I insisted on cleaning the house as a team every Sunday morning.

I adopted a leading-by-example approach. For instance, never using the quad bike for personal convenience, only when equipment or provisions needed collecting or if there was a disturbance issue that urgently needed attending to. Indeed, if there was not a work-related need to use the quad, I requested that my understanding, patient partner walk either along the ridge from Cley, or even across the harbour at low tide, when visiting me. This actually added romance to our relationship, building excitement and making a great story to tell. As time went on, however, there seemed to be more of a desire for new team members to frequently use the quad bike, listen to Radio One and heat frozen ready-meals for dinner. My romantic vision of old-fashioned life had become dated and the time came when I was ready to move on from communal living to set up home with my fiancé.

I like to think that history lives on. I do not believe in the supernatural, but I did have an extraordinary experience one night. I woke in the early hours to what I was convinced was the sound of women and children who had just been rescued by the Blakeney lifeboat. I could hear the crew too, feet shuffling on the wooden floor, children crying, but an overall sense of relief that lives had been saved. It was clearly a dream, but it felt so vivid and realistic, as if I was witnessing an event that had happened in history.

Some assistants have had a fear of staying in the Lifeboat House on their own overnight. Some people wonder why anyone would want to work and live out there at all. I remember once being on a health and safety training course where the leader said that only mad people would want to work out on Blakeney Point. Some people think that too much time working on a place like the Point will drive you insane. I must admit, it seemed to me that most of the former long-serving wardens' time on the Point ended with an element of difficulty and suffering.

After the four wardens who worked between one and four decades on the Point in the twentieth century, no one has worked there for more than nine seasons in the twenty-first. I doubt anyone ever will again. There seems to be a much greater turnover of staff due to people generally changing jobs more than they did in the previous century, myself included.

I remember sitting in an armchair by the log burner alone in the Lifeboat House one autumn evening and watching the fiftieth anniversary episode of *Doctor Who*. It featured a scene with all of the doctors over the fifty years, which made me think of all the Blakeney Point wardens: Bob Pinchen, Billy and Ted Eales, John Green, Ronnie Pimm, Joe, Dave, Eddie and myself.

Very few people remember Bob and Billy, but many have memories of Ted: the longest-serving warden, spanning half a century, if you include the decade he spent assisting his father. Besides caring for Blakeney Point, I probably have relatively little in common with Ted Eales – except that both of us went on to have careers in wildlife television.

Quite early on in my time at Blakeney, Channel 4 asked to feature the Lifeboat House in a programme about unique homes on the coast. I was interviewed by presenter Charlie Luxton as I showed him around the building, slipping in a conservation message about ground-nesting birds. The experience was a pleasure, as was receiving positive feedback following its broadcast and numerous repeats. But it was my appearance with the seals on *Winterwatch* that set the ball rolling.

A couple of years later, I was invited to Minsmere to appear on the live *Springwatch: Unsprung* show presented by Chris Packham, having been remembered from my *Winterwatch* appearance. It was an excellent opportunity to promote little tern conservation and spread key messages such as keeping dogs on leads. The other guest turned out to be singer, Will Young. I later found out the episode had the highest rating of the series. I got a real buzz from the live television experience. Funnily enough, I was filmed for television again the very next day, this time on a seal ferry with Neil Oliver for the popular BBC *Coast* series.

A couple of months later, I was out on a seal trip with a television crew again. This time, it was for *Secrets of the National Trust*. By now, I was considering getting more involved in wildlife television presenting, constantly being told what a natural I was. In the Morston Anchor, after the shoot, I chatted to presenter Suzannah Lipscomb about how she had started out. Like me, she had done a succession of television news interviews. The next step was to get an agent.

I rang David Foster Management, who represent Chris Packham, Bill Oddie and Iolo Williams. David himself answered and agreed to represent me. Television work then began to come in: first, a couple of quiz shows, then co-presenting the primetime BBC documentary *Inside the Bat Cave* and going on to work with the Natural History Unit as part of the *Springwatch* team.

While on the set of *Inside the Bat Cave*, I spent almost as much time chatting to co-presenter Professor Kate Jones about Blakeney Point as I did about bats. As a professor at UCL, she had stayed in the Old Lifeboat House.

For part of the programme, I was flown up to Edinburgh from Norwich Airport. (I now try to avoid flying for environmental reasons.) Towards the end of the return journey, the cloudy sky cleared, revealing the coast below. A familiar hook-shape came into view and I felt an incredible sense of excitement to be looking down on the Point. I had seen countless aerial photographs but now I was actually over the Point. 'I thought I'd never get over the Point!' I laughed to myself.

In truth, I never will get over Blakeney Point. I have so many treasured memories and have made some wonderful friends there. When you fall in love with a place as special as the north Norfolk coast, it remains in your heart and mind forever. I will always feel immensely proud to be part of the history of Blakeney Point.

Few things compare to the sound of a bustling tern colony. Whenever I hear the distinctive calls of terns, I am transported back to Far Point in summer: the excitement, the drama, the responsibility, the absolute joy.

Marilyn and Graham wrote the following lines about my time at Blakeney:

It's been great working with you for several years[*]
Knowing that it's with someone who cares
From first volunteer days to running the reserve
The progress was nothing less than you deserve

* Norfolk pronunciation: 'yares'.

We both knew that on you we could rely
That is something no one could deny
Take a moment to think of the variety of work done
Some great times, some tough times, but mostly fun.

Reginald Gaze summarised the place nicely in his 1947 book, *Bird Sanctuary*:

To know Blakeney Point, one must live with her in all her moods and know that, like a fickle maiden, she is never twice the same, but always lovable.

For me, it is the changing light and changing seasons that are perhaps the most special. When the migrations of terns and wildfowl overlap. When first light breaks in spring, rendering the sand golden as the dunes fill with sweet skylark song. When dusk paints the autumn sky with the colours of fire to a soundtrack of curlew calls from the harbour.

Once you have got to know Blakeney Point and been involved in its conservation, it will always be part of you. For some, the present and future can't possibly match their treasured memories of days gone by. For me, the Point remains a very special and extremely important place that never fails to bring me immense pleasure whenever I visit. It is the privilege and responsibility of the relevant people to protect the wildlife and habitats as well as they possibly can for future generations and it is the responsibility of *everyone* to treat nature with respect. Nature continues to face numerous threats and compromises, but our understanding continues to grow in tandem with our appreciation for peace, space, seal-crammed beaches and bird-filled skies.

Bibliography

Allison, H., and J.P. Morley, *Blakeney Point and Scolt Head Island* (National Trust, 1989).

Bicknell, J.E., Mason, L.R., Peach, W.J., and J. Smart, *The Impacts of Non-Native Gamebird Release in the UK: An Updated Evidence Review* (RSPB, 2020).

Blakeney Point Management Committee, *Blakeney Point in 1913: The Report of the Committee of Management* (National Trust, 1913).

Blakeney Point Management Committee, 'Minutes: 1946-79' (National Trust, 1946-79).

Brownlow, A., et. al. 'Corkscrew Seals: Grey Seal Infanticide and Cannibalism May Indicate the Cause of Spiral Lacerations in Seals', Public Library of Science One, 11(6) (2016).

Büche, B., and E. Stubbings, 'Grey Seal Breeding Census, Skomer Island 2014' (Wildlife Trust of South and West Wales, 2015).

Chestney, B., *Island of Terns: Warden of Scolt Head* (Quiller Press, 1993).

Collinge, W.E., *An Investigation of the Food of Terns at Blakeney Point* (Norfolk and Norwich Naturalists' Society, 1925).

Eales, W.E.R., *Countryman's Memoirs: A Warden's Life on Blakeney Point* (Jim Baldwin Publishing, 1986).

Gaze, R., *Bird Sanctuary* (Faber and Faber Limited, 1947).

Green, J., Pimm, R., Reed, J., Wood, D., and Stubbings, E., 'Blakeney Point Warden's Reports: 1980-2012' (National Trust, 1980-2012).

Gurney, J.H., *A Catalogue of the Birds of Norfolk* (Lea Wertheimer and Co., 1887).

Harwood, A.; Berridge, R.; Perrow, M., 'Summer use of estuarine and coastal waters around Blakeney Point by a diverse fish assemblage' (ECON Ecological Consultancy, 2016).

Joyner, S., and A. Stoddart, *The Birds of Blakeney Point* (Wren Publishing, 2005).

Latham, J., *A General Synopsis of Birds* (Leigh and Sotheby, 1787).

Lockley, R.M., *Grey Seal, Common Seal* (Andre Deutsch Limited, 1966).

McCallum, J., *The Long, Wild Shore: Bird and Seal Seasons on Blakeney Point* (Silver Brant, 2012).

Norfolk and Norwich Naturalists' Society, 'Norfolk Bird and Mammal Reports: 1954–2010' (Norfolk and Norwich Naturalists' Society, 1955-2011).

Perrow, M.; Davies, M.; Harwood, A.; Tegala, A., 'Little Terns Breeding at Blakeney Point: Understanding the Past Informs the Present', *British Birds* 113: 398–411 (2020).

Pinchen, R.J., *Sea Swallows: Reminiscences of a Bird-Watcher* (Green and Company, 1935).

Porter, R., *An Atlas of the Plants of Blakeney Point* (National Trust, 2013).

Reed, J., 'Blakeney Point Property Manager's Reports: 1995–1999' (National Trust, 1995–99).

Reed, J., and R. Tidman, Seals: Their Lives and Legends (Sterna Publications, 1987).

Rivere, B.B., *A History of the Birds of Norfolk* (H.F. and G. Witherby, 1935).

Rowan, W.M., *Annotated List of Birds of Blakeney Point* (Norfolk and Norwich Naturalists' Society, 1917).

Rowan, W.M., 'The Blakeney Point Ternery', *British Birds* 8: 250–66 (1918).

Sayers, G., *Once Upon A Tide* (Whitefox Publishing Limited, 2014).

Seebohm, H., *The Birds of Siberia* (John Murray, 1901).

Stoddart, A., *Shifting Sands* (self-published, 2013).

Stubbings, E., 'The Birds of Blakeney Point: 100 years of National Trust Ownership', *British Birds* 105: 497–554 (2012).

Taylor, et. al., *The Birds of Norfolk* (Pica Press, 1999).

Tegala, A., and L. Newman, 'Blakeney Point and National Nature Reserve Breeding Bird Reports: 2013–20' (National Trust, 2013–20).

Tegala, A. et. al., 'Norfolk Coast with the National Trust', online blog (2012–2018, accessed 2020): www.norfolkcoastnationaltrust.blogspot.co.uk

Turner, E., *Bird Watching on Scolt Head* (Country Life, 1928).

White, D.J.B., *An Annotated Checklist of the Birds of Blakeney Point* (National Trust, 1981).

Appendix 1

List of Blakeney Point's Breeding Bird Species

Between 1901 and 2021, a total of forty-seven bird species have been confirmed breeding (defined by the laying of eggs) on Blakeney Point:

Greylag goose (Anser anser)
First bred 2003, with one to three pairs nesting in ten to twelve of the nineteen years since.

Shelduck (Tadorna tadorna)
Has bred most years since 1901, the number of pairs typically ranging between thirty and sixty-five.

Gadwall (Anas strepera)
Between one and eight pairs have nested each year since 2003.

Mallard (Anas platyrhinochos)
First bred in 1952, with between one and eight pairs recorded breeding most years since.

Shoveler (Anas clypeata)
Breeding suspected since 2003, first confirmed a decade later, with one pair most years since.

Red-legged partridge (Alectoris rufa)
Bred sporadically in the early twentieth century, peaking at twelve pairs but usually far fewer.

Grey partridge (Perdix perdix)
Bred sporadically in the twentieth century, increasing from a pair in 2008 to a peak of eleven.

Pheasant (Phasianus colchicus torquatus)
Has bred since 2012, with one to five territories recorded each year.

Kestrel (Falco tinnunculus)
Bred only once, in the Lifeboat House roof in 1974, fledging four young.

Oystercatcher (Haematopus ostralegus)
Returned to breed in 1906 and has done ever since, ranging from 50 to 200 pairs since 1952.

Avocet (Recurvirostra avosetta)
Has bred since 2012, with between nine and seventeen pairs nesting each year.

Little ringed plover (Charadrius dubius curonicus)
Bred in 2006 and 2016, failing in the former year and fledging a single chick in the latter.

Ringed plover (Charadrius hiaticula)
Has bred every year since before 1901, number of pairs ranging from 180 to 9, declining.

Kentish plover (Charadrius alexandrines)
Bred once in 1983 but was predated. A lone male held a territory in 2007.

Lapwing (Vanellus vanellus)
Bred first in 1961, then again in 2014 and 2019, fledging two young in both 1961 and 2019.

Redshank (Tringa tetanus)
Has bred most years since before 1901, usually ten to twenty pairs, but sometimes higher.

Black-headed gull (Chroicocephalus ridibundus)
First bred in 1925, numbers fluctuating greatly but often over 1,000 pairs, peaking at 3,000.

Mediterranean gull (Larus melanocephalus)
Has nested most years since 1992, peak nesting pairs reaching fifteen.

Common gull (Larus canus)
Has bred some years since 1964, peaking at ten pairs but usually three or fewer.

Lesser black-backed gull (Larus marinus)
First bred in 1978, number of pairs fluctuating greatly, peaking at 180, but often none.

Herring gull (Larus argentatus)
First bred in 1972, number of pairs fluctuating greatly, peaking at 240 but often fewer than ten.

Kittiwake (Rissa tridactyla)
Bred just once, with two nests recorded in 1958.

Little tern (Sternula albifrons)
Has bred every year since before 1901, number of pairs ranging between ten and 200.

Sandwich tern (Thalasseus sandvicensis)
First confirmed breeding in 1920, regular breeder with great range in pairs, peaking at 4,120.

Common tern (Sterna hirundo)
Has bred every year since before 1901, number of pairs ranging from 2,370 to 63, declining.

Arctic tern (Sterna paradisaea)
Has bred most years since 1922, number of pairs usually ranging between one and twenty.

Arctic x common tern (Sterna paradisaea x hirundo)
A female Arctic bred with a male common from 1973 to 1976, fledging one in 1976.

Roseate tern (Sterna dougalli)
One to two pairs bred in some years from 1921 to 1957 and 1994 to 2002, but have not since.

Stock dove (Columba oenas)
Bred in the early twentieth century. Up to four pairs since 1987, usually just one pair.

Wood pigeon (Columba palumbus)
Has bred most years since 2003, peaking at six pairs, but usually one or two.

Cuckoo (Cuculus canorus)
Juveniles were recorded in a skylark nest in 1966 and being fed by a meadow pipit in 1986.

Skylark (Alauda arvensis)
Has nested every year since before 1901, ranging from twenty to sixty pairs.

Sand martin (Riparia riparis)
Bred just once, in 2007, one or two pairs nesting in an eroded sand dune face.

Barn swallow (Hirundo rustica)
Occasional breeder since at least the 1920s, usually one to two pairs, maximum of seven.

House martin (Delichon urbicum)
Only records are of one pair breeding in 1915 and two in 1916, has not bred since.

Meadow pipit (Anthus pratensis)
Has nested every year since before 1901, ranging from twenty to over 100 pairs.

Pied wagtail (Motacilla alba yarrelii)
Around six to eight pairs bred in the early twentieth century, usually a pair or two since 1995.

White x pied wagtail (Motacilla alba alba x yarrelii)
A female white bred with a male pied in 2009 and 2010, fledging two broods both years.

Wren (Troglodytes troglodytes)
A pair first bred in 2002, with four to fifteen pairs recorded breeding each year since 2006.

Dunnock (Prunella modularis)
First recorded breeding in 1961, around five to ten pairs have bred each year since 2003.

Wheatear (Oenanthe oenanthe)
Two to three pairs bred each year in the early twentieth century, has not bred since 1956.

Stonechat (Saxicola rubicola)
First bred in 2020, with three pairs recorded in both 2020 and 2021.

Blackbird (Turdus merula)
One to three pairs bred each year from 1971 to 1979 but have not done since.

Sedge warbler (Acrocephalus schoenobaenus)
A pair were suspected in 2010 and 2011. Singing male in 2014. Confirmed breeding in 2019.

Carrion crow (Corvus corone)
Single pairs nested in the Plantation in 2009, 2011, 2014 and 2016.

Starling (Sturnus vulgaris)
Occasionally between one and six nests on the Lifeboat House until 1986, plus one in 2015.

House sparrow (Passer domesticus)
Between one and six pairs bred on the Lifeboat House between 1961 and 1987.

Linnet (Carduelis cannabina)
Generally between twenty and thirty pairs have bred every year since before 1901.

Reed bunting (Emberiza schoeniclus)
First bred in 1960, usually around twenty pairs have nested each year since 1999.

The following species has built a nest but did not go on to lay eggs:

Marsh harrier (Circus aeruginosus)
A pair made two unsuccessful nesting attempts in 2019 before abandoning.

The following two species have been suspected breeding but remain unconfirmed:

Canada goose (Anser canadensis)
A pair held a territory in 2004, but no nest was located and no young were observed.

Grasshopper warbler (Locustella naevia)
Two singing males recorded in 2007, but no nests were located or young observed.

Unpaired individuals of the following two species have built nests on Blakeney Point:

Laughing gull (Leucophaeus atricilla)
A lone bird built a nest on Near Point in 1999 and tried to mate with black-headed gulls.

Magpie (Pica pica)
A solitary bird built three nests in spring 1979 before being found dead.

Appendix 2

List of Blakeney Point's Notable Wardens

Between 1901 and 2021, the following watchers, wardens and rangers –
excluding assistants – have worked on Blakeney Point for a minimum
of three years:

Bob Pinchen: 1901–29
The Point's first watcher, employed each breeding bird season until retiring in
1929. He went on to write *Sea Swallows* about his experiences.

Billy Eales: 1930–39
Watcher for nine seasons, until his death in early 1939. He had worked alongside
Bob Pinchen during the 1929 season to learn the job.

Ted Eales: 1939–80
Succeeded his father in spring 1939, whom he had assisted for a decade. The
Point's longest-serving warden, he retired in March 1980 and went on to write
Countryman's Memoirs about his experiences.

John Bean: 1966–80
Filled in for his cousin, Ted Eales, working as the winter warden for thirteen seasons.

Joe Reed: 1981–2002
Took up the post in December 1981, following two short-lived wardens. He
became property manager in the mid-1990s, became mainland-based by 2002
and retired the following year.

Dave Wood: 2002–06
Became Point warden in April 2002, having been a seasonal assistant in 2000 and 2001. Became mainland-based head warden in autumn 2006, holding this post until October 2011.

Eddie Stubbings: 2006–13
Took on the Point warden role in November 2006, having been an assistant during the 2006 season. He held the position until February 2013.

Ajay Tegala: 2013–18
Became Point ranger in March 2013, having been a seasonal assistant in 2012 and volunteer in 2009 and 2010. He became primarily mainland-based in 2017, until August 2018. Went on to write *The Unique Life of a Ranger* about his experiences

Leighton Newman: 2018–21
Took on the Point ranger role in February 2018, holding the position for exactly three years until February 2021.

In addition to the above, the following assistants worked on the Point for more than six seasons: Reginald Gaze (1946-1964), Richard Gilbert (1987-1995) and Paul Nichols (2007-2015).

Appendix 3

List of Ajay Tegala's Media Appearances

Ajay has made several appearances on national television, many of them filmed on Blakeney Point:

2012: *Countryfile:* 'Summer Special' (BBC One)
     Autumnwatch (Series 7): 'Episode 4' (BBC Two)

2014: *Walking Through History:* 'North Norfolk' (Channel 4)
     Homes by the Sea: 'Norfolk' (Channel 4)

2015: *Winterwatch* (Series 3): 'Episode 1' and 'Episode 2' (BBC Two)

2016: *Springwatch: Unsprung* (Series 8): 'Episode 7' (BBC Two)
     Coast (Series 11): 'East Anglia' (BBC Two)

2017: *Secrets of the National Trust* (Series 1): 'The Lake District' (Channel 5)
     Curious Creatures (Series 1): 'Episode 7' (BBC Two)

2018: *Celebrity Eggheads* (Series 8): 'The Theory of Nothing' (BBC Two)

2020: *Inside the Bat Cave* (BBC Two)

2021: *Springwatch* (Series 17): 'Episode 10' (BBC Two)

Ajay has also starred in the following popular radio programmes:

2014: *Living World:* 'Grey Seals of Blakeney' (BBC Radio Four)
     Listen online: https://www.bbc.co.uk/programmes/b03sr5qx

2022: *Ramblings:* 'Wicken Fen with Ajay Tegala' (BBC Radio Four)
     Listen online: https://www.bbc.co.uk/programmes/m0014pgh

The destination for history
www.thehistorypress.co.uk